CW00544320

HINE'S VARIETIES

SOME OTHER TITLES FROM FALCON PRESS

Christopher S. Hyatt, Ph.D.
Undoing Yourself with Energized Meditation and Other Devices
Techniques for Undoing Yourself (audios)
Radical Undoing: Complete Course for Undoing Yourself (videos/audios)
Energized Hypnosis (book, videos & audios)
To Lie Is Human: Not Getting Caught Is Divine
Secrets of Western Tantra: The Sexuality of the Middle Path
Hard Zen, Soft Heart

Christopher S. Hyatt, Ph.D. with contributions by
Wm. S. Burroughs, Timothy Leary, Robert Anton Wilson et al.
Rebels & Devils: The Psychology of Liberation

Christopher S. Hyatt, Ph.D. & Antero Alli
A Modern Shaman's Guide to a Pregnant Universe

S. Jason Black and Christopher S. Hyatt, Ph.D.
Pacts With the Devil: A Chronicle of Sex, Blasphemy & Liberation
Urban Voodoo: A Beginner's Guide to Afro-Caribbean Magic

Antero Alli
Angel Tech: A Modern Shaman's Guide to Reality Selection
Angel Tech Talk (audio)

Peter J. Carroll
The Chaos Magick Audios
PsyberMagick

Phil Hine
Condensed Chaos: An Introduction to Chaos Magic
Prime Chaos: Adventures in Chaos Magic
The Pseudonomicon

Joseph Lisiewski, Ph.D.
Ceremonial Magic and the Power of Evocation
Kabbalistic Cycles and the Mastery of Life
Kabbalistic Handbook for the Practicing Magician

Israel Regardie
The Complete Golden Dawn System of Magic
New Wings for Daedalus
The Golden Dawn Audios
The World of Enochian Magic (audio)

Steven Heller
Monsters & Magical Sticks: There's No Such Thing As Hypnosis?

**For up-to-the-minute information on prices and
availability, please visit our website at
http://originalfalcon.com**

HINE'S VARIETIES

Chaos & Beyond

by
Phil Hine

Foreword by
David Southwell

THE *Original* FALCON PRESS

Tempe, Arizona, U.S.A.

Copyright © 2019 C.E. by Phil Hine

All rights reserved. No part of this book, in part or in whole, may be reproduced, transmitted, or utilized, in any form or by any means, electronic or mechanical, including photocopying, recording, or by any information storage and retrieval system, without permission in writing from the publisher, except for brief quotations in critical articles, books and reviews.

International Standard Book Number: 978-1-935150-76-3
ISBN: 978-1-61869-760-8 (mobi)
ISBN: 978-1-61869-761-5 (ePub)
Library of Congress Control Number: 2019945655

First Edition 2019
First eBook Edition 2019

Cover by Maria Strutz & Phil Hine

The paper used in this publication meets the minimum requirements of the American National Standard for Permanence of Paper for Printed Library Materials Z39.48-1984

Address all inquiries to:
THE ORIGINAL FALCON PRESS
1753 East Broadway Road #101-277
Tempe, AZ 85282 U.S.A.
(or)
PO Box 3540
Silver Springs NV 89429 U.S.A.
website: http://www.originalfalcon.com
email: info@originalfalcon.com

TABLE OF CONTENTS

TANTRA

SEXUALITIES

HISTORIES

FICTION

"Write, and find ecstasy in writing!"
— Liber AL, 2.66

Acknowledgements

Thanking everyone who has ever encouraged me to write or shaped my ideas over the last forty years or so would be a lengthy task indeed, but I would like to express my thanks and appreciation to the following individuals without whose friendship, support and inspiration this book would not have come about:

Jenny Alexander, Gavin Brown, Alexander Cummins, Joseph De Lappe, Gyrus, Amy Hale, Lou Hart, Ben Joffe, Christopher Josiffe, Patricia MacCormack, Gordon MacLellan, Mike Magee, Christina Oakley-Harrington, Rodney Orpheus, Estelle Seymour, Michael Staley, Andrew Stenson, Nicholas Tharcher, and Caroline Wise.

In particular, I would like to thank Maria Strutz for her love, patience and unerring ability to remove the dead wood from a passage of text, and David Southwell for his clarity of thought, inspiring conversations (plus delicious bread pudding), and his generous foreword.

FOREWORD

In aging, I have become wary of any inducement to time travel. To journey down your own timeline is at best emotionally messy. At its worst, dealing with all the what-if nexus points, all the inevitable previous versions of yourself you encounter, is the harshest of harrowings.

It tends to be even more dangerous for writers. As soon as we step a few pages back into our past, we become so dismayed at what we find, there's usually an overwhelming urge to burn the bygone down. Make all our words of yesterday a reduction of ash and resulting paradox. Nothing more quickly demolishes the defences of nostalgia, erodes all comfort of misremembering, than the actuality of having to reread your old work.

Few authors have the courage to take the timeline trip Phil has here. Even fewer could return to the *now* with such good material. Beyond the practicalities of gathering pieces you'd normally have to hunt for in attic boxes of old occult magazines and dubious PDFs scattered across the Net, this book chronicles and contextualises. I hope it's not the closest we ever get to an autobiography, but if it is, it does a bloody good job of documenting not only Phil's life within paganism, but the evolution of the wider esoteric landscape during the last 40 years.

Phil's written work has always mattered because it has never been lazy, refusing easy commentary or being satisfied with dull synthesis. It has never fallen into the trap of playing magical status-games, smugly alluding to the fact that he knows more than you and is now going to present you with a 3,000-word article to prove it. He's always given his audience the massive compliment that he trusts them to be as smart as he is. Readers feel his genuine joy at sharing insight and information. Phil's historical work is erudite and accessible, managing to balance intellectual clarity and entertainment. Being schooled in the arcane is rarely more fun than the essays on Lobsang Rampa and Elizabeth Sharpe included here. Few provide better paths to Tantric understanding that both the scholar and the newly curious can walk together than Phil offers in his essays and talks.

As is demonstrated throughout this collection, Phil is adept at using humour to defeat any possibility of pomposity, undercutting any attempt by a reader to project guru status onto him. Phil's wit also plays a role in crafting material that allows lightning leaps of realisation in the reader through feeling as well as fact. Most occult writing is sterile, content to impress at an intellectual level, but rarely moving us the way magic itself does. This text is typical of Phil Hine's writing as it provides powerful, connective emotional tissue.

Many of the pieces included here were first released into the wild during a time when linking to and learning from the wider occult community was much more difficult than anyone who was born a citizen of the Net can imagine—especially for a kid out in the squatted spaces of suburbia. Zines were devoured, every smudge of ink scraped for potential wisdom or useful instruction. Isolated from mentors and friends with more knowledge, I read these publications wanting to learn, wanting to connect with those who understood the marginalised places my own magic practice occupied. Wanting to hear from those who truly understood how magic felt, not just how it worked.

Phil was one of the key voices I discovered on day trips up to London and Camden's Compendium Books to buy as many issues of *Nox* or *Pagan News* as I could find. Phil's words came from the bits of bruised and broken landscape that I recognised, he poked fun at the class-based attitudes I bristled against. He carved out permissive emotional spaces to think about and practice magic in that few else offered. This collection more than ably demonstrates why his work clicked with me and so many others, why it mattered so much. It also proves that when it comes to making the past sing to the now, when it comes to either opening gates of the sublime or extracting the urine to keep you grounded whilst reality warps around you, his voice remains undiminished and unmatched.

— David Southwell, London, April 2019

INTRODUCTION

I have been writing about the occult in general and the practical aspects of various approaches to magic for forty years now, so 2019 seems like a good point to celebrate this with a selective anthology of essays on a range of subjects. Although I'm most well-known for my three books on Chaos Magic (*Condensed Chaos: An Introduction to Chaos Magic; Prime Chaos: Adventures in Chaos Magic*; and *The Pseudonomicon,* all from The Original Falcon Press) all of which were written during the 1990s, I thought this would be an opportunity to highlight some of the writing I did which preceded and has post-dated those books. Much of this early material was published in the kind of small press occult magazines which flourished in the 1980s, and which, for the most part, have been killed off by the rise of the worldwide web.

Coming up with a selection of essays in itself would have been relatively easy, but I wanted to do something more. I wanted to show, through presenting this material, how my ideas and thoughts on a particular subject have changed with intervening years. For each section I have tried to select essays that reflect, to a degree, shifts in ideas and emphasis over time. I also wanted to take this opportunity to reflect on what motivated me to write a particular essay—what was happening in my life at the time of writing, and to provide some autobiographical insights into my passage from Wicca to Chaos Magic and beyond.

I have come to view writing as an important magical process. For me, it is a grounding—a kind of full stop in any magical endeavour—a chance to pause, reflect, or try to make sense of something which can, at last, be articulated in a way that makes it sensible to others. Although writing can be intensely frustrating at times, it is also soothing, and in rare moments, it seems that the writing happens by itself, without much conscious input from me.

A word about the title. *Hine's Varieties* is a parodying riff on the famous "Heinz 57 Varieties" slogan of the H.J. Heinz Company. Due to the apparent similarity of my name with the company, being compared to one or another of Heinz products was a constant source of amusement for other children throughout my early years, so it is a small gesture of defiance for me to reclaim that association.

Beginnings in Magic

How did I become interested in the occult in the first place? What prompted me to take an interest in magical practice? I had no time for the occult at all until I was in my late teens, although I had become interested in the works of Carl Gustav Jung. One day in the school library, I was idly leafing through a copy of *Man, Myth and Magic* looking for photographs of naked witches (as you do) when I came across a reproduction of a painting by the occult artist Austin Osman Spare. This painting struck a chord with me. It seemed to recall some of Jung's ideas that I'd been reading about, and I began to get interested in the occult—something which I had, up until then, dismissed.

I spent hours in the local library, the occult shelves of which were, for the most part, stocked with Dennis Wheatley novels, spiritualist classics and a good deal of Theosophical literature—the writings of Madame Blavatsky, Annie Besant and Charles Webster Leadbeater. The first book on practical magic I managed to get hold of was David Conway's 1972 classic *Magic: An Occult Primer*.

My first act of practical magic was a curse. I was, at that time, an avid fantasy wargamer, and after suffering a particularly ignominious defeat at the hands of one of my friends after which he jeered at me, saying something along the lines of "What are you going to do, cast a spell on me?" I replied hotly that I was going to do just that. I took inspiration from a recent television programme which was a modernized retelling of M.R. James' classic tale, *The Casting of the Runes* (ITV Playhouse, 1979). One of the scenes showed a woman being menaced by a thought-form of a giant spider, and I stayed up the entire evening visualising a shadowy form looming over the bed of my friend. I saw him a couple of days later and he said something to the effect that he wondered if I had "done something" as that night he had had terrible nightmares. I took some satisfaction in hearing this, which gives a major clue to my state of mind at the time.

Later that year I left my home town and moved to Huddersfield, West Yorkshire, to pursue a three-year degree in Behavioural Sciences (Psychology, Sociology and Philosophy) at the Polytechnic. It was this move away from home which brought me into contact with the wider occult subculture in the UK.

The degree course I had signed up for attracted a lot of mature students, and some of these turned out to have occult interests. One of my fellow students had been, briefly, a member of the Order of the Cubic Stone, a British-based Magical Order which specialised in Enochian magic—and he had an older sister who was still involved in the group. The Order had a postal correspondence course—a kind of basic training course after the completion of which, prospective candidates could apply for membership proper. I undertook the course in 1980, and was soon practicing the Middle Pillar and Lesser Banishing Ritual of the Pentagram in the basement of the student house where I was living.

I had already joined the Theosophical Society by this time, and it was through visiting the Theosophical Society in nearby Leeds that I found myself attending public Pagan Moots and visiting what was then one of the few occult bookshops in the country—the Sorceror's Apprentice in Leeds.

The shop with its blacked-out windows and visored door had from the outside a forbidding air, tinged with the kind of backstreet seediness associated at that time with sex shops. Soon I was a regular, visiting as often as I could and spending my student grant on acquiring a library.

It was via the Sorceror's Apprentice that I first came across two slim volumes which would, some years later, come to be seen as two of the foundational texts of the Chaos Magic movement—Peter J. Carroll's *Liber Null*, and Ray Sherwin's *The Book of Results*. I was soon experimenting with Sherwin's method of drawing sigils, and was roundly ticked off for doing so by the person mentoring me through the Cubic Stone's coursework, who said that this kind of magical practice was dangerous and should not be attempted by a beginner. He also told me off (in red pen on my letter, with several exclamation marks) for spelling magic as "magick", saying that this was something only Thelemites did, which the Order of the Cubic Stone was not! I continued to experiment with sigils nevertheless. I could not believe that sigils—or in fact magic in general for that matter—could be in any way dangerous, which was probably a belief I'd formed through studying psychology.

My first experience of ritual magic weirdness was my attempt to evoke the Great Old One Yog-Sothoth on the top of a hill. I'd discovered the fiction of H.P. Lovecraft, and one aspect of Lovecraft's writing that really resonated with me were his descriptions of countryside and of landscape. I was by that time fond of solitary walking, and decided to take advantage of my living in proximity to a range of mountains by summoning one of the Great Old Ones. It's safe to say that I had no real idea of what I was doing, and my magical diary of the time does not record the exact details of the night-time ritual. What I *do* recall seeing was a beam of light coming down out of the stars and striking one of the low stones on the hilltop where I stood...at which point, I simply ran away. Fragments of memory persist; running, panic-stricken down the hill, trying to avoid tripping over rocks. My torch swinging about, occasionally illuminating the faces of sheep. I ended up, gibbering slightly, at the house of a student friend who lived on the other side of the village. He told me, with a smug air, that he thought something like this would happen.

Nowadays, Lovecraftian magic tends to get classed by some people as a sub-genre of chaos magic, but this is not how I thought of it at the time. I hadn't really got my head around the idea that there might be different styles or approaches to magic—it was all too new and exciting.

Early in 1981, after completing the degree, I returned to my home town. Idly leafing through some occult magazines one day, I came across an advertisement for a Wiccan coven recruiting for potential members with a local telephone numbers. Throwing caution to the wind, I rang the number and was invited to a meeting. This was to be a turning point in my occult career, for not only did I meet the High Priestess of the Wiccan coven I was later initiated into, but also Richard Bartle-Bertelli (aka "The Dewsbury Magus") who became, some years later, a mentor to me.

K., the High Priestess of the coven, lived with her husband and her two children in a large house in a secluded area. Throughout that year, I visited her several times a week, and she began to teach me the basics of Craft—how to set up an altar, how to draw a magical sword from its scabbard, and how to cast a circle. Whenever she wanted to impart something particularly important, K. would take me for walks along the beaches or sand dunes on the seafront, or sometimes, we would hide in the bushes of her overgrown garden. I started to keep a book of Shadows and did various exercises to develop a relationship with the elements. I showed K. both *Liber Null* and *The Book of Results* and she encouraged me to keep on experimenting with these new approaches to magic. I had just read Luke Rhinehart's novel *The Dice Man,* and experimented with dice to determine courses of action or magical exercises.

It was during this time that I wrote my first article for *The Lamp of Thoth* magazine, which was published by The Sorceror's Apprentice. The editor (and owner) Chris Bray sent me a letter encouraging me to do more writing—the first positive feedback I'd had. The article, entitled *The Dark Night of the Soul* was a brief account of how to deal with bouts of spiritual dryness and depression. This early article can be found all over the web, although it is now, through those strange processes by which articles make the leap from paper to digital, commonly attributed to one Fra. Apfelmann, who originally transcribed it or uploaded it to a bulletin board.

Later that year, I was formally initiated into the coven. I recounted this event, and the subsequent twist to it, in *Prime Chaos.* Basically, I was initiated into the coven and then, a few days later, informed that the initiation had been a mistake, that I was not temperamentally cut out for magical practice, and that I should not attempt to do any further magical work.

It is hard to convey the shock and disappointment I felt on hearing this, and it was not long after that I left the UK to work on a Kibbutz in Israel. I continued my magical studies in Israel, finding remote areas in which to practice rituals, and working through both the Order of the Cubic Stone's introductory material and Liber MMM, the training programme in *Liber Null.* I also wrote some short articles which appeared in *The Lamp of Thoth* magazine.

Being in Israel during that period was both exciting and unnerving at times—the Falklands War between Britain and Argentina kicked off whilst I was there; and on one occasion, a Kibbutz I was visiting near the border with Lebanon came under a rocket attack. There were areas that were unsafe to walk because of unmarked minefields, and I became inured to seeing soldiers everywhere. I might have stayed longer, but for the invasion of Lebanon in 1982, which was a cue for me to return to the UK.

In 1982 I was living in a small village in Lincolnshire. It was here, despite my intention to take a break from all things occult, that

I had my recurrent dream-meetings with the Tantric Goddess Kali (see Introduction to the Tantra section). I spent much of this year visiting non-occult friends, hitch-hiking around the UK, but it felt as though the Kali dreams were drawing me back to the occult world. From Lincolnshire, I moved to Nottingham to begin training as a Psychiatric Nurse. I continued to write, and in 1983 achieved another milestone in actually being paid for an article, combining my occult interests with my love of Fantasy Role-Playing games in an article for Games Workshop's *White Dwarf* magazine, entitled "Sorcerous Symbols"—an attempt to place Austin Osman Spare's sigil methodology within the game mechanics of Advanced Dungeons & Dragons. Whilst I was in Nottingham, I became involved in an experimental drama group which at various points called itself "The Theatre of Voodoo". We did some interesting work with masks and possession, inspired by Keith Johnstone's 1979 book *IMPRO* which to my mind, is still a fantastic resource for anyone interested in creative ritual, and in particular, working with masks. Although some of the work in this group would later flow into my practice, at the time I did not really grasp the connection between freestyle drama and magical ritual.

Later in 1983 I switched from Psychiatric Nursing to Occupational Therapy training in York. By this time, I was back in contact with K. and her coven. They had moved to Macclesfield in the North of England. I had an out-of-the-blue letter from K. asking did I want to continue working with the coven? My "failed" initiation, she later said, had been a deliberate test to try to shake me out of my then all-consuming obsession with all things occult. In retrospect, I'm not sure it was wholly successful, but it was probably what I needed at the time. I came back to the coven with much more confidence in my own developing abilities, and recognising that I had stopped thinking about magic in mostly psychological terms and begun to strike out in my own direction. I began to visit the coven regularly, and started to attend various Psychic Festivals in the region. These were not exactly occult or pagan gatherings, but usually attended by local Wiccans to exchange news and gossip, and it was through these events that I began to meet other pagans and occultists. This was significant, as in widening my circles of acquaintances, I also encountered people with different perspectives.

Given my later association with Chaos Magic and gaining some degree of notoriety for magical innovation (or at least challenging sacred cows) it now seems odd that I spent the first few years of my occult life not doing much to challenge the received wisdom of books or teachers. Whilst I found the world of magic tremendously alluring and exciting, I lacked the confidence to strike out on my own. I was also fairly isolated, having only a limited circle of contacts to talk with, and most of the people I did know seemed vastly more experienced and knowledgeable than I felt myself to be. I knew only one or two people that I felt I could relax with and talk as equals. But this isolation was in some ways, beneficial. Nowadays, any fledgling magician who wants to seek advice from their peers before embarking on a magical experiment can do so via the internet. When I began to participate in discussions on occult forums such as Barbelith or Liminal Nation, I often noticed that requests for advice led to some interesting discussions on the advisability of performing a particular ritual. However, it struck me on more than one occasion that people asking advice were effectively discouraged from trying things out. If the internet had been available in the early 1980s, I would probably have been talked out of trying to summon Yog-Sothoth in the hills of West Yorkshire. Lacking anyone to tell me *not* to try it though, I just went ahead and did it—an attitude to experimentation which has since served me well.

CHAOS

Introduction

Phase I: from Wicca to Eris

As mentioned earlier I first encountered the works of Peter J. Carroll and Ray Sherwin in 1980, but apart from doing the odd bit of sigil magic, I really didn't do much with it until some years later. By 1985 I was living in a punk/hippie commune on the outskirts of York and studying to become an Occupational Therapist. Both of these situations were, in their various ways, influential on how I came to practice Chaos Magic. Although I was still, for the most part, heavily invested in Wicca at the time, I was beginning to pull away from it.

Through the communal space in York I began to meet people involved in the UK's alternative scene. Old hippies, young punks— "alternative" people with brightly-coloured hair and a playful attitude to life that was markedly different from most of the people I had met through Wicca. For the most part, they were white working-class folk who, despite their occult interests, were otherwise rather conservative in their outlook. The coven that I'd been initiated into in 1981—then thrown out of—and later been allowed to return to was *secretive* in the extreme. For example, I was told not to keep any of my occult books on open display. I was enjoined not to talk about my occult pursuits with non-occultists, to the extent that if other people tried to engage my interest in the occult, I was to deny all knowledge of the subject and avoid them. For a time, I went along with this, but increasingly, I began to chafe under such restrictions, and discovered gradually, that I actually *enjoyed* talking to people about the occult. After all, it was something I was passionate about— it was so central to my self-identity that eventually, I couldn't help but talk about it. And for the most part, the people I talked to were really positive in their responses. They may not have shared my ideas, but they didn't run away screaming either.

It was during this period that I read the *Illuminatus!* trilogy by Robert Anton Wilson and Robert Shea, and some of Wilson's non-fiction work. This led me to obtaining a copy of *Principia Discordia,* and the idea of a playful goddess of Chaos—Eris—really resonated with me. At the Autumn Equinox of 1985, I managed to talk the coven into helping me do a ritual to invoke the Goddess Eris. The next day, whilst waiting at Stockport train station, I received a chan-

neled 'communication' from Eris, *The Stupid Book.* For the first
time, I began to feel that I was "going somewhere"—although I
wasn't sure where that somewhere was, or where it might lead. More
rituals with Eris followed, and although these were, for the most part,
structured according to the style of ritual magic I'd been taught in the
coven, I was beginning to "experiment"—later bringing in a pentagram formed from curves (the "spiral pentagram" mentioned in
Condensed Chaos) and energetic movement sequences from Tai Chi.
At the same time, I was spreading the word of Eris as it were,
amongst my friends in York's alternative scene, most of whom—
even if they thought occultism was dry and boring—had no problem
accommodating the idea of a zany, capricious goddess of chaos, who
might be petionable via random acts of silliness. One of my friends
had her bike stolen from outside the Student Union building. She put
up a notice declaring that she was an "Erisian Witch" and her bike
was her familiar. In a college with a large and powerful Christian
membership, this was a brave move, but the bike reappeared in no
time at all. That same year I took part in a performance piece in a
York Nightclub where another friend was declared to be the Discor-
dian Papess of York, and given an impressive set of documents to
prove it. I was getting to grips with another important lesson which
would later feed into my approach to Chaos Magic: playfulness, the
art of not taking magic—and by extension myself—too seriously.

I want to return to the Occupational Therapy course itself, as I
feel that the principles that I was taught to use within a clinical
setting also shaped some of my ideas about Chaos Magic. It is true
that my interest in group dynamics and creative ritual were heavily
influenced by the training I had from occupational therapy in running
groups. For a few years I did workshops in the UK, Europe and
America which drew heavily on this background. I basically took
drama-therapy exercises from my clinical training and repurposed
them into "occult" exercises. But there's more. Occupational therapy
uses a multidisciplinary approach to the resolution of a particular
client's problems. For example, a therapist might have a client where
the optimum approach to engaging with that client's problems might
be a psychoanalytic method, and have another client where behaviour therapy might be the best option. Both methods of treatment

have their own strengths and weaknesses—and the skill comes in knowing in what settings to apply them.

There is also an important emphasis on assessment—being able to evaluate the practical results of treatment and how effective the therapist has been in delivering that treatment.

I think all of these themes are very apparent in both *Condensed Chaos* and *Prime Chaos*. Although by the end of the three-year training course I decided that I didn't want a career in occupational therapy, much of the training (which included a wide range of practical skills ranging from woodworking to using a computer) did come up later in my magical work—be it in facilitating groups or workshops, or dealing directly with magical clients.

The events that finally caused me to move away from the coven came in November 1985. There was a ritual in which the coven leaders had made some heavy emotional investments. Some of the people who were invited to the ritual spent the previous evening being both verbally and physically aggressive, casting about accusations that others present were "black witches" or "possessed by the devil." This did not produce an atmosphere which I at least, felt was conducive to good magical work. I really did not want to perform any ritual work in such a setting, but felt I had no choice.

Immediately after the ritual I sought escape from the more or less immediate resumption of hostilities once the ritual had concluded. I lay down in one of the bedrooms and tried to pathwork myself into a kinder space. Some time later I was suddenly jerked back into the present to find one of the other people who been in the ritual sitting astride my head, waving an athame in my face. Apparently, my lying down in a bedroom alone and not being very responsive to verbal summons was interpreted that I was "under attack by demons." I spent the rest of that evening in another house, bouncing between confusion and utter rage.

That should have been enough, but no. The next day I left to return to York as early as possible, flatly refusing to attend a further event which had been planned. The trust that I had held for the coven had absolutely been shattered, and I wanted no more occult drama. A couple of days later, I received a letter informing me that the other members of the coven had received an astral message that I'd come under attack by demons *again*. They'd actually pulled their car over on the motorway and done some kind of impromptu ritual by the side of the road as my astral body was in imminent danger of being destroyed! There was lots of 'advice' too about how my interest in chaos, Kali, etc. was leading me into dangerous waters... But I'd stopped listening at that point. Fortunately I had a friend—the late Richard Bartle-Birtelli—who was something of a mentor for me. He always shrugged off any suggestion that he was a teacher to me, we were just two magicians sharing thoughts and ideas. Richard was gentle, down-to-earth and didn't suffer from taking himself too seriously. Moreover, he knew most of the other people who'd been involved in this chain of events. After explaining the situation, my feelings and the weird letter, he basically said "They're mad. You don't need this. Stay away from them." And that's pretty much what I did.

Phase II: Leeds

In 1986, I moved to the Northern City of Leeds. In the mid-1980s Leeds was a melting pot of magical potentialities. Not only was there a thriving, if loose, "chaos scene," but there was also the presence of members of groups such as the Arcane and Mystical Knights of Shambala (AMOOKOS); the Esoteric Order of Dagon; and the Typhonian O.T.O. Much of this activity flowed around the Leeds University Occult Society. The various groups were not isolated from each other, and there was a vibrant social scene which I threw myself into. Leeds also had an alternative scene too—there were various networks of squatters, people involved in setting up communal spaces. Anarcho-punks rubbed shoulders with indie musicians, goths and vegan activists, and as many people were unemployed, there was a widespread network of people were specialists in helping a newcomer such as myself navigate the labyrinths of government bureaucracy. But admittedly, it could be frightening, too. A few days before I moved to Leeds, the bands Chumbawamba and Conflict had done a gig at the University which had ended up in a riot, and I spent my first evening in Leeds in a friend's basement whilst various people regaled each other with stories of fighting the police with bricks and bottles—and I wasn't quite prepared for that. What impressed me very much about the squatters, though, was that *they got things done,* and some of them were doing interesting things too, with street theatre and parody. As much as I found myself in the midst of a thriving occult scene, I was also on the fringes of the loose anarcho-punk squat scene, and there was some degree of interchange between the two communities.

By this time three more books which had emerged from authors whose names became synonymous with Chaos Magic—Peter J. Carroll's *Psychonaut* (1982), Ray Sherwin's *The Theatre of Magick* (1982), and Paula Pagani's *Cardinal Rites of Chaos* (1984). There were also more small press occult magazines starting to circulate such as *Chaos International, Formaos, Nuit-Isis* and *Nox*—as well as established zines such as *The Lamp of Thoth*—in which the parameters of Chaos Magic, as a self-consciously 'new' magical current were being explored, debated, and in some cases, resisted. Some authors seemed to be appalled at the very word 'Chaos'. William Gray, for example, in his 1989 book *Between Good and Evil: Polarities of Power* likened Chaos Magic to be a spiritual equivalent of AIDS, and declared Chaos Magic to be "Nuclear Nastiness."

Other authors took issue with the suggestion that magical work could be done with deities and figures drawn from fiction as opposed to "proper" mythology or seemed concerned that the "chaos kids" were abandoning traditional morality. There were dark mutterings about the influence of "Black Adepts from Atlantis" and groups not being "properly contacted." It was not unlike what happened in wargaming circles when fantasy miniatures arrived. Wargamers in the 1970s tended to feel that they were engaged in the serious hobby of historical re-enactment and not—as the wider public tended to perceive them, as "grown men playing with toy soldiers." You can imagine, I hope, their horror when suddenly, in the late 1970s, there was an influx of mostly teenage boys turning up at wargaming clubs with boxes of elves, orcs and dragons. Within the occult "scene" it seemed that suddenly, many sacred cows were being poked at.

One of the earliest manifestations of this new wave of chaos thought I encountered was *The Chaochamber* by P.D. Brown and Rodney Orpheus (with whom I later co-founded *Pagan News). The Chaochamber*—subtitled, rather grandly, *A Quantum Sorcery Pathworking for Manipulative Magicks*—was a science fiction approach to the notion of an Astral Temple. Instead of the usual post-Golden Dawn method of building an astral temple, the user whirled through the aethyrs in a weird, steampunk-like spaceship, sucking up raw chaos power into their own being. It was creative, clever and cool, and very much had a "Do It Yourself" feel to it. Again, it showed me the possibilities of bringing elements from beyond the immediate horizon of what was considered "properly" occult into my magical world.

My first entry into chaos-related "publishing" came later in 1986, with a group collaboration—*Apikorsus: An essay on the diverse practices of CHAOS MAGICK from the Lincoln Order of Neuromancers (L.O.O.N)*. At least some of impetus for Apikorsus came from a grimoire from the Satanic order, the Order of the Nine Angles, which bore the stern warning that anyone attempting to photocopy the manuscript would be automatically death-cursed. We decided to reverse this notion, and release a freely-circulated "chain book," the idea being that if you liked the content, you should add something yourself to it, and pass it on. Of course, unlike most chain messages, there was no kickback if you didn't—we just thought it was a fun way of passing some information around, along with having a bit of fun. We also came up with the idea of a chaos magical order, the Lincoln Order of Neuromancers, and there was a brief flurry of articles written under a variety of pseudonyms from apparent members of this group, which appeared in various magazines around the time that we started sending out copies of Apikorsus to various friends in distant and exotic locations—such as London. How influential any of this was is difficult to say, although I am somewhat amused that the Lincoln Order of Neuromancers now features in at least two historical accounts of the rise of chaos magic (Nevill Drury's 2011 book *Stealing Fire from Heaven* and Gary Lachman's 2018 *Dark Star Rising: Magick and Power in the Age of Trump)*. This do-it-yourself, keep-things-low-cost, make-works-accessible ethos was another key element in my developing ideas about chaos magic. Although I tend to feel now that the comparisons sometimes made between chaos magic and the UK punk scene are overstated, there was a kind of "anyone can do this" ethos around at the time.

It was also whilst I was in Leeds that I began to work on the writing project that eventually became—through various iterations—*Prime Chaos,* as well as the first version of *Condensed Chaos* (originally a short chapbook) although I was so poor by that time I could not afford to even self-publish it using the low-cost approach through which much of my early work was circulated.

Phase III: London

In 1991 I moved from Leeds to London, which kicked off the final phase of my entanglement with Chaos Magic. London also had a vibrant and thriving occult social scene, and by that time I knew a fair number of people who could help me find my feet. I became involved with magical organisations such as the Fellowship of Isis, the Temple of Psychic Youth (TOPY), and the Illuminates of Thanateros (IOT). It was via the latter that I was able to run workshops in continental Europe and later, America. It was largely thanks to the late Robert "Bob" Williams, former section head of the IOT in North America, that I ended up being published by Falcon Press, and having the opportunity to spend an afternoon in the company of William S. Burroughs. I'd been reading Burroughs' work since my late teens and written the occasional article about his magical ideas, and the prospect of meeting him was both exciting and anxiety-making. It didn't help having Bob chanting "Phil's gonna see Will-IAM" over and over again as he drove us from the airport to the Burroughs residence in Lawrence, Kansas. I was so nervous that when Burroughs addressed me directly for the first time, I could do no more than squeak out a stammering reply. Eventually I relaxed into an easy conversation and the rest of the afternoon passed rapidly, but memorably.

As the 1990s progressed though, I was becoming increasingly critical of some of the propositions of Chaos Magic which I had accepted earlier. The rekindling of my interest in Tantra led me to question the notion that all the techniques of magic were universal, with the implication that cultural or historical context didn't really matter. Also, having written two books on the subject plus a short book examining approaches to Lovecraftian magic from a chaos perspective *(The Pseudonomicon),* I had really come to feel that I had said all I felt I wanted to say on the subject of Chaos Magic, and it was time to step away and do something else.

THE STUPID BOOK

[*The Stupid Book* is a channelled communication, "received" by me whilst waiting for a train on Stockport Station, England, on 22 September 1985. It was the morning after one of my first major rituals directed at invoking the power of the goddess Eris. In hindsight, the influence of Crowley's *Liber Al* and similar "received writings" is all too obvious. Although I found this communication personally significant for a few years, I've been loath, until now, to put my name to it.]

———◦———

0. This Dumb Book is the Utterance of Eris. Speak me not aloud, for only in the silences between spaces may I be heard.
1. My priest is mute, for he is enraptured by my kisses. My lips are ice, the fire (glyph of Shin) of my tongues burns upon his brow.
2. The past knows me not. Each moment is a new beginning. The future is written on the folds of my gown. And I have shed my gown; the possibilities of all things not yet born.
3. In all things adore me. The love-play of agonies and ecstasies. Be here with me. Now. Forever.
4. Matter is my playground. I make and break without thought. Laugh and come UNTO me.
5. My priest knows my secret name.
6. Lust, I tell you, but not after result, for thereby you are bound. naked I come to you. My body is outlined in the stars.
7. Seek me not without, seek me not within.
8. I am dancer and the dance. Let all things unite in nought.
9. The passion play of sight and sound: All things come to you as I refuse nothing!
10. I am the whole and the none. All Qabalahs are equal. think not to bind me in one; fore I am none.
11. Think not to worship, for I shall strip you of all weight. You are but a peacock's feather in my hair. understand this!
12. I am the root of all that is to come!
13. You are the apple of my eye; gold and silver.

14. The fool is already mine. Let the Magus become a juggler in the streets. this is more honest.
15. Let my priestess be the whore of the Gutters.
16. There is no message in this book!
17. My trees bear a strange fruit: share and share alike.
18. All is revealed in my secret name.

FRACTURE LINES

[*Fracture Lines* was written in 1987 and first published in *Nox* magazine, edited by Stephen Sennitt. As might be obvious, it was written in the wake of a particularly disastrous love affair which was complicated by my having developed an obsessive crush on the subject of my affections; so that by the time the affair began, I had all kinds of unrealistic expectations and fantasies which—naturally enough—were dashed. This is me trying to articulate the coping strategies for dealing with this kind of situation and trying to reflect on the nature of fantasies and obsessions.]

"If Will stops and cries Why, invoking Because, then Will stops & does nought."
— *Liber AL*, II,30.

I lay possessed by a demon. Obsession. Twisted by talons; self-love & hatred knotting my guts. Howling frustration into the night, the broken dream heaped around my bed.

Later.

A shaft of light burns through the brooding darkness; my cloak of night, my self-sewn shroud. Knowledge. Insight. Wild laughter. A strange way into gnosis. A self-wounding, stretching back into my personal time. I crawl into my centre, my circle, and with my pen etch a triangle. And force the monster into it; to loosen the skeins of form; moments of weakness, wanting and waiting, desire ignited by imagination. Manufacturing my own junk, my own addiction.

If this is wading through "qlipothic muck" then so be it. But out of this muck I wove a conversation, a story with no chance of a happy ending. A story which clouded my will, which blurred my eye.

I made this monster; a golem born of my own longings & shortcomings, and now I will take it apart, piece by piece, draining the pus from knotted passions. We are but knots in a cord. Untie them and we slip easily across the aeons into nebulous dreams.

Emotional Engineering

We are bound by our own past, bound to repeat patterns; programs written long ago. Flowcharted in an infant's crabbed hand; meshed like kitten-pulled wool; a language of critical moments in our personal histories. Years later, a gap opens in the world, and creatures of free will and freedom that we think we are, our sudden vulnerability surprises us. Caught off guard we pause, and in that silence, ancient-innocent fingers deep within us pluck at strings, so that we jerk awkwardly in the grip of self-spawned monsters of the mind-obsessions.

Defence Mechanisms

The more value that we place on upholding a emotional pattern, the more likely it is that all ambiguous signals will be perceived as supporting it. Evidence which counters it will most likely be overlooked or rationalised into a more malleable form. Conflict arises when dissonance occurs between desires and existing mental constructs (have you ever feared the strength of your own desires?) To cope with such conflicts, a variety of Defence Mechanisms can be adopted:

Aggression

A typical response to frustrated desire and loss of control; loss of devouring dreams. We can direct it at the source of our frustration, or direct it onto others.

Apathy

Loss of control—loss of face and self-worth. The machine stops.

Regression

Adult, who me? A return to a child-like mien. Cry hard enough and someone will come and comfort us. Perhaps we have learnt that through tears, we can control others.

Sublimation

In other words, putting a brave face on it. Re-directing the energy into a more acceptable form. But demons are cunning. Kick them down the front stairs and they will come sneaking round the back, waiting with spider calm until you leave the door of your mind ajar.

Intellectualisation

Displacing feelings with words. A quick lie for the aesthetic becomes a fast buck for the lay analyst.

Such strategies are normal; that is until they become obsessive: a locked-up loop automatic as breathing. Out of control.

Fantasy

Fantasy is the cornerstone of obsession, where imagination is trussed up like a battery-farmed chicken; catharsis eventually becomes catastrophic. Walter Mitty lives in all of us, in varyingly-sized corners. We use Starter fantasies to weave meaning into a new situation, Maintainer fantasies to prop up a boring task, and Stopper fantasies to persuade ourselves that it's better not to...

A fantasy has tremendous power, and in a period of high anxiety we can imagine a thousand outcomes, good and bad (but mostly good) of what the dreaded/hoped for moment will bring us. The fantasy exists in a continual tension between the desire to fulfil it, and the desire to maintain it—to keep from losing it. Of course, any move to realise it threatens its existence.

A closed loop is the result, shored up by our favourite defence mechanisms, whipped on by fear of failure and lust of result. The obsession clouds all reason, impairs the ability to act, makes anything secondary to it seem unimportant. It's a double-bind tug o' war. The desire to maintain the fantasy may be stronger than the desire to make it real.

In classical occult terms I am describing a thought-form, a monster bred from the darker recesses of mind, fed by psychic energy, clothed in imagination and nurtured by umbilical cords which twist through years of growth. we all have our personal Tunnels of Set; set in our ways through habit and patterns piling on top of each other. The thought-form rides us like a monkey; its tail wrapped firmly about the spine of a self lost to us years ago; an earlier version threshing blindly in a moment of fear, pain or desire.

Thus we are formed; and in a moment of loss we feel the monster's hot breath against our backs, its claws digging into muscle and flesh. we dance to the pull of strings that were woven years ago, and in a lightning flash of insight, or better yet, the gentle admonitions of a friend, we may see the lie; the program.

It is first necessary to see that there is a program. To say perhaps, this creature is mine, but not wholly me. What follows then is that the prey becomes the hunter, pulling apart the obsession, naming its parts, searching for fragments of understanding in its entrails. Shrinking it, devouring it, peeling the layers of onion-skin.

This is in itself a magic as powerful as any sorcery; unbinding the knots that we have tied and tangled; sorting out the threads of experience and colour-coding the chains of chance. It may leave us freer, more able to act effectively and less likely to repeat old mistakes. The thing has a Chinese puzzle-like nature. We can perceive only the present, and it requires intense sifting through memory to see the scaffolding beneath.

The grip of obsession upon us has three components:

Cognitive—our thoughts & feelings in relation to the situation. These must be ruthlessly analysed and cut down by Vipassana, banishing, or some similar strategy.

Physiological—anxiety responses of heart rate, muscle tone and blood pressure. The body must be stilled by relaxation and pranayama.

Behavioural—what we must do (or more often, don't do).

Often, our obsessive behaviour is entirely inappropriate and potentially damaging to others. Usually it does take other people to point this out. Analytic techniques such as *I Ching* or Tarot may prove useful here.

The wrath of the monster left me gasping and breathless, feeling trapped. All paths littered with broken glass.

Desperation drove me to a friend. There is magic enough in reaching out to ask another for help. An *I Ching* reading suggested action and non-action, negating the momentary trap of self-doubt. Pranayama banished the physical tension (well, most of it). The monster shrank and skittered on spindly legs through years of frozen memories, dissolving finally into a heap of mirrored shards.

Clues. I'm still fitting them together, but the pictures they hint at aren't frightening any more.

CTHULHU MADNESS

[*Cthulhu Madness* was written in 1995 and was originally published in the second edition of the Creation Press anthology *Starry Wisdom: A Tribute to H.P. Lovecraft,* and later incorporated into the second edition of my book on Lovecraftian magic, *The Pseudonomicon.* I was trying to convey the emotional entanglements and disorientations which, in my experience, are all too common in magical practice. Obsessions can be creative, but can all too easily tip into emotional disorientation and a sense of loss of self. Surfing the edge of trips to the edges of sanity can be difficult at times, yet ultimately, can be immensely rewarding—providing of course, one manages to come out of the other side of the event.]

———◆◆———

Each god brings its own madness. To know the god—to be accepted by it—to feel its mysteries, well you have to let that madness wash over you and through you. This isn't in the books of magic. Why? For one thing, it's all too easily forgotten, and for another, you have to find it out for yourself And those who would sanitise magic—whitening out the wildness with explanations borrowed from pop psychology or science—well, madness is something that we still fear—the great taboo. So why did I choose Cthulhu? High Priest of the Great Old Ones. Lying dreaming "death's dream" in the sunken city, forgotten through layers of time and water. It sounds so simple to say that I merely heard his 'call'—but I did. Gods do not, generally, have a lot to say, but what they do say is worth listening to.

I recall one evening staying in a friend's flat. I'd been 'working' with Gaia. No new-age mommy with a channeling about saving whales or picking up litter. I felt a pressure inside my head building up—something huge trying to pour itself into me. Sensations of geological time—layers sleeting through my awareness. The heat of magma; slow grinding of continents shifting; the myriad buzz of insects. Nothing remotely human. This sort of experience helps me to clarify my feelings on Cthulhu. Alien but not alien. A vast bulk stirring somewhere around the pit of my stomach. A slow, very slow heartbeat crashing through waves. Lidded eye peeling back through darkness, back through the world, the cities, the people walking outside, peeling back slowly. Peeling back through my entire life, all memories and hopes crashing into this moment. Waking from the dream of this to feel a stirring—a nagging disquiet; the absolute fragility of myself thrust back at me through crashing waves of silence. This is the sense of Cthulhu madness.

Cut to walking through a forest. It is pouring with rain. The trees are bare of leaves, slimy, mud churning underfoot. I'm seeing them as clutching fingers attempting to snare the sky; as winding tentacles. Cthulhu is all around us. It is a squid-thing, bestial, dragon-winged— a theriomorphic image, but such things are all around us, as trees, insects, plant life, and within us as bacterium, brooding viruses; born momentarily through the alchemical transformations taking place in my body even as I write. Hidden. Dreaming. Carrying on without our cognisance. Unknown beings, with unknown purposes. This thought builds in intensity, and it throws me sideways into realisation. That Nature is alien to us. There's no need to look for hidden dimensions, higher planes of existence or lost worlds of myth. It's here, if we but pause to look and feel.

The old Gods are everywhere. Their features outlined in the rock beneath our feet. Their signatures scrawled in the fractal twisting of coastlines. Their thoughts echoing through time, each lightning storm an eruption of neural flashes. I'm so small, and it (Cthulhu) is so vast. That such an insignificant being becomes of the focus of that lidded eye peeling back across aeons of time—well, it puts me in my place, doesn't it? My carefully-nurtured magician-self ("I can command these beings, I can!") goes into momentary overdrive and then collapses, exhausted by the inrush of eternity. Run away. Hide.

Having tried to break out of the mould, I have only succeeded in breaking down. I scream inwardly for my lost innocence. Suddenly the world is a threatening place. The colours are too bright and I can't trust them anyway. Windows are particularly fascinating, yet they too become objects to be suspicious of. You (I) can't trust what comes through windows. We can look out of them, but other things can look in. I press my hand to the glass. What secrets are locked into these thin sheets of matter? I would be like glass if I could, but I'm afraid to.

Sleep brings no respite. The eyelid begins to peel back even before I sleep. I feel as if I'm falling, tipping like a child's top into something... I don't know what. All pretence at being a magician has failed. This thing is too big. I can't banish it and even if I could, I have a strong sense that I mustn't. I have opened this door and unwittingly stepped through it, like walking deliberately into a puddle only to find that I'm suddenly drowning. Cthulhu's pulse-beat echoes slowly around me. Cthulhu is dreaming me. I was unaware of this, and now I am acutely aware of it, and wish to hell I wasn't. I want to sink back into unconsciousness. I don't want to know this. I find myself developing rituals of habit. Checking plug sockets for stray outpourings of electricity; avoiding particularly dangerous trees; you know the kind of thing.

I thought I was a rising star, yet I'm reduced to the four walls of my room. But even they won't keep these feelings out. Slowly, some self-preservation mechanism kicks into gear. Madness is not an option. I can't stay like this forever—another casualty of what is never mentioned in the books of magic. I begin to pick up the patterns I've let slip—eating regularly (at more or less the right times), having a wash, going out for walks. Talking to people—that kind of thing. I feel the sensation of the lidless eye peering out of abysses of time and memory, and I find I can meet that eye ("I") steadily. The environment ceases to be a threat. The self-protection rituals (obsessions) fall away, and after all, what is there to protect? The dreams change. It is as though I have passed through some kind of membrane. Perhaps I have become glass, after all. The thoughts of Cthulhu stirring down there in the darkness are no longer fearful. I find that I can, after all, ride the dream-pulse. What was that lidless eye but my own "I" mirrored through fear and self-identifications? I'm no longer haunted by strange angles. All resistance has collapsed, and I've found myself a measure of power in its place.

Of course, this theme is familiar to one and all—the initiatory journey into and out of darkness. Familiar because of the thousand and one books that chart it, analyse it, and, in some cases, offer signposts along the way. Which brings me back to why I chose Cthulhu, or rather, why we chose each other. There's something very romantic about H.P Lovecraft. The same romance which brings people towards magic by reading Dennis Wheatley. As Lionel Snell once wrote "When occultism dissociated itself from the worst excesses of Dennis Wheatley, it castrated itself for the worst excesses of Dennis Wheatley are where it's at." There's something gut-wrenching, exciting, awe-ful—romantic—about Lovecraftian magic. Contrast it with the plethora of books available on different magical 'systems' which abound in modem bookshops. Symbols everywhere—everything has become a symbol, and somehow, (to my mind at least), less real. Awesome experiences have had all the feeling boiled out of them, into short descriptions and lists—always more lists, charts, and attempts to banish the unknown with explanations, equations, abstract structures for other people to play in.

Lovecraftian magic is elemental. It has an immediate presence, and resonates with buried fears, longings, aspirations and dreams. The Great Old Ones and their kin can only ever be fragments of the mysterious, never to be codified or dried out for scholars to pick over. Yes, you can bounce gematria around until you've equated this god with that concept, and I do feel that gematria, if used appropriately, can become a thread with which you can begin to weave your own Cthulhu madness, tipping yourself into sub-schizoid significances. There are no Necronomicons—okay, I'll amend that, there are several *published* Necronomicons, but none of them for me do justice to that sense of an 'utterly blasphemous tome' which sends you insane after a thorough reading. If it does exist, it's in a library somewhere where you will have to go through madness to get the key, only to find that what works for you, probably won't make much sense to everyone else. After all, to some people, *Fanny Hill* was blasphemous. The whole point of the *Necronomicon* is that it is a cipher for that kind of experience which twists your whole worldview and, whilst the insights of that illumination are dancing around your head, impels you to act upon it—to do what 'must' be done in the fire of gnosis—whether it be Dr. Henry Armitage setting forth to Dunwich or Saul's conversion of the Greeks, the flames of his vision on the road to Damascus dancing in his heart. This experience, this core, out of which *magis*—power—bursts forth, for me is the core of magic—the central mystery, if you like. Gnosis of the presence of a god rips away the veils and leaves you gasping, breathless. Character armour is blown away (until it slowly accrues into a shell once more) and briefly, you touch the heart of that unknowable mystery, coming away with a shard embedded. It drops away, it works its way in, it becomes a dull ache, so we have to go back for more. Most of the 'set' magical rituals that I've done or participated in don't even come close to this. Yet all the magical acts which I have done, responding to external circumstance, the crash of events or some burdening inner need have thrust me into the foreground of the mystery. I can still remember seeing a witch priestess 'possessed' by Hecate. The eyes…weren't human. This year, in answer to my plea out of confusion and torment, the wild god Pasupati stooped down low and peered down at me, a vision of blazing whiteness, the after-burn of which is still glowing at the edges.

Real magic is wild. I can feel the near-presence of the Great Old Ones at night. When the wind rattles the window-panes. When I hear the growl of thunder. When I walk up a hillside and ponder on the age of that place. To feel them near me, all I would have to do is stay there until night fell. Stay away from the habitations of men. Away from our fragile order and rationality and into the wildness of nature, where even the eyes of a sheep can look weird in the moonlight. Outside, you don't need to 'call things up'—they're only a breath away. And you are nearer to Cthulhu than you might otherwise think. Again, it's a small thing, and rarely mentioned, but there's a difference between a 'magician' thinking he has a right to 'summon the Great Old Ones,' and a magician who feels a sense of kinship with them, and so doesn't have to call. Anyone can call them, but few can do so out of a nodding acquaintance born of kinship. There's a great difference between doing a rite, and having the *right*. But once you've faced a god, letting its madness wash through you, and change you, then there is a bond which is true, beyond all human explanation or rationalisation. We forge bonds with the gods we choose and with the gods which choose us. It's a two-way exchange, the consequences of which might take years to be manifest in your life. But then, gods tend to be patient. Cthulhu dreams.

Analytic Techniques for Sorcery Interventions

[*Analytic Techniques for Sorcery Interventions* was written in 1996, and as far as I can recall, wasn't published anywhere until it got onto one of the early incarnations of my first website. It is rooted in some of the magical work I did in the late 1980s and early 1990s with friends in Leeds, and later, London, to develop approaches which would help magicians to think more carefully about sorcerous interventions—particularly in respect to working with other people's problems and issues. The importance of this kind of approach is, I think, fairly well recognised now, but at the time we were thinking about these issues, there wasn't anything much available.]

———◆———

I sometimes think that attempting to influence a situation by sorcery is something akin to acupressure—hit the right spot, and you will get the desired-for result. The problem is though, that the 'right spot' isn't always immediately obvious, may shift from moment to moment, and isn't likely to be the same spot the next time you try to do something similar.

There is a natural tendency for magicians, when faced with a situation which seems to merit some kind of sorcerous intervention from us, to act on our fairly immediate impulses. This can result in a situation where we end up 'rushing in' and attempting to alter the situation without knowing as much as we could about it. Since fore-warned is often forearmed, I believe that using a range of analytic techniques to build up as complete a picture of a situation as possible, is beneficial to acts of results magic—it can mean the difference between 'firing blindly' and an aimed shot at what you want to bring about.

A few years ago, I was approached by a client and asked to attempt to magically favour an individual who was going to court on a number of charges. I was given a basic sketch of the person's situation and asked to aim for the 'ideal' of all charges being dismissed. Feeling that somehow I wasn't being told the full story, I asked a friend who was a shit-hot diviner, to do some tarot readings about the situation, in the hope that we might discover some 'hidden variables' in the situation. Out of my friend's readings came a good deal of information, all of which was later verified by my client, and, in my view, made the probability of all charges being 'dismissed' highly unlikely. Subsequently, I aimed for an outcome which I felt to be more reasonable, given the circumstances of the case.

What I am trying to get at here is that situations are often much more complex and less clear-cut than we often give them credit to be, particularly when we start reaching for our wands. I feel that a key to effective sorcery is not so much applying 'magic' into a situation, but at what point you apply leverage, and how you apply it.

A mutual friend of myself and Frater GosaA went into a depression after the break-up of her relationship of some years standing. She stopped going out and seemed to us to have lost much of her self-confidence. We thought it would be beneficial for her to have some new, interesting people in her life, and decided to enchant for this outcome. If someone isn't going out socialising, the likelihood of them meeting 'interesting people' is going to be very slim. Also, if they are feeling emotionally vulnerable and lacking self-confidence, they are unlikely to make the best of any opportunities to make a good impression. We made our first priority a progressive spell which 'tickled' our target's self-esteem and once a particular level of self-esteem had been developed, the spell began to work in other directions, unfolding into several different variables of the situation at once.

Using Divination Techniques

Divination systems can be extremely useful when preparing to intervene/influence a situation by means on an act of sorcery. The areas where their use is particularly worth considering are:

a) One's Own Self-Motivation

It can be very useful to examine one's own motivations to intervene, particularly if other people are involved in the situation—if you're working on behalf of someone, for example. I've occasionally found out, by questioning my own perspective of a situation, through a series of divinations, that my desired-for-outcome has, in actuality blinded me to alternative possibilities—both in terms of what particular approach I was taking to the situation, and over the question of whether it was appropriate for me to get involved in the first place. I remember once receiving an anguished call from an ex-partner who claimed to have received a 'runic curse' through the post from another ex-partner. Being fully immersed in using the Lesser Key of Solomon at the time, I fired off a batch of demons in the direction of the supposed source of the runic-curse, without stopping to consider the situation in more depth. Only later did I discover that the facts of the situation were not exactly in accord with what I'd been told and the conclusions which I'd leapt to!

b) The Situation/Event

There are numerous ways which divination can expand your information concerning a situation. You can, for instance, use the tarot to scan for 'hidden aspects' and then do subsequent readings on what is turned up. You can discover how different aspects of a situation sometimes relate in non-obvious ways, and what the probable outcomes of the situation are likely to be in different scenarios. if you're feeling particularly brave you could always ask if your magical intervention is likely to influence the outcome favourably.

c) Personality Profiling

If you have only minimal details about the key individuals who are involved in a situation, you can build up a 'personality profile' using divination systems (natal astrology may well be useful here), which can be used to make projections about a person's behaviour, attitudes, etc. This kind of profiling may come in very useful if you are probing for psychological weak spots.

Other 'Magical' Approaches

Apart from Divination systems such as Tarot, Runes or I Ching, there are other magical techniques which can become sources of analytic discrimination.

Intuition

I have found, over the years, that my sense of Intuition is fairly developed, and that I discount it at my peril. However, over-reliance upon one's intuition can be perilous. Having an intuitive feeling about what is the best approach to a situation shouldn't become a barrier to considering other perspectives and possibilities. Also, (and like much else of magical practice, this is a personal thing), I like to be able to work out (sometimes with a little bit of hindsight) the 'reason' for the explanation. Your intuition can be trained to work more effectively for you and stepping back from a situation and examining it dispassionately (rather than remaining entangled in it).

Oracles
You can seek oracles in many forms—from metaprogramming your dreams using sigils or servitors, to speaking with Spirits in vision, or questioning an entity astrally or through a human agent. I have (admittedly, only rarely) been given 'clues' on how I might conduct a particular working from a spirit familiar, but I wouldn't like to rely solely on such a source.

S.W.O.T Analysis
The SWOT acronym stands for: STRENGTHS, WEAKNESSES, OPPORTUNITIES, THREATS. It can be useful to analyse a situation in terms of these 4 points.

Strengths
Here you look at the Strengths of your position viz. the outcome—anything that is present in the situation which will help in manifesting your 'Mission Statement.'
Information you can particularly focus on here includes anything you know/can infer, etc. about the emotions/behaviours/attitudes of any individuals involved, how timescales may play a role in the situation (i.e., will leaving the situation alone for a month be more effective than working immediately?), or how tangential events on the fringe of the situation might be helpful.
Another point to consider is that, given your Mission Statement, what pathways are available for the outcome to manifest along? If you are about to bring about the collapse of a multi-national corporation which is very interested in turning your local sacred site into a car-park, have you pinpointed possible weak areas in its structures which, if slightly 'tipped,' could escalate into its downfall? Or, on another scale, if you're enchanting to meet the boy/girl/penguin of

your dreams, are you doing anything to enable such a paragon to walk out of your dreams and into your life?

Weaknesses

Under Weaknesses, you should consider anything which 'weakens' the likelihood of the outcome you are working for, coming about. This is a good point to maybe examine your desired-for result and consider whether you may be setting your sights too high, if only initially. Is for example, the scale of what you're attempting too large? Is it unfeasible to expect an instant outcome, when the constraints of the situation tend to point in the direction of a slowly progressive outcome? Is it perhaps unreasonable to try to influence another person in a way that is widely at variance with what you know about their personality? It may well be the case that the way you have defined your Mission Statement is, in itself, a weakness.

Opportunities

Under Opportunities, consider any strategies which can help you fine-tune the enchantment or open an 'opportunity window' for you. Is the target of your displeasure about to go into hospital for a 'minor operation'; is the person you're magically assisting to detox from heroin about to go into a clinic? Do you have a material link to the person you're trying to heal or a photograph which might help other people help you in your attempt?

Threats

Here, you consider what possible consequences there might be if your spell goes awry. Also, what might happen if there is a sudden change in the situation which you haven't previously bargained for. You may well find that only very occasionally can you conceive of any possible 'Threat' scenarios, but it does have some bearing for example, on malefic magics. I knew of one magician who seriously considered a death-curse on a relative, but who backed out when he was told that "a quick car-crash" wasn't very likely, but that terminal cancer, given the target's medical history, was much more likely to yield a successful outcome. The 'Threat' here, was that the sorcerer realised that he could not live with the consequences of giving a relative terminal cancer!

Conclusions

Whatever techniques you use to 'flesh out' your knowledge of a situation—to 'zero in' on a particular point of influence (or several, for that matter)—you may well find that your Mission Statement changes considerably in the light of what you find out.

I do find generally that intelligence-gathering is always useful and that there are comparatively few situations which can't wait a day or so whilst I poke at them from different angles. Asking people their advice is sometimes useful, as is playing 'devil's advocate' to yourself, if there is no one else who can do it for you. I have noticed that there is a tendency amongst occultists (as much as anyone else) to fall into a very black/white viewpoint of a situation in which they 'know best' (because they are a magician, of course). It's a common human tendency to simplify everyone else's situation other than our own, so I feel it is particularly important to approach every potential sorcery intervention as a complex, unique situation. After all, if someone out there was poised to start magically re-arranging *your* lifestyle for you, you'd want them to get it right, wouldn't you?

Summary Points
- Think before you Enchant!
- Ask Questions
- Gather Intelligence
- Analyse the Situation from different angles/perspectives
- Reform your Mission Statement if necessary
- Seek Clarity
- Then Act

Stirring the Cauldron of Chaos

[*Stirring the Cauldron of Chaos* was written in 1997 and was first published in *Chaos International* No. 15. Whilst a great deal of my chaos magic-oriented writing was concerned with the exposition of particular techniques and my own personal explorations, this essay is more reflective. By this time, I think much of the initial enthusiasm I had for chaos magic was beginning to wear off. The little aside about things not yet having been "painted...black and arranged...around a Chaosphere" is a reference to the increasing way that the eight-rayed star of chaos was being used in much a similar way to the Kabbalah's Tree of Life, or the ubiquitous seven chakras: as a means of arranging and ordering phenomena. My basic argument here is that magic and mysticism are complementary to each other rather than binary opposites, and that much of contemporary magical practice is very much framed within what I would later come to understand to be the Protestant work ethic. In this essay, I am very much coming down on the side of the Playful, rather than the Instrumentalist, approach to Chaos.]

Chaos Culture lacks an overall vision of progression into a shared future. Civilised progress is running out of steam, whilst pluralism & divergence twist the contemporary landscape into a fractal surface seething with new possibilities. Fragments of pasts & present rearranged by the blind hands of the new gods—fashion, style, entertainment; plundering the past to support an immediate now. This is the dizzying dance of Maya. Everything is Permitted because Nothing is True. Think about that for a moment.

No Direction Home

Critics of Chaos Magic have pointed out that Chaos Magic does not have any stated goal to strive for. Unlike other magical philosophies, which are spun around 'New Aeons', future dreams, or still cling to crypto-transcendentalist structures, Chaos does not have, at least on the surface, any overall goal. Other magical philosophies tend to have goals, be they 'spiritual' progression or a more humanistic ideal to which to spur the individual on. For Chaos there remains just the constant sharpening of technique & ability, the recreation and recuperation of new paradigms, the 'empirical' testing of new ideas, and whatever hidden agenda each practitioner of Chaos might choose to uphold.

It could be argued that, having dumped the concept of an overall future, we are free to dream and design any number of possible futures. Hence the Pandemonaeon: a Chaos future, which to a large extent, has already happened—the problem being, of course, that we lack the required cognitive systems to make the best adaptation to it. This idea in itself, throws the whole issue of a 'direction' for Chaos Magic into sharper relief; the ways in which we can cast forth future projections are couched in terms of present knowledge, present viewpoints, and the patterns through we structure information.

In attempting to disentangle contemporary magic from the trappings of religiosity or transcendentalism, advocates of the Chaos Current have taken up a pretty hard-line stand on the subject of Mysticism. They're having none of it, basically. So, while it is okay to applaud Crowley's practical magick, a hard-line Chaoist is likely to deplore his mystical writing. Of course, one might also consider the view that Crowley was a piss-poor magician but a superb mystic. But enough of mysticism. For now, anyway.

Gnosis

That peculiar experience of consciousness known as Gnosis is the key to all practical sorceries and magics. A good deal of magical practice revolves around developing the ability to enter Gnosis, and perhaps, in some cases, to recognise Gnosis. Gnosis is generally understood to be the 'peak' moment of any trance-inducing exercise whereon desire may be successfully phenomenized. But, I ask, is Gnosis merely that which is attained after half an hour's whirling, chanting or wanking over a sigil? All that dancing around just for that one brief, momentary lapse into else-where?

Gnosis can also be read as 'Knowledge of the Heart'—knowledge that is difficult to express immediately in words; a gestalt projection which might take years to filter down through layers of connectivity before it surfaces into words on a screen. The magical universe is, of necessity, a finite space. Gnosis may well propel us, momentarily, beyond its confines. And as William Burroughs has it, you cannot take words into space.

Gnosis, as the term is generally applied in Chaos Magic, is merely the visible tip of a vast range of numinous experiences which have, apart from a few intrepid researchers in Psychonautics, been viewed as the domain of mystics. While it is arguable that Mystical practices can lead to all kinds of word-viruses (such as religion), it is also worth considering that merely regarding Gnosis as that which is entered briefly, in order to phenomenize a desire, is an underestimation of the wider potentialities of this experience.

Work and Play

I will offer a simple distinction between Magic and Mysticism. Magic is about Work, whilst Mysticism is Play. These are not 'opposite' states, but complementary experiences. How so? Let us take an example of two acts of Sexual Magic. In the first case, we see a couple fiercely shagging, minds ablaze with a sigil, sweaty bodies humping towards that almighty release—orgasm—where sigilized desire is hurled into the void. Second case, a couple spend hours rolling around each other, lazily tasting, stroking, joking even, with no particular urgency to orgasm, the question of whether or not orgasms will happen at all, being not particularly important. Which do you think is the more magical of the two scenes?

The first scene reflects the general approach to sex-magic in Western Culture. Work: doing something to get something. The second scene is closer to a Mystic view of sex: relaxed, sensuous, pleasure-centered. Play.

We have to work at Magic. Doing training programmes, learning the symbols & languages, learning new skills; analyzing, refining, enchanting—it's all work. This is all very necessary, as we have to learn to Work before we can learn to Play, at least, as far as this subject requires. Here, Work and Play are experiences of the World, each complementing each other.

Again, another simple example. Again, sex. Chatting someone up, relating to a Significant Other, Copping Off—whatever you want to call it. One way to achieve this desire is through Work—which in this case might be practising chat-up lines into a mirror, or perhaps, invoking Jontrav-Olta as the patron spirit of smooth-talking sex-machines, to project the appropriate glamour in order to pull. This is Work, and I hope that all readers are at least familiar (if only in theory) with this kind of situation. The Play mode here is on one level simple, yet on another, complex in the extreme. Here, you merely make brief eye contact with someone else, and suddenly you Know with absolute certainty that somewhere in this unfolding event, two paths will converge and end up waking up in the same bed together. What is marvellous about this experience, as I expect most *Chaos International* readers will know, is that when that flood of certainty dashes itself through your mind, you are so confident about what is going to follow that initial moment, that you no longer have to Work to make something happen. You can afford to Play. And a person who is playing is free of attachment to the fulfilment of desire, and so may take more risks than a person who walks in terror of losing his cool and looking stupid.

These are two distinct, but not dichotomous experiences of the world. You can either work to make things happen, or Play and let things happen. But alas, it's not that simple. In practising Magic as Work, we prepare ourselves for Play. And the key factor which links both Work and Play is Gnosis.

Each time you attempt to phenomenize desire requires a burst of Gnosis-consciousness. Gnosis can last for a split second or propel you into a state of altered perception which can go on for days, weeks or even months. The effects of Gnosis are cumulative. Gain enough momentum and Gnosis begins to affect you in various ways: illuminations, waking dreams, hallucinations, voices, clairvoyant vision, the awakening of capacities which no one has taught you (and which did not come from a book, yet are there at your finger-tips). There is more. Heightened perception of self, of connections between disparate experiences and concepts, new gestalts. The surface content of these altered states is not as significant perhaps, as what is going on in the Central Nervous System. Peaks of Gnosis rewrite the neural paths, taking the mind's software up to a new version, geared for high-speed processing. Whilst the magician remains, to a large extent, centered in Work mode, this process remains as a hidden agenda. Indeed, it seems sometimes that you have to put a great deal of Work in before you can get to grips with the potential of Play.

So here I am arguing that Magical Work prepares you for Mystical Play. The difference can be understood in terms of manipulating reality to be one thing or another, as opposed to enjoying the dance in all its forms.

The problem with Mysticism is that the result of cognition whilst within a highly-accelerated state of consciousness can be perceived as some great, universal Truth. Also, it is necessary that the experiences one has are re-integrated and assimilated successfully when, as is inevitably the case, one returns to a more 'stable' sense of reality. Gravity hugs the free-flying psychonaut back into the well of Paramount Reality. At least, to a working approximation of such, as the magician progressively becomes something other than human. This is where previous Work experience becomes important. The ideational contents of the Mystical flight are useless unless they relate to the magician's extant mind-set. If the experience results in the ability to go beyond previously held beliefs and concepts and produce something new, then its validity is questionable. So gnostically-induced experiences of Play enable the magician to Work more effectively. By the same token, we need to have done a certain amount of Work to explore the possible value of Play.

Playing with Chaos

The Chaos approach to Magic has reversed the general view that magical abilities are merely the by-products of the Mystical quest. The emphasis is placed instead on Work, in manipulating Maya. In some ways, the idea of Mysticism's end-goal, as one of overcoming or transcending Maya, is a western misperception of a process which upholds the statement "Nothing is True, Everything is Permitted." From the experience of Play, success might well be easy, but 'failure' is certainly no harder.

I would posit further that the experience of Play leads us into new magical realms. That is to say, they are probably quite old ones, it's just that no one has yet painted them black and arranged them around a Chaosphere. Here we encounter the mysteries of our own internal cycles of change; cycles which have been buried away from the flames of perception; habits of thought and emotional response—

demons, if you like, which have so far crept quietly along in the cellars of selves-dom. Here we might choose to focus attention on those 'hidden gods' which around much of our interpersonal experience is based—love, fidelity, possession, curiosity—the undefinable words are suddenly eased into sharp relief and looked at from new angles. Yes, the Play state may be used for enchantment and the like, but only fleetingly as, in intense states of Play, the attachment to any particular desire is likely to be at best, fleeting. If such magic is done, it is done from a condition of Do Easy (*vide* Burroughs).

One of the best applications of the Play state I have found so far is the Creative connection and analysis of ideas. Anything from various Work practices (magical or otherwise) to less definable areas of experience: desire, cognitive habits, language. The relationship is a simple one—enough Work builds up momentum for Play. Play jumps us into a state where we can radically modify our experience of Work. Yet the background Work helps us to understand the dynamics of Play, and also opens up new areas for exploration.

To rewind back to the question of an overall goal for Chaos Magic. I would suggest that the goal is present, although yet hidden. Chaos Magic is a process of Mutation. Cumulative Gnosis remaps the neural pathways—mutation. The deconstruction of Identity from the beleaguered Ego into the legion Selves requiring only Self-Love—mutation. The search for the most effective and adaptive Work techniques so that reality becomes effectively, a playground—mutation. The seeding of culture with novel ideas, styles, fashions; the replacement of Truth with the permission to do—Mutation. But mutation into what?

Well, that's another story.

Paganisms

Introduction

If I have to describe myself using a label, it would be "Pagan". Regardless of whatever kind of magic I've been doing at any time, be it Wicca, street shamanism, Chaos Magic or Tantra, "Pagan" feels like a default setting.

My involvement with Pagan Activism didn't really kick off until the mid-1980s, when I moved to Leeds and became involved with PaganLink network. PaganLink was a kind of grassroots network with the aim of bringing Pagans in the UK together, starting local Pagan Moots, getting involved in political action, and so forth. There are various people who are now tagged as the "founders" of Pagan-Link, but my contact was the late Rich Westwood, who was the proprietor of an occult bookshop in Birmingham, *Prince Elric's*. I had met Rich at a psychic festival in Manchester and we chatted about PaganLink. Rich was a friendly and passionate man who strongly believed that to declare oneself to be a Pagan was a political act, and that part of that political sensibility was local and regional community-building through networking. At the time I was very keen to meet more people and was very willing to help Rich bring about his vision.

When I moved to Leeds I became PaganLink regional coordinator for West Yorkshire, which was just a fancy title for someone who was willing to give their address out, and help other local Pagans get in contact with each other. One easy way to do this was to revive the Leeds Pagan Moot, which had been active in the late 1970s—it even did a zine called "The Griffin", named after the Griffin Hotel in Leeds, where the Moot was held. One of the first things I did was to help revive the Moot and advertise it through the various magazines that were starting to spring up around the country. Other local moots followed suit.

Then came *Heal the Earth*. Heal the Earth was a mass ritual, aimed at getting Pagans in different localities to perform a ritual or magical act (we didn't specify what form it should be) on the day of the Summer Solstice, 1987, between 12 and 2 pm in the aid of raising people's awareness of the global ecological crisis. We discussed the idea of specific political issues, but in the end decided to aim for a general raising of awareness: "a ripple across the human planetary mind" as one person put it. I did learn some very important lessons in helping to get the event off the ground, principally, that other people's enthusiasm was essential in gathering impetus. Just being in a group of people throwing ideas around was a great experience, and then taking those ideas to other groups, and getting them all enthusiastic too was wonderful. I had been in a closed group which forbade open discussion of occult topics and ideas for so long that this was a really liberating experience.

Sheila Broun, a magical artist and teacher, let us use an image she'd created of the Ace of Cups as an image to focus on, and we worded the leaflet to make it as succinct as possible. The leaflets were displayed in shops, snuck into books and magazines, and distributed at festivals up and down the country. The Leeds group alone distributed about 7,000 leaflets—not bad for people mostly on low incomes—and we later found out that over 20,000 had been distributed. Was the ritual a success? I don't know. What is important for me, in hindsight, was the realization of how shared enthusiasm can quickly become a force for change.

One of the people I met through helping get *Heal the Earth* up and running was Rodney Orpheus, a Leeds-based musician who was really into computers. It was through Rodney that I had my first glimpse of the Bulletin Boards which were the precursor to the Internet, and it was with Rodney that I started up a free local Pagan-Link newsletter—*Northern PaganLink News.* The first issue of *Northern PaganLink News* (NPLN) was issued in March, 1988. It was four pages long and we ran off 25 copies and distributed them at local pagan events and through friendly shops. By May of that year, we were up to 200 copies an issue, and by June it had gone up to six pages and we had acquired publishing software and a high-end laser printer. We sent out the pages and encouraged other people to make their own copies and distribute them. The newsletter featured local moots, updates on PaganLink-related events and other events of interest to Pagans. By that time though, something had come along which we were increasingly devoting column space to—the Satanic Child Abuse panic.

The so-called Satanic Child Abuse moral panic ran, in the UK at least, from 1987 to 1992. In 1988, this early phase of the panic mostly took the form of anti-occult articles in the popular press, and the appearance of various experts in the media who were raising concerns about the growing popularity of occultism in society. For example, an article published in *The Sunday Express* newspaper (15 May 1988) named the Ordo Templis Orientis as an organisation which has "brought misery and degradation for hundreds of children" and urged the Home Secretary to investigate "evil cults." There was also some discussion in the popular press and parliament for reviving the UK's laws against Witchcraft.

In September 1988, Rodney and I took the momentous decision to drop the "Northern" and the "Link" from the title of the newsletter (as the distribution was wider than the North of England by now and the focus had enlarged from just doing PaganLink-related material) and *Pagan News*, "the monthly newspaper of Magick and the Occult," came into being, with a price tag of 30p for 8–12 pages. The printing was done by AGIT Press of Leeds, which was run by members of the band Chumbawamba. We managed to keep *Pagan News* going, first monthly, then bi-monthly, until 1991. We were helped enormously by a number of volunteers who helped us distribute the zine to local shops, by the few occult-oriented businesses that paid us to carry their adverts (our main source of income), and by the various columnists who agreed to write for us. *Pagan News'* editorial ethos was to be as eclectic as possible. We published articles on any aspect of the Occult/Pagan spectrum as long as it met our editorial guidelines for particular sections, which gave maximum word counts and set out our approach to editing. Our ethos was that Paganism could encompass a wide range of beliefs and we frequently expressed it in terms of the Vulcan philosophy of "infinite diversity in infinite combination" (we were both *Star Trek* fans). Occasionally we drew flak from readers for taking humorous digs at various sacred cows or for publishing "Left-Hand Path" material.

We were also resolutely against giving any credence to the "reality" of the Satanic Child Abuse scare, for which we were also occasionally criticised and lost subscribers. There were those within the nascent Pagan and Occult communities who wanted to distance themselves from those elements which they were suspicious of, such as anything related to Aleister Crowley, Thelema or whatever could be bundled under the rather broad umbrella of the "Left Hand Path." It was not unusual, during this period, to find self-professed 'White

Witches' grabbing their own fifteen minutes of media fame by claiming that whilst the majority of Pagans were good, law-abiding citizens, there were some "darker elements" that needed to be weeded out.

When I talk to people now about what it was like to be openly Pagan during the period of the Satanic Child Abuse scare, it is often assumed that this was a grim and horrific period in British Pagan history in which nothing much went on in public and people kept their heads down. This wasn't my experience. After all, it was in this period that the first large Pagan conferences were held. A two-day event at Leicester University in 1988 had over 5,000 attendees, for example. Occult art exhibitions were being held in public libraries. Pagans *were* becoming more public, and unfortunately, this was a time when some members of the Conservative government saw this as a threat to "traditional" Christian values, which in part, generated some of the anxieties which emerged during the Satanic Panic.

This was also the period when, thanks partially to the development of relatively low-cost personal computers and desktop publishing applications, there was a mushrooming of small Pagan and Occult magazines across the UK, from generalised, news-oriented zines such as *Pagan News,* to those that catered for particular occult traditions. As I became more confident in writing, I began to write for a wide range of publications, ranging from Rich Westwood's Pagan-oriented *Moonshine* magazine, to *Nox,* a "Left-Hand Path" journal for 'hardcore' occultists. On one memorable occasion I wrote a short 'biography' of Satan intended for *Nox,* but decided to see what would happen if I submitted it to *Moonshine,* whilst sending a piece on Shamanic practices—originally intended for *Moonshine,* to *Nox.* The editor of *Nox* was quite happy with the Shamanic essay, and *Moonshine* did use the piece on Satan, although later I heard through the grapevine that the editors were less than enthusiastic about it, and that anything further of a similar vein would not be accepted. I also heard from one of my friends that he'd been asked if there were two "Phil Hines" as some folk found it difficult to accept that the same person could write about shamanism and Pagan issues as well as the more *outré* areas of occultism.

Labels are odd things. Over the last forty years of my occult life, I have worn—and in some cases been given by others—many labels:

Wiccan, Pagan, Chaos Magician, Tantric practitioner, Urban Shaman, Independent Researcher, to give but a few. Labels can give a handle, or a way in to understand the parameters of an individual's orientation or mode of practice, but they are frequently constraining, too. I see Paganism very much in terms of a permissive space within which many ideas and attitudes—some conflicting—can flow.

POLITICAL RITUAL RECONSIDERED

[*Political Ritual Reconsidered* first appeared in issue 8 of *Moonshine* magazine, at the Winter Solstice of 1987. This short article was written at a time when the idea of doing mass ritual actions was gaining some traction in UK Pagan circles. Perhaps unsurprisingly, some people were of the opinion that this sort of thing could be done safely in the confines of one's bedroom (or "on the astral"). This essay was a call to direct action, both in terms of organising community events and street theatre, and to take seriously the idea that direct magical intervention in a situation could be efficacious.]

———

The injection of a political dimension into Western magic has had a number of encouraging side-effects, these being:

1) Mass ritual generates community and raises the scope for further collective action.

2) It helps draw together people of differing orientation through the commitment to bring about change.

3) It is empowering: re-emphasising the inner certainty that we can act to make a difference.

4) Feedback from participation in such rites is directly proportional to the initial input given to power the rite or build its organisational structure.

Having made these positive points about our enterprise it is necessary to look critically at the process and look for ways and means of extending the politicization of magical activity. A first point to make is that it does matter what kind of power-raising technique you utilise for the ritual. The most convenient technique is solo meditation, but solo meditation is not the most effective means of raising energy: drumming, dancing, chanting, hyperventilating—the more energetic ways of raising power are preferable. When this is done by two or three people, better yet.

The site of the ritual is also important. The back bedroom is probably the easiest, but again, ease is not the prime consideration here. To go outside is preferable, particularly some high place where you can see a large tract of land about you. Obviously, the more effort you take in organising something, choosing a site, getting people together and deciding what is to be done, then the more special the event becomes. And special the event must be if it is going to be effective in any way. Remember that this is a Sacred act being performed—which is not to say that it must be totally serious, just don't go about it in a half-hearted fashion.

Since the targeting of present political ritual is the group consciousness of the world at large, or at particular sections of the populace, the results of such workings are going to be subtle and long term. There is no reason why we should be content with this situation, so it is necessary to look for other ways in which we can intervene as a magical act.

Our Christian brethren are in this respect way ahead of us. When the more militant Christian sects get wind of something they find morally reprehensible, they organise a pray-in to stop it going on. A small group, empowered with daring and will (and a little knowhow) can throw quite a number of "spanners" into the machinations of the state and the corporate "idiot-gods."

Out Demons Out

This is the sharp end of political ritual—selective psychic terror waged against those institutions and dogmas which maintain the current levels of psychic/physical pollution.

The first point to make is that targeting these rites of resistance is of the utmost importance. It must be in an area which is going to bring about some kind of result. Trying to "waste" individual figures is rarely any good. To use the 'beast' analogy—chop off a head and five more grow in its place. So, put away the pins and Ronald Reagan image dolls.

More useful is the idea of cursing institutions rather than individuals. Complex and delicate data networks have been shown to be highly susceptible to magical interference, and there are a wide range of electro-elementals and gremlins who can easily be persuaded to go and play around with the hardware of some company who's been messing you about.

Magi-Prop

The most subtle forms of opposition are those which are not immediately recognisable as such: those which are aimed not at the waking awareness, but the deep mind. The best example of this kind of Sorcery is the advertising media. Its very banality lulls us into a false sense of security whilst the real message sneaks in unawares. To counter this, the politically-inspired magician must be equally, if not more, cunning. The least effort for maximum effect, using secret weapons: humour, superstition and chaos, to counteract stupidity and narrow-mindedness.

Assuming you have some kind of code or identifiable ideals, print them on a broadsheet and hand them out to local shoppers. You never know, someone may be illuminated by your words.

Such is the role of the shaman—to inject chaos into order and shatter reality for an instant, opening the gateway to liberation. In other words, be sneaky. Leave a false name, proclaim a new age of enlightenment, not to your friends, but to total strangers. Become a legend in your own lunchtime. Don't hang around to quibble, exit stage right! But most of all, don't get caught.

THE REACHOUT REPORT

[*The Reachout Report* appeared in the May 1990 issue of *Pagan News*. This editorial comment was written two years into the "Satanic Panic" which gripped the UK. I was trying to draw attention to the point that the media attacks on Pagans and Occultists fuelled by Christian fundamentalists should be taken as elements of a much wider campaign to restore conservative 'family values' in the UK.]

Two years ago the anti-occult campaign inspired by fundamentalist groups started the press hysteria, led by 'have a go' MP Geoffrey Dickens and the gutter press. It hasn't stopped since, and shows every sign of getting worse. Groups like *The Reachout Trust*, and *Christian Response to the Occult* have orchestrated a countrywide campaign to 'inform' national and local press alike about the 'dangers' of the occult. using powerful emotive hooks—the Family, and children 'in danger.' People have tried to dismiss them as a few cranks and extremists, but it's not that simple. It's not just pagans & occultists who are under fire. The last few years have seen a steady erosion of civil liberties in the UK. Britain has its own 'Moral Majority'—a collection of peers, knights, ministers, academics, journalists and other professionals. They have influence on industry, the government, and the ear of the press. Bodies like *Family and Youth Concern, The Conservative Family Campaign, Family Forum,* and *The National Family Trust* all believe that "the family must be central to all political thinking." They are the people who inspired Section 28 and have successfully applied pressure on central government to abandon its AIDS campaign. Dame Jill Knight, whose 'unofficial' parliamentary committee on 'satanic child abuse' is presently gathering information, is one of the people who helped promote *Family and Youth Concern's* video "The Truth About AIDS", which they tried to force every school in Britain to take. The Campaign for Real Education submitted detailed proposals to the Secretary of Education, some of which have ended up in the new syllabus. This should give you an idea of how much influence these groups have—and how much they can achieve.

Groups such as *Reachout* are now instructing their members to campaign to try to get *Prediction* magazine removed from the shelves of chain distributors like W.H Smith & Sons, and Menzies. They have at least learnt that scripture-quoting and banner-waving tends to put people off. Instead, they are going for the approach of being 'concerned parents.' With rank-and-file members complaining to local shops, and with the *Evangelical Alliance* applying pressure at director level, this approach suddenly doesn't sound so ludicrous, does it? *Reachout* are now claiming that they have managed to pressure W.H. Smith into issuing an internal directive ordering that *Prediction* be stacked on the top shelves where pornographic magazines are usually placed. They are also complaining to the Director of Education about subjects which have 'occult elements' and have harassed teachers that they have discovered to have a pagan background. They are well-versed in the art of manipulating the press through complaints to TV stations and newspapers. In a tape entitled "How to Deal with the Occult in Your Area", Maureen Davies boasts of how she has picketed Transcendental Meditation meetings, and even presented a case to hospital management about why TM is dangerous to health. TM and similar techniques are widely used in the National Health Service as part of relaxation training for people with a wide variety of problems—but as far as the Fundamentalists are concerned, it's a doorway to Satan. Anyone who teaches it, therefore, is suspect. Now as we all know, TM is a fairly innocuous practice, so one wonders what chance more in-depth approaches have of surviving the fundamentalist onslaught?

Maureen Davies tells her followers to go 'right to the top' when complaining—that's to senior management—who are usually very concerned with the threat of bad press and will cancel an event or meeting—or take other action in line with fundamentalist demands. Apart from a few notable exceptions, the major response that the pagan community has managed to come up with is along the lines of 'it's not us who's to blame, it's someone else'—which is not very convincing or helpful.

I'll keep on repeating it till it gets through—they are out to suppress all minority beliefs and practices which they see as being a threat to their conception of how society *should* be. We need to be building bridges with other minorities that are at risk, not trying to hide behind barriers, hoping that they'll go and bother someone else. They won't, and they've got the resources for a long, and escalating campaign. As was reported last issue, they are buying magazines like *Pagan News* to find out names, addresses and phone numbers of local contacts. In their newsletter, *Reachout* recently asked subscribers to 'pray' for the 'enlightenment' of misguided people like myself and the editors of *ORCRO* (Occult Response to Christian Response to the Occult) magazine—a form of cursing, perhaps?

Assessing the success of the anti-occult campaign so far is difficult. While it remains true that the general public tends not to be concerned one way or the other, fundamentalists have been successful in that they have created a press barrage and the appropriate hysteria that allows them to bring pressure onto government bodies, where they already have a great many allies—people of influence who have the ear of ministers and Whitehall mandarins. The implication is that right-wing and fundamentalist pressure groups are 'steering' the policy-making of central government, and officers within the Department of Health are already complaining that they cannot control the influence of fundamentalist-motivated groups. They are so highly-connected, however, that they cannot be ignored. The proof of their power, in the case of Pagans, will be the appearance of fundamentalist-inspired legislation against us. Are we going to sit back and wait for it to roll over our heads? Probably. A recent letter to *Pagan News* gave the view that 'any good magician has nothing to fear'—so much for 'community spirit,' eh? It's not just a question of 'Pagan rights,' but the erosion of human rights. How easy is it to have an outdoor gathering these days? How many psychic fairs have been subject to last-minute cancellations? Let's face it—so far Pagans and Occultists have been a soft target for the fundamentalists; good copy for the gutter press; a nice carrot to rope in respected groups like the National Society for the Prevention of Cruelty to Children; easily divided against each other; no ability to lobby or organise counter-information as a whole; plus an innate tendency to ignore 'material' affairs and politics. They don't see us as individuals—just a homogenous group of evildoers masquerading under a variety of guises. A couple of years ago, some U.S. senators tried to sneak a bill through Congress which 'defined' witchcraft, in order to pass anti-occult legislation. Thanks to the Bill of Rights and well-organised lobbying, it was thrown out, but there is no such safety net here. Our government recognises only Christianity as a legitimate religion, and individual 'rights' have no protection whatsoever.

So where do we go from here? Keep quiet and hope it all goes away? Some of us don't have that option, and in writing this article I've probably added a few lines to a file on some shadowy fascist database. So far, the only organised response is via the *Sorceror's Apprentice Fighting Fund* and the *Pagan Federation* who are actively involved in countering and lobbying against the fundamentalist aims. Making links with other groups who are having their freedom constrained would also be helpful—the Fundamentalist ethic wants women chained to the sink, Lesbians & Gays back in the closet, and anyone who aspires to 'alternative' lifestyles suppressed. If anyone's got any good ideas, I'd like to hear them. A basic tenet of Pagan philosophy is that morality and ethical responsibility comes from within, but if we're not careful and attentive to what's happening, we will very soon find ourselves hamstrung by an imposed definition of what we are in the eyes of those who make policy. Sure, they cannot take our beliefs and values away from us, but they can make it more difficult for us to live. Life could be made very difficult for anyone who is running a small business related to the occult. Some pagan families are already having problems from people who've reported them to social services and police. Our freedom to gather together is being restricted. How much worse does it have to get? It's easy to become apathetic or frustrated, but we must persevere. Use your magical skills not to lash out, but to ground yourselves so that you can act—with calmness and persistence. Adversity such as this could be a great opportunity for us to reach out to each other (despite differences in path or lifestyle), and give support where it's needed. If the only thing which unites us in action is the desire to preserve our freedom to live as we wish, without interference, then let this be our clarion call!

Magic in the Great Outdoors

[*Magic in the Great Outdoors* was written in 1994 and delivered as a lecture at the London Eco-magic Conference of that year. This essay is a series of reflections on the various ways that Pagans and Occultists relate to Nature—from idealised romanticism to treating outdoor spaces as just a larger version of an indoor temple—and cultivate a readiness to both acknowledge and discard preconceived ideas.]

———•◦•———

Pathworkings and Guided Visualisations are a very popular form of magic. But have you ever noticed how, when you're being led along a path through a sacred wood that you never step in any cow-pats? That when you sit down next to a sacred spring to hear the wisdom of some inner-plane guide, you're never plagued by ants or wasps? This is an example of what I feel to be the tendency to idealise Nature which can be discerned in elements of contemporary Paganism and the occult.

It's so insidious that we don't tend to notice it. It seems to me that although there is much writing about elements, faeries, spirits and sacred places, we are often looking at Nature through rose-tinted spectacles—and the messy, awkward and occasionally downright dangerous aspects of Nature are omitted, or at least ignored. In some ways, this is understandable. Many of us live in urban centres and the desire to escape them and experience Nature more directly is very strong. Yet at the same time, it's easy to underestimate the power of Nature. I grew up in a seaside town where the awesome power of the sea struck me forcibly at an early age. One memory which will never leave me is being taken to see a trawler which had been literally hurled up onto the sea-wall during a storm. I learned to swim in the sea and thought I could handle it until I was nearly killed a couple of times, and it was not unusual for each holiday season to be punctuated by a couple of deaths of holidaymakers who did not realise how capricious the sea can be. And this I feel is true every time we wander into the wilderness. A couple of years ago, a simple trek around the foothills of Snowdonia led by two experienced mountaineers suddenly became, for me, a near-death experience. In the wild lands, anything might happen, and in my experience, does, particularly when you think you're 'safe.' Safety can itself be a complex issue, particularly when we do magic with other people and when we go outdoors.

In my own experience, even doing guided visualisations set outdoors can have unpredictable results. In the mid-1980s I was training as an Occupational Therapist and working in a psychiatric hospital in York. I was sitting in on a group therapy session where the facilitator was using guided visualisation to help the group members explore their feelings about being with other people. Part of the journey involved the group wandering into a forest until they could not see each other for the trees. Suddenly, one of the participants jumped out of his chair and shot out of the room. I followed him to find out what the problem was. It turned out that the last time this person was in a forest, it was during the British retreat from France just prior to Dunkirk. He had become separated from his unit, but could hear their screams as they were hunted down and shot by the enemy. An extreme example perhaps, but something worth bearing in mind.

Coming back to magic, I've never been happy about doing 'formal' rituals outdoors. Rituals which feel okay within a temple, cellar or spare bedroom just seem to feel out of place in the middle of a woodland glade. All that stuff about casting a circle or 'banishing'—which is basically about establishing boundaries—just feels plain wrong. I've often felt that there's a tendency, particularly amongst modern magicians, to take an 'indoors' ritual and perform it outdoors without any awareness that being outdoors might require a different approach and some basic respect of the different space that one has moved into. At times this has led to some ludicrous situations. A few years ago, whilst I was doing a three-day seminar in Austria, I attended a session being led by another facilitator, wherein we were asked to visualise being in a forest. Nothing wrong with that in itself, but the venue we were at, an ex-Knights Templar castle, was surrounded by about 15 acres of prime forest! Another time, I was outdoors with a group and one of the rites which had been decided upon beforehand called for people to hide themselves behind trees and bushes—the problem being that where we were, there weren't any. So instead of calling off the rite, it went ahead, and I recall feeling somewhat bemused by it all. In retrospect, I see this as an example of a group imposing its preconceptions onto the outdoors space, rather than trying to work appropriately within it.

Some years back, a friend and I decided to go into the depths of one the larger parks in Leeds to see if we could establish contact with the local spirits of place—the genius loci, if you like. Rather than taking the established magical route of doing some kind of ritual, we simply walked into the woods and found a spot by a stream and sat quietly, attempting to widen our perceptions to feel a brush of contact, no matter how faint. After a few hours, we both agreed on feeling a sense of something tentatively reaching out to us. Gradually, we began to discern a shape—huge, shaggy and mossy—not a water elemental or an earth elemental or even a tree spirit (those are terms, after all, which we impose onto the world), but something which was an encapsulation of the place where we were. The contact was fleeting, wary, but overwhelmingly one of sadness and yearning, something we both found difficult to put into words yet which touched us deeply. This for me was an important experience showing the value of 'throwing away' the rulebook, as it were, and learning to trust feelings in respect to contacts with 'spirits.'

How we look at spirits is, in itself a key issue. There is a great deal written about 'nature spirits'—elementals, devas, faeries, etc.— but they are often made out to be nice or at least controllable or amenable to contact with us. There are two issues within this. One is that whilst modern pagans have accepted 'Nature' spirits, it seems to me that there is a block about accepting that there might be other kinds of spirits such as the impish spirits which lurk around overloaded electrical sockets, the vindictive ones who hide your house keys, or the spirits who flit around the underground late at night. We walk in the woods, yearning to meet dryads or faeries, but would we expect to encounter a troll in the backstreets of Birmingham? We are learning to get to grips with the genius loci of outdoor spaces, but perhaps not giving enough attention to the 'souls' of the cities where we live yet are equally deserving of our attention.

The other issue is this whole 'spirits are nice' kick. In my own experience, many 'nature' spirits are just plain angry. Angry at what humans have done to their places. Angry at our unthinking invasion of their spaces. Really pissed off about being patronised, ignored for so long, or even at times, 'invited' by pagans & magicians into spaces which they already regard as their domain, thank you very much. Just like us, some are okay, some aren't, and will, if given the chance, let you know in no uncertain terms how they feel, one way or another.

Having ranted thus far, I find I don't want to offer any prescriptions for how I feel one should take magic outdoors, except perhaps to say this: It comes down to respect. If, as pagans we say that we respect the land and its inhabitants, we have to act from that premise at every moment. This requires, for me, forgetting much of the book-received 'knowledge' about spirits, sacred places, etc. that I have accumulated over the years and experiencing Nature as it is, rather than perhaps how I'd like it to be. Recognising that whenever I go outdoors with magical intent in mind, that I'm moving into someone else's territory where what I want to do isn't necessarily important, and being ready for being informed that they'd rather I did it someplace else. Of being aware that a place that felt welcoming during the day can be downright forbidding in the dead of night, and that whatever I think of myself as an 'experienced' or adept magician, this might count for nothing with *them*.

MUST WE LOVE THE GOLDEN BOUGH?

[*Must We love the Golden Bough?* was written in 2010 and appeared on *enfolding.org*. This essay is a reflection on the popularity of Frazer's classic work *The Golden Bough*, and the tendency for occult authors (myself included) to indulge in sweeping generalisations and "top-down" theories which are not rooted in experience or based on evidence.]

⤙⬦⬥⤚

What is it about Pagans and *The Golden Bough*? It seems like every time I open a book written by a Pagan or Magician, there it is, casting an inescapable shadow over the text, like the monolith in *2001: A Space Odyssey*. Recently, in exploring a quotation that paraphrased some of Frazer's "data," and delving into some of his secondary sources, I found myself reflecting (and not for the first time) on why Frazer's work—which contemporary anthropologists, folklorists and mythographers have been at great pains to distance themselves from—still remains popular in Pagan & occult texts. In a way it is not surprising given the influence that Frazer's mammoth work has exerted on the twentieth century. Indeed, Robert Brockway professes that:

> "...it is no exaggeration to say that everyone interested in myth from the turn of the century to World War II was initially inspired or strongly influenced by reading *The Golden Bough.*"
>
> — Robert Brockway,
> *Myth from the Ice Age to Mickey Mouse* (p.157)

Frazer's work had a direct influence on Yeats and Margaret Murray, to name but two prominent names in the history of modern occultism, as well as Freud, Jung, Eliade, and Campbell.

Chas C. Clifton, in his contribution to *Researching Paganisms,* laments the continued presence of Frazer (and others) in contemporary Pagan writing:

"Thinkers whom the contemporary academy regards as exhibits in the museum of ideas, such as the anthropologists Frazer and Bachofen, or Margaret Murray as historian of witchcraft, still loom large in contemporary Pagan writing, despite the critiques of academic Pagans. For example, the scanty bibliography of a rather vapid new work entitled *Philosophy of Wicca* lists Frazer's *The Golden Bough*, Robert Graves' *The White Goddess*, and of course Margaret Murray, but not Ronald Hutton, Carlo Ginzberg, or any other deeply rooted contemporary historian. This author is not unique, unfortunately, and it is easy to conclude that an attitude of 'don't confuse me with new ideas' is at work." (p.93)

Whilst I'd agree, to some extent, with what Clifton is saying, I don't think it is quite as simple as the conclusion he offers. I don't want to get into a sustained critique of Frazer; that's been ably done by better people than I, although my principle problem with *The Golden Bough* is the way Frazer blithely and uncritically lifts aspects of culture out of their social and historical contexts which give them meaning, as Ruth Benedict highlighted:

"Mating or death practices are illustrated by bits of behaviour selected indiscriminately from the most different cultures, and the discussion builds up a kind of mechanical Frankenstein's monster with a right eye from Fiji, and a left from Europe, one leg from Tierra del Fuego and one from Tahiti, and all the fingers and toes from still different regions. Such a figure corresponds to no reality past or present..."

— *Patterns of Culture,* 1934

Yet, at the same time, I'd argue that this is precisely what makes Frazer's work attractive to Pagans and Occultists, and that a great deal of occult writing is distinctly Frazerian in style (although often without his citations, which make it hard for a reader to chase up an author's sources). Frazer is often criticised as being an "armchair anthropologist"—writing from the lofty position of an ivory tower, disengaged from having to deal with actual, living people. It strikes me that a lot of occult writing (in which I include my own work) uses a similar strategy, making sweeping generalisations (without Frazer's acknowledgement of partiality) from the panoptic perspective of "occult truth." What's also attractive about Frazer is that he doesn't burden the reader with what may be perceived as the unnecessary complications of modern anthropology; the discussions of theory; the all-too-often opaque language; the constant referencing of other theorists one is expected to be familiar with in order to get to grips with the author's work. It's easy to detach Frazer's "data" from his own views and treat it as self-evident evidence for one's own argument.

A key theme underlying Frazer's writing is that all "savage peoples" are pretty much the same. His impetus for writing *The Golden Bough* was to document savage people's beliefs before they all died out in the triumphant march of civilisation. Much of nineteenth-century anthropology is pragmatically oriented towards the concerns of colonial administrators—the people who need to understand the quaint beliefs of the primitive folk they are in charge of to manage (and civilise) them more effectively. For Frazer and his colleagues, such as his mentor Tylor, the notion of sympathetically engaging with the conceptual framework of a different culture—one where people believed in magic, spirits, etc.—was quite alien, and to them, an impossibility.

Frazer's work is also heavily symbolic, showing the influence of Herbert Spencer's assertion that the reality of nature is radically inaccessible to the human intellect. All that we can know of the world are the "feelings" which it somehow generates in our perceptual apparatus—perception therefore has nothing in common with that which provokes it: "the sensations produced in us by environing things are but symbols of actions out of ourselves, the natures of which we cannot even conceive." (Spencer, 1862). For Frazer, social life is a kind of institutionalised expression of symbolism—a representation of something else, and his mission is one of decipherment or interpretation. *The Golden Bough* is like a never-ending hall of mirrors, with symbol being linked to symbol by analogy—a continual deferral of meaning. A symbol is always explained in terms of other symbols, which bear no relation to any real-world referent. Frazer openly acknowledges that the explanations he offers will never be definitive, they will always be conjectural, partial: "All our theories concerning him [primitive man] and his ways must therefore fall far short of certainty; the utmost we can aspire to in such matters is a reasonable degree of probability." It brings to mind the old joke that if all the sociologists in the world were laid from end to end they would never reach a conclusion, and certainly plays well to the exponents of cultural relativism in contemporary occulture, often expressed, as did a correspondent last year to me in terms of: "all we can do is speculate." A great deal of occult writing uses the analogical mode in a similar way to Frazer—Kenneth Grant being just one example, with his fantastic leaps between gematria, fiction, mythology, symbolism and "initiated" occult commentary.

What's strange about contemporary Pagan deployments of Frazer, is that he's generally antithetical to magic, although again, it is not quite that simple. In his preface to the second edition of *The Golden Bough* (1900) he presents his view that magic is fundamentally distinct and opposite to religion and also, "I believe that in the evolution of thought, *magic as representing a lower intellectual stratum,* has probably everywhere preceded religion" (my italics). He also stresses that both magic and science share a similar worldview: "In both of them the succession of events is perfectly regular and certain, being determined by immutable laws, the operation of which can be foreseen and calculated precisely, the element of chance and of accident are banished from the course of nature." Like many of his contemporaries, he believed that European "civilisation" was superior to all other cultures—particularly "savage" ones. He thought that magic was misguided "savage science" and that all cultures progressed from a magical worldview to a religious, and ultimately rational, scientific mentality. I can see that Frazer's diametric opposition between magic and religion plays well to Pagans and Occultists who are equally keen to keep a distinction between the domains, and equally, his assertion that magic and science share a similar worldview (although he does think that magic is fundamentally a misunderstanding of scientific laws, and that savage peoples do not entertain any ideas about how magic "works").

I mentioned, at the beginning of this post, that I'd been chasing up some of Frazer's sources—particularly the group of Russian anthropologists whose accounts of shamanism, like Frazer, are widely referenced and cited, particularly in texts that seek to establish the global antecedents of shamanism.

Again, whilst these authors are heavily cited in passing, if you actually read their reports you get quite a different picture of their views on shamanism. Imagine this scenario: a group of anthropologists breeze into your local Pagan community, and later publish their findings along the lines of, "Well there's people called witches. A lot of them are neurotic and hysterical and given to strange fancies, and some of them are, well, sexual perverts. They believe in magic and spirits, but no one can take that seriously, so we have to conclude that any effects from their magic is basically trickery or fraud." Somehow, I can't see that kind of analysis getting cited in contemporary occult texts, yet that's pretty much the tone I read from anthropologists such as Vladimir Bogoraz.

So then, are we still enthralled by the dazzling patterns of light displayed on the monolith, or can we—whilst acknowledging its influence—look past it towards the dizzying complexities of the world around us? Do we celebrate difference and diversity or blot them out in favour of finding safety in superficial comparison? It's too easy to be dismissive of Frazer, but equally, it's too easy to continually recycle him. Pete Carroll's apt phrase "I'm sick of occult ideas which pass from book to book without any intervening thought" springs to mind.

PRACTICE

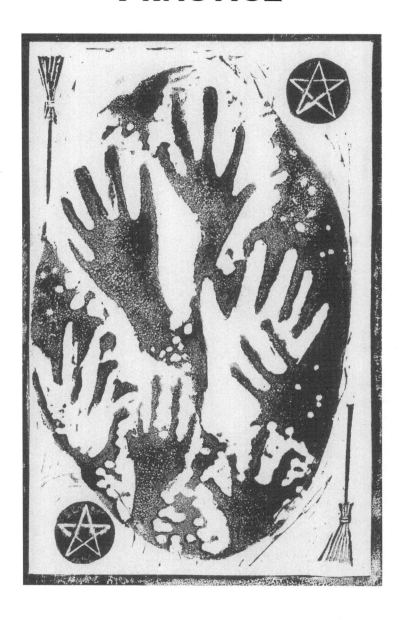

Introduction

A good deal of my written output over the last thirty-odd years has been directed towards exploring and reflecting on various aspects of magical practices. I was first encouraged to write about practices by one of the Wiccan High Priestesses I was training under. Her opinion was that writing about a practice was an excellent way of checking that one had understood it well enough to communicate it effectively to someone else. Of course, there was the added benefit that the written material could be then passed on to another person who was beginning the practice. I wrote a good deal of this kind of "how to do practice x" material in the early 1980s, most of which I haven't kept.

What constitutes a Practice? When I first began reading occult how-to books in the late 1970s, practices were things that you set aside time for—that were different to your day-to-day life. You set out (or were given) things to do on a regular basis, did them, and recorded the results in your magical diary. Simples. But then, perhaps not.

I find that writing about practice tends to lead me into reflections regarding the nature of practices. One thing that interested me early on is the relationship between practice and theory—particularly how they are seen to be opposed. Generally, "Theory" is conceived as being abstract and impersonal—it is concerned with explaining the world, rather than acting on or in it. From theories are derived "rules" which can be applied to practical situations. Yet there is a widespread perception of a theory-practice gap where students often feel that the theory they've been taught in universities and other institutions has no direct relevance for their practice. Equally, in practice-oriented disciplines, there is sometimes a suspicion of those who appear to veer too far towards the "theoretical." In some of my early work on Chaos Magic, I wrote that what attracted me to the Chaos Magic ethos was the emphasis on practice—the idea that it was more important to get down and "do" magic—and that one didn't have to imbibe huge drafts of "theory" before getting down to doing something practical. Of course, this suspicion of theory is widespread in contemporary culture. But gradually I came around to the idea that theory *informs* and shapes practice.

This was a side effect, I feel, of my engagement with Indian material. I'd been put off by the "theoretical" approach to Indian religiosity due to my early readings of Theosophical material and later, the books of Sir John Woodroffe. Something that struck me early on, as I began to read translations and ethnographic accounts of Indian religious and magical practices, was that some of the things we tend to take for granted in the West—such as the idea that there is a hard divide between mind and body, or that imagining the presence of something is inferior to it actually being there—just doesn't seem to operate in the same way. I realised that I had been approaching Tantra from a Western mindset, essentially viewing it as similar in its underlying assumptions to the Western ideas I had grown up in, and not even considering that the philosophy underpinning the practices might be quite different. One of the things which is repeated time and time again in popular works on Tantra is that it is *practice-oriented.* It is not theoretical or philosophical in its nature. Whilst it is largely the case that, in general, Tantric texts have more to say about ritual than philosophical hair-splitting, this does not mean that Tantra does not have a theoretical basis or that Tantrik practitioners in India did not write philosophical works. Frequently, they did.

This also led me to reflect on the relationship between theory and practice in my earlier experience of Wicca, Ceremonial Magic and Chaos Magic.

I have spent a lot of time writing about what is sometimes disparagingly referred to as "Basic Practices". The notion of a hard distinction between "Basic Practices" vs. "Advanced Practices" is something of which I've become quite critical. I've met people who've undergone courses in "Basic Practices" and then never revisited them again, or who have skipped over the boring basics, and gone straight for what they consider the "Advanced" practices in a tradition. Nowadays, I tend to think in terms of "Core Practices" rather than "Basic Practices." Core Practices are foundational—they are those applications which we constantly return to.

Another important aspect of Practice for me is the experience of being in a magical group. I have been involved with—and occasionally facilitated—a wide range of groups, from the formal hierarchical structures of magical orders to fluid and informal groups of friends working together. There's frequently an assumption made that a competent magician will naturally make a good group leader, but I found that this is rarely the case, and that leadership is a skill that requires hard work and the cultivation of insight. Although magical groups do share in the dynamic processes of groups in other settings, they do have some unique characteristics—as you might expect when magic is added to the sometimes volatile mix of getting people together to perform a task.

Rites that Go Wrong

[*Rites that Go Wrong* was written in 1992 and given as a lecture to the London Philos-o-forum discussion group. It is basically a string of anecdotes and quips organised around exploring the idea that magic, contrary to how it is sometimes written about, does sometimes go wrong or result in surprises (even scary ones) of various kinds and how magical mistakes can be instructive.]

———

I am indebted to the indomitable Reg for suggesting the subject of tonight's talk. Magicians are all too eager to hold forth about the rituals that work—the superb invocations, the powerful evocations and the money-working spell after which you find a tenner lying in the street. But what about the rituals that don't come off as planned—the invocations when the deity doesn't manifest, the Results Magic that doesn't come up with the goods, and the workings which leave you with a sense of 'was that it?' Tonight, I'll be looking at some of the magical 'wobbles' that I've experienced and discussing how they changed my life—or perhaps didn't—and some 'wrongs' that have occurred to colleagues. On re-reading, it looks like yet another Hine excuse for multiple anecdotes, but what the hell, eh?

Why Rituals don't Work

Reading Pete Carroll's mathematical exegesis of magic, I sometimes get the impression that if a ritual goes wrong, it's because someone got a decimal point wrong somewhere. The explanations that we often use to describe how magic works—you know, morphic fields, butterflies flapping their wings, and so forth, are all very well, but reading them, I often get the impression that magic shouldn't, all things considered, miss the mark. In some circles, occultists fall back on the argument of 'ah well, the tides were against that particular working' or 'it wasn't my Karma for that spell to work.' Spot the cop-out clause? Under these arguments, if your rite works, then it's ego-stroking time; if it didn't, then it's the fault of some cosmic agency.

And anyway, what do I mean when I use the phrase 'Rites that go Wrong'? In the case of Results Magic (Sorcery) this would refer to spells to bring about a specific condition that haven't manifested yet. In which case I might argue my way out of that one and say that 'the Universe is still working to manifest that one'—i.e., the cheque's in the post. For Invocations, 'going wrong' might be when the deity being summoned fails to turn up. Well, I'll go into that one in a while. Of course, a lot of magic doesn't require hard-core results; subtle stuff like personal development & so forth, where you can only judge the 'results' over time.

Results Magic

Results Magic or Sorcery is concerned with bringing about specific changes in your conditions. One of the simplest approaches to Sorcery is using sigils. The important thing about sigils, I would stress, is getting your intent as precise as possible; vague 'wishing' tends to give rise to vague results, in my experience. However, there are other factors to bear in mind as well.

Right then. Sex.

Hands up everyone who's ever done a sigil to get laid.

Me, too.

Works doesn't it? Well, most of the time.

A while ago, I did a Temple of Psychic Youth sigil with the intended result of bringing about a much-desired sexual fantasy, and no, I'm not telling you the details. Needless to say, it hasn't worked...yet. And for what it's worth, I'll treat you to my own reasoning behind this. A core part of the sigilisation process is allow-ing the desire to become latent—that is, you don't allow it to resur-face into consciousness. Seeing as the sigil was for an extremely powerful desire—an obsession, even—I'm probably too bound up with that particular scenario to let it become 'latent' and so manifest. To do so, I'd probably have to rework some of my lust-complexes. If I did, and then the opportunity arose to 'manifest' the result. I might no longer be interested. Then again...

A 'traditional' magical line is that you shouldn't place too much strain on the Universe. There is the old adage of a magician who does a spell for money and waits for the multiverse (like Santa) to provide. He doesn't do anything to 'help' the desire manifest, and so his result manifests by him getting insurance compensation after tripping over a loose stair carpet in the dole office and breaking both legs. A successful result, but not in the way he expected it. Which if nothing else shows that the Multiverse has a slappy sense of humour.

Invocations

I've often been at group rituals where the deity being called upon descends, not into the chosen priestess or priest, but into someone else. This can be embarrassing for all concerned, especially as in most of the rites where I've seen this occur, the whole thing as gone ahead as normal, whilst one of the celebrants is standing/sitting there totally zapped. Only afterwards do you get the mutters of 'Kali was in me, not so-and-so,' etc. The other point to mention is that after an invocation, not all entities will obligingly go away. Some refuse point-blank, and have to be cajoled, threatened or plied with alcohol. This isn't so much 'failure' though, as an unexpected level of success. Magicians should beware the unexpected. A friend of mine once did some conjurations of 'Dark Gods' in his flat. Good Chaos Magician that he was, he banished with laughter. However, 'something' was still around and whatever it was, it literally kicked him out of bed. Laugh that one off.

York, 1985 and I was performing an invocation of Baphomet with the High Priestess of the coven I was then half-in. Again, 'something' in the room objected. Whatever it was pulled a heavy poster off the wall—it didn't just slide off, oh no, it looked for all the world like someone was peeling it back from the wall, at a right angle. After that went, my stereo speaker plinth started rocking. We took the hint, banished, and went down to the pub.

Sometimes, I have thought that a ritual had gone wrong, when in fact it hadn't. Two illustrations spring to mind here. The first is when a colleague and I attempted to get through to the wizard Amalantrah—one of Aleister Crowley's inner-plane contacts. We were setting up a new magical group at the time (Dark Star), and, flying in the face of discussions in the zines about Holy Guardian Angels, etc., decided to have an 'inner-planes adept' or two heading the Order. I recall the rite fondly, as a circle of fairy lights and a chocolate Easter egg were part of the temple props. To cut a long story short, we got through to old whatzis-face, but he wasn't interested in sponsoring our temple, as it were.

The second one was an invocation of Thoth—again, during an attack of Thelema. The whole thing went smoothly, except Thoth didn't manifest in any discernable way: no 'inner voices,' no visions, nowt. What a let-down. Except the next night, I was asked to do a tarot reading using the Thoth deck. It went on and on—for about five hours—and I realised that I had a lot of realisations about the cards, etc. Again, the unexpected.

Talking about 'unexpected results' there's Eris to consider. She's got one helluva odd sense of humour. We did a working once on behalf of someone with Eris as the powering current. The rite worked for that person, only they got a whole heap of shit with their result to work through as well. As for me, the following day, I locked myself out of my top-floor flat, necessitating a climb over the roof (it was raining) to get back in; my computer monitor suddenly 'died' on me; and a condom split, causing a few days of anxiety for myself and the other person concerned. Hail Eris!

Nowadays I tend to more-or-less hold the belief that if I do a working, it's *going-to-bloody-well-work*! Having said that, I'm careful to only attempt things which have a good chance of coming off—not straining the fabric of the wossname too much.

I can recall, many years ago, doing a pentagram ritual and thinking "oh shit—I just did all the pentagrams wrong—and, like, nothing noticed." And if they did, I haven't been stitched up by something nasty—yet. In the first proper group I was in, I was brought up to believe that if you crossed a ritual circle once it was set up, then it gave you a nasty turn. Later, I was somewhat taken aback when I was visiting another group one time, and they were in and out of the circle like yo-yos. Still, I suppose it was good practice in disciplining people to do their wee-wees before the ritual and not halfway through the invocations...mind you, for some people that is their idea of ritual.

But this isn't answering the question of why do Rites Go Wrong? I think Group Dynamics, or perhaps, the lack of awareness of, can explain some occult gaffs. A typical example is the instance where no one really knows what they're doing, but is either too nervous to voice this, nor do they wish to look a prat in front of their colleagues.

To maintain magi-cred, it's not usually considered good form to say "Erm, I don't understand why we're doing this bit." Mind you, if it turns out that nobody else does, then this could mean trouble all 'round.

Not Having the Right Attitude

Not having the right attitude is probably responsible for a few gaffs. There was this time we did a Mercury ritual. Tricky bastard, Mercury is. (Mind you, aren't they all?) There was this couple—not taking it seriously—probably still hoping that after this ritual there would be an orgy after all. Everyone else got their desire manifested. They got their house broken into. So what is the 'right attitude'? Difficult to define, but I think playful seriousness probably sums it up for me. Get too serious and you tend to get pompous. Get too playful and you'll get on other people's nerves—possibly including the entities you're working with.

Not Bothering to Banish

Not bothering to Banish is always good for a few sticky moments. Okay, there are times when you don't have to banish anyway, but you need to develop a sense for this, and I have met numerous people who have started off by saying that they 'never bother with banishing' and have gone off their heads. One acquaintance burnt all his magical books, cut a pentagram into his chest and was last seen being held down by burly nurses.

This is a good point to mention Loonies. Yes, we've probably all met magical Loonies. The scene is full of them. The Maguses; reincarnations of Aleister Crowley; people who have astral battles with imaginary black lodges; and the ones who think they're gods. In my book, going loony is a magical mistake. Well, it's supposed to make you a better person, isn't it? So, if you end up boring people stupid then you've done a whoopsy somewhere. Simple guideline: if you go loony and pull out of it, then it was an 'initiation.' If you stay a loony then it was a mistake. You might think that you've crossed the abyss, kicked the crap out of Satan and discovered a whole new set of initiation titles for yourself, but if everyone else thinks you're a prat, then it's tough shit. It's easy to do your head in with magic. If you consistently invoke the same deity, it's quite likely that you'll end up obsessed by that deity. Sure, invoke often, but variety please.

One of the Leeds magia a few years ago did too many invocations of Pan and was last heard of wandering around Newcastle city centre displaying a proud erection, and declaiming himself to be the person-ification of the male principle and where was his Priestess? What he did get was a manifestation of spirits clad in blue with accompanying sirens.

Over-Confidence

With magic, it pays to have a certain amount of confidence—if you're not sure what you're doing, I think that this can sometimes lead to a working going awry. But with confidence, you can have too much of a good thing. If you're totally confident about how some-thing's going to work out, then you're less likely to adapt quickly if something doesn't happen as you think it should.

1981 and I am part of a group watching a Priestess go into trance. Lie still, relax, mumble mumble. Fine. Nothing we didn't expect. Suddenly she starts twisting and groaning and generally doing things that we thought weren't supposed to happen. Somebody sprinkles consecrated water on her. Someone else draws a pentagram over her—she gets worse. By this time people are panicking and who's going to volunteer to go out and ring an ambulance? General consternation. What do we do? Eventually she comes back, and is not pleased. Didn't we know that she was fighting a demon and our well-meaning efforts were getting in the way? Minus 10 million points of karma and stand in the corner of the temple 'til you've memorised the laws of Witchcraft.

Likewise, what do you do when someone won't come out of trance? Leave them to it? Call their name gently? Tickle their feet? Throw a bucket of water over them or slap 'em round the chops? Books on how-to-do magic don't tend to mention this sort of occur-rence—you give the license to depart and off goes the entity back to wherever-it-was they manifested from. You hope.

Sometimes rituals go wrong because something that sounded okay during the planning didn't actually come out right when being done. Some friends of mine planned to do an Odinic working. I forget the details, but it involved hanging someone in a tree. The arrangement of ropes did something horrible to the volunteer's circulation and he had to be taken down. That rite was aborted.

Similarly, the problem with becoming over-reliant on other people's ritual scripts is that it's hard to improvise if you're not used to it. One group I was in was on one occasion doing that old Wiccan favourite, 'The Descent of the Goddess into the High Priestess,' after which the Priestess would declaim the Charge of the Goddess. That was the plan anyway. However, after stumbling over the first two lines, the next thing we heard was, "Oh shit, I've forgotten the rest" followed by a fit of giggles. Okay, we all forget our 'lines' now and again, but if you can't improvise in such moments, then it can lead to a sudden 'deflation' of any ritual atmosphere that's been carefully built up.

Being Wet

I think a key point about doing ritual is that if you're going to do it, do it with a bit of jazz or style. Imagine you're an actor on stage and put a bit of life into it. You may not believe that the Gods you're invoking are real—but if you were up on some lofty spiritual plane, would you bother dragging yourself all the way down to the lower astral for some drip who erred, ummed, and declared the invocation with about as much enthusiasm as Robert Maxwell answering back to the tax inspector? And call those pentagrams...? Magic works very much on the principle of nothing in, nothing out. If you can at least act as though you're summoning up powerful forces from beyond space and time, you might get somewhere. If you're into ritual at all, then it's quite likely that, somewhere amongst your legion of selves, there's a drama queen screaming for recognition. So be flamboyant. Put on a good show and the gods will reward you, give good reviews, come back for more and tell their friends about you.

And this brings up something else: asking gods to do things for you. This can be tricky. Asking Kali to blat the guy in the next flat who plays his stereo too loud when you're trying to meditate is a bit like using a tac-nuke to swat a fly with. It is said by some that gods have a different sense of time than we do and our sense of 'now' is a lot different to theirs. I got the impression, when doing some work with Isis a few years ago, that she wouldn't actually get around to doing anything for a few thousand years at least. Elementals are easier by far. Though, again, they can be tricky. I blame all this magical psychology. It lessens the impact of all the entities and let's face it, if someone came up to you and said, "You're only a subpersonality of me, so do this sharpish mate" would you go for it? No, you'd punch them in the face (hopefully) and half the time I think that entities feel the same way about all these jumped-up magicians saying "do this, do that" without so much of a please, thank you or a decent sacrifice.

If, at gatherings of the occult hoi-polloi, you actually admit to a working going wrong, some clever dick is bound to point out a flaw in your research. Like, "Oh you didn't invoke the wossname through the right portals, nor did you have the right colours on the temple banners and you did the dance widdershins." That kind of thing. After discussing our abortive Amalantrah working with a member of a certain O.T.O. faction I was given the clue: "Well, you see, the inner-plane adepts are in a period of silence at the moment," which presumably meant they were all 'out to lunch' or having a quick nap. Ergo, it followed, the entity who we got through to, and claimed it was Amalantrah wasn't; it was something else posing as an inner-plane adept. It was the chocolate Easter egg that screwed thing up, I know it. Needless to say, I pointed out that we had gone through all the usual tricks to test the validity of the entity. Did the fact that we had done it without a Scarlet Woman zonked on ether make a difference? End of conversation.

I'm not a great fan of this kind of explanation. Most 'systems' seem to have whopping great contradictions in them. For example, no one has ever been able to give me a good explanation of why the sphere of Hod in the Qabalah is given the elemental association of water. I never spotted it until we did a series of Hod workings last year, and no one has come up with a satisfactory explanation since. Still, I digress.

Nevertheless, there do seem to be some ground rules in certain types of magical operation. Take Goetia. Ooer, yes, summoning demons. A couple of years ago we did a whole series of evocations from the Lesser Key of Solomon. For the first working, we thought "why bother with all this circle & triangle on the floor stuff—we'll just visualise 'em instead." The main result of that was that we both suffered nausea and a 'drained' feeling for a couple of days afterwards—a sort of dark hangover of the soul, I suppose. And the demon didn't come through very clearly. It turned out that Goetic demons have fairly 'traditional' ideas about how they like to be invoked. None of this trendy stuff for them. Either we did it properly or we'd have a strike on our hands.

Dreamweaving
This is a nice trendy-sounding name for what often amounts to little more than intense fantasising so that you continue to dream about what you were thinking about before you drop off to sleep. What often happens is that you drop off to sleep anyway. This can happen with pathworkings, too. You're leading a pathworking with the whole group laid out in front of you, you're using your best 'pathworking' voice and then suddenly, there it is...snoring. I recall dropping off in a pathworking once. Everyone else had wonderful visions to report. Then it was my turn. "Well, actually I was so knackered from the drive down here I just fell asleep." Cue look of faint disgust/superiority from everyone else present. I used to worry about my tendency to drop off to sleep whilst practicing 'astral' banishings in bed. No problem, as it turned out.

It seems to be a part of magical learning. Whilst you class yourself as a neophyte, you sort of 'expect' things to go wrong and are continually over-stating the consequences of what 'orrible thing might appear if you do something wrong. Once you've knocked around for a bit, you're more confident about what you're doing and when something does go wacky, you're often less prepared for it. These days I try to go for a mix which is: if I do this working then something will happen, but I'm not 100% sure what. Magic involves taking risks. If nothing else, getting into a sticky situation will give you a new perspective on things.

1979. I'm doing Psychology at Poly. Doing some work with Tattva cards & elementals. Magic is just an extension of psychology is what I'm thinking. Ha bloody Ha. I wake up one night. There's a red mist in the room and it feels like someone has dumped a suitcase full of concrete on top of me. ...oh sh*t.

I can't move. I can't speak. What the f**k do I do. Heavy.

Eventually I projected a banishing pentagram outwards. The feeling of weight vanished, as did the mist, and I promptly went into gibber mode. For about two days. Okay, so I had one of those experiences when you think you're awake but you're not. At the time though, it really threw a scare into me, and it gave me a deeper respect for magic. So that was okay, in the end. Ah the days of youthful folly.

Not long later I did my first attempt at evoking Yog-Sothoth. You know, one of the most 'orrible of the 'orrible Great Old Ones. Being on the edge of the Peak District, I had some good mountains to choose from and chose one of the highest in the district. It was snowing, too. I took a torch with me and can still remember the eyes of sheep reflecting red in its beam. Spooky. I don't quite remember the details, but I do recall seeing a beam of light coming down from space onto the stones I was sitting on. The next thing I can recall is getting the hell out of there in a blind panic and turning up at a friend's house. More gibbering. I don't know whether that was a failure or a success, but once again I managed to scare the shit out of myself. Perhaps at the time, it's what I needed.

It may be that we learn far more about magic and ourselves when things don't quite go according to plan. If magic was as easy as some people make it out to be, we'd probably find it too pedestrian and we'd be a secret cabal of Christians plotting the downfall of the Pagan Aeon or something. No. Magic, like life, is wacky, weird and wonderful. It's never ceased to amaze me that by standing in a room, waving your arms about, and spouting awful verse, you can change the atmosphere, how you feel, and possibly set off a stochastic process that will result (more or less) in what you want to happen, happening. We can theorise, argue and woffle pedantically all we like, but the core of the mystery I don't think will ever be pinned down.

I think it's extremely difficult to judge magical results entirely in terms of success and failure. My experiences with doing magical sigils for example, have shown me that quite often the results don't manifest until I've thought, "Well bugger this, that was a waste of time"—and then they pop up. Some magical approaches do in fact recommend that you work occasionally for a negative result—and the opposite will come along in due course. Any magical act should be instructive, especially when it doesn't go the way you planned. Let me finish then, with some magical axioms to bear in mind:

1. Invoke Often
2. Banish Often
3 Do it with Style
4. Keep a sense of Perspective
5. When caught out, Improvise

MASTERS, MENTORS, TEACHERS AND GURUS

[*Masters, Mentors, Teachers and Gurus* was written in 1997 and made its first public appearance on an early incarnation of my first website. It is an examination of the role of the mentor in esoteric pedagogy, as opposed to more traditional teacher-student relationships.]

———

We can learn about magic in a variety of different ways. For most of us reading books is probably the primary source. Other routes to learning include correspondence courses, workshops, receiving instruction within a group, and entering into a one-to-one relationship with a teacher. When information on magic was relatively scarce, teachers were in much demand as keepers of knowledge that was otherwise hard to come by. Nowadays, of course, this is no longer the case, due to the plethora of occult books, magazines and the World Wide Web. In fact, some would argue that on this basis, there is no need for individuals to seek out teachers when information on magical techniques and practice is (relatively) widely available.

There is also a recurrent discussion over how many self-styled teachers, spiritual masters, and gurus are only concerned with boosting their own egos at the expense of their students, and fucking around with them (often literally!). There is a great deal of suspicion directed at individuals who appear to want others to perceive them as teachers. Having said this, occult contact sheets ring to the pleas of people who are looking for teachers. Why? One factor, which needs to be understood are the general beliefs concerning initiation. Many books which deal with Western forms of magic hint, to varying degrees, that to attain magical proficiency, the student needs to find a proficient teacher—someone who will initiate a student into 'the mysteries.' In some circles, there is a measure of status ascribed around whether a person is initiated by a recognised teacher, or merely self-initiated—that is to say, self-taught. I recall during my stint in a Wiccan coven that the elders would occasionally refer to one person or another as self-initiated, the implication being that these self-initiates were something of second-class citizens in comparison to people who had been initiated into a coven. The idea still persists that to be a 'proper' magician, witch or shaman, you have to have been initiated by someone else or have studied under a master. Related to this is the popularity of non-western esoteric systems, be they from the Orient, Africa or the Americas. When one looks at the pseudo-ethnic magical systems, such as the various brands of shamanic practice, the pan-African traditions or the various Oriental esoteric systems, the link between personal progression and being initiated/finding a guide becomes even more explicit. What should be remembered here is that in the cultures from which these systems are drawn, attitudes toward esotericism, teachers, etc., may well be markedly different from western perceptions. Westerners, in their zeal to appropriate non-western (or pre-industrial) magical systems, may well forget or overlook the background culture in which these systems are rooted. For example, the term "Guru" in India is associated with a filial relationship between teacher and student that is somewhat alien to modern westerners, where rebellion against the previous generation (i.e., the move towards individualism) is a far stronger cultural imperative than obedience and veneration for one's elders, and by extension, for a received historical tradition.

The relationship between teacher and tradition is important, as many contemporary occultists are seeking a strong relationship with a sense of tradition, a feeling of continuance between modern practice and what the ancients did. It should also be recognized that teachers can be something more than keepers of knowledge. In our information-rich culture, the role of the teacher shifts from someone who doles out knowledge to someone who may be able to help us steer a path through that information by helping us to sort out what is relevant for us, and how to make it meaningful to our lives. I remember an elder magician that I used to visit for chats about magic. I regarded him as a teacher, but he always said that we were "equals—sharing information." On one occasion, I asked him for advice on using a pentagram made out of curves—something which I'd thought up, but was unsure about. He said something along the lines of "Interesting. Go and try it out and let me know what happens." This gave me the confidence to go and try out my own ideas. Things that weren't in books, which is largely all I had to go on. It is this kind of relationship which makes a teacher valuable to the learning magician and is vastly different to the popular view of magical teachers as individuals who, by virtue of their 'Higher Initiation' have a license to spout pretentious bullshit in return for adulation and slavish obedience.

Those of us who have been immersed in magical activity for a number of years sometimes forget, I feel, how weird it feels to be taking one's first steps into the magical world. It's fairly understandable that when we find ourselves moving in a direction which is new and relatively unknown, we look for others who can assist us, and magic is no exception to this. Feelings of uncertainty and risk are considerably diminished if we have someone we know we can turn to for encouragement and help, particularly if things get sticky or strange. Handling uncertainty is different for everybody. There is likely to be a marked difference between someone whose only contact with the occult world has been to read a few books and from them gained the conviction that they need to find a teacher, and an individual whose opinions on the subject of teachers and magic as a whole has been widened by contact with the occult milieu through magazines, discussion groups, or the internet. So, in general, I am in favour of people forming learning relationships providing, of course, that all parties concerned are aware of what the relationship is about and what is going on. To clarify these issues, I will explore the role of the Mentor.

The word *Mentor* originates in Homer's *Odyssey*. Mentor was the teacher of Telemachus, the son of Odysseus. The Mentor-figure is a key image in Greek Myth, seen for example in the initiatory relationship between Achilles and the Centaur Chiron, and over the ages the word Mentor has become synonymous with friend, trusted adviser, guide, counsellor, teacher and initiator. There are also numerous examples of Mentor relationships in history, such as Freud and Jung, Socrates and Plato, and perhaps Aleister Crowley and Alan Bennett. What is special about the Mentor? The original Mentor's task was not just to raise and educate Telemachus, but to prepare and develop him for the responsibilities he would have to face as the heir to a kingdom. A Mentor, then, is much more than just a teacher: a Mentor is someone who offers knowledge, insight or perspective that is especially useful to the other person. The essence of Mentoring is difficult to pin down as it is part intuition, part feelings, arises out of the given moment, and is composed of whatever materials are at hand. Mentoring requires the capacity to be flexible. The Mentoring relationship is one which leaps beyond other formal relationships. Helping someone cope with a personal problem is not necessarily Mentoring. But even a casual remark, if it sparks a new understanding or perspective on a problem, revealing previously unknown aspects in a flash, could be considered Mentoring. Magical history is replete with examples of such flash illuminations, from the legends of Zen, Tantric and Taoist sages, to the meeting between Crowley and Theodore Reuss, during which Crowley intuited the secrets of sexual-magic. One of the tasks, then, of a magical Mentor is to illuminate the student. For me the major difference between a mentor and a teacher is that whilst the teacher says "Do this," the mentor is more likely to say, "What do you want to do?" Teachers can tend to dispense rules and take over the process of interpreting metaphors on behalf of the student. Mentors, however, act to assist us in the conscious recapitulation of experiences, so that we are no longer blindly following someone else's rules or squashing the world into limited metaphors long past their sell-by date.

The central focus of Mentoring is the empowerment of the student through the development of his or her abilities. To do this effectively requires that the Mentor respects the uniqueness of that person. We can see the results of dysfunctional teaching when we meet so-called magicians who appear to be little more than mirror-reflections of their teachers, who lack independent voices, and hold the world at bay with their belief-systems which (as Peter J. Carroll once quipped) "act not even as crutches for the feeble, but broken legs for the incapable." The tendency to teach magic to others cookbook style, rather than encouraging individuals to twist techniques and theories so that they are relevant to their immediate life experience, is responsible for much of the blinkered, narrow thinking of many modern occultists. I suspect that this is due to the fact that many teachers have a position to cling to which involves keeping students around them rather than letting them go off and pursue their own interests. Some of the best Mentors, in comparison, are those who view the mentoring process as a learning experience for themselves.

The idea of ageless wisdom, passed down from Mage to Neophyte is an endearing one, but is inaccurate in a world of constant, accelerating change. Mentoring requires both work and responsibility for both parties in the relationship. It is a partnership between Mentor and student, based on mutual respect. Both Mentor and Student contribute and gain equally from the relationship.

However, having said this, it must also be recognised that both Students and potential Mentors need to be clear about what expectations they bring to the relationship. For the relationship to be effective, these expectations must be made explicit.

Mentoring is based on a friendly, informal relationship, and any attempts to extract firm promises from either side is likely to end badly. This is not to say, however, that some form of agreement between Student and Mentor is not useful. If both parties have made their expectations from the relationship explicit, then an agreement can act to remind both parties of specific objectives which have arisen from their mutual work, and secondly, it can be drawn on occasionally to clarify the boundaries of the relationship.

This latter point is particularly useful in magical Mentoring where it is easy for the Mentor's influence to extend beyond the boundaries of the immediate magical relationship—which it often does under a variety of guises and justifications. The desire for this can come from Mentor or Student, or may arise unbidden from the sharing of intense magical experiences. Similar issues are not unknown between therapists and clients, nurses and patients, or teachers and pupils.

Over the years I have done a good deal of magical Mentoring. Gradually, I have evolved an agreement for these relationships which is along the lines of: "This is a meeting of my previous magical experience, with your inexperience and insight (which stretches me to attempt things I have never tried before), which will bring something out which is new and valuable for both of us. What I want out of this relationship is that at some point in the future, when you excel in one aspect of magic beyond me, you will come back and teach me about it." I am happy to report that nine times out of ten this has largely been what has happened.

This sort of code can be seen as a general agreement, as something which a Mentor can make explicit at the beginning of a relationship, and bring up only when the situation befits. There are also more specific agreements, which relate to objectives and goals set between the Student and Mentor, and which can be adjusted, periodically evaluated, and are, of course, subject to change.

A key theme in understanding the value of the mentoring relationship is that of dealing with change. Change takes place within an ever-shifting personal and social environment. Giving up familiar and comfortable beliefs, behaviour and, occasionally, relationships tends to be accompanied by a sense of loss. There is also fear of the unknown, or possible failure to contend with. Change is, of course, central to magic. Often, the hardest thing to get to grips with is our resistance to change, or the refusal to admit that we, and our lives, are changing almost on a daily basis.

The key to this process is that of Context Shifting—which can be understood as an adjunct to, or an extension of, Belief Shifting. If you can clearly imagine what you and your world will be like once the desired-for change has been accomplished, you will begin to do things which will move you towards that goal. This contextual adjustment needs to be framed in positive terms. Here, the challenge for the Mentor is to enable the student to shift perspective from today's problems to tomorrow's success. It should be recognised that change is not instantaneous. The way that many people expect magic to work is, of course, sudden, positive change without any stress or unpleasantness. Another important aspect of assisting students to cope with change is in the provision of coping strategies for stress.

It is important to bear in mind that the Mentoring relationship is one of mutual trust and respect which, if well-founded, will maintain itself despite interpersonal differences and disagreements. Success, for a Magical Mentor, is watching a student come into their own power, excelling and mastering areas of magic which may be beyond the Mentor's own immediate interests and ability. This powerful form of bonding should not be underrated, particularly in a discipline as given to disputes over magical differences and personality clashes as Chaos Magic. Mentoring is not simply concerned with the transfer of skills, theories or opinions, but is a process whereby one person encourages another to find out what works for them, in the most effective way possible, by the application of knowledge and ability into their own unique circumstances.

In many ways, finding an effective Mentor is much harder than approaching a teacher. Mentoring relationships tend to arise informally and require (for me anyway) a face-to-face interaction. I can't do it by letter or e-mail. Like a friendship, it happens slowly and (grin) chaotically. Also, and I think significantly, the mentoring relationship isn't entirely focused around magic, at least in the sense of discussing the technical aspects of practical magic, but more about how magic reaches into our lives. So don't fall into the trap of looking for a mentor in the same way that people already advertise for teachers. Seek friendship instead.

Leaving Magical Groups

[*Leaving Magical Groups* was written in 1998 and appeared in *Talking Stick* magazine. It is a reflection, based on some of my own experiences, on group dynamics in respect to departing (or being kicked out of) a magical group; how to handle it, and why it can be, for all those concerned, traumatic.]

——•◦•——

Introduction

The dynamics of Magical Groups and organisations has for some years been a field of increasing interest for me. In this essay, I want to explore what is often a turbulent issue—the processes attendant to an individual leaving a magical group after some years of association and intense magical exploration. My contention is that it's not always as simple as sending in a resignation letter and walking away from the group; that there may be varying degrees of psychic and emotional 'fallout' to deal with, both on a personal and, sometimes, interpersonal level. I will also discuss some of the group processes by which members are identified as transgressors within the group and how they tend to be dealt with.

Experiences of Leaving Groups

In 1980, after some years of being a lone magician, I made contact with a Wiccan coven in my home town. Having previously only met two other practising magicians, you can imagine my joy at having finally met some other folk who were serious about the occult in the same way that I was. I began to work with this group on a weekly (sometimes more frequent) basis, doing the 'year-and-a-day' training. As is recounted elsewhere (in my book *Prime Chaos: Adventures in Chaos Magic,* Falcon Press) following my initiation into the coven, I was summarily dismissed from it (this being, as I found out much later, part of the initiation!) I dealt with the shock of this by going abroad for eight months. But dreams followed me across the water—dreams of doing rituals with the group, and of talking to its members, and I also had to work through a good deal of hurt and anger at being rejected by the group after such an intense bond had been built up. It was this experience which first led me to dwell on the psychic and emotional consequences of 'leaving' a magical group. To cut a long story short, I subsequently returned to this group and worked with them for three years before leaving again (on my own initiative this time) in somewhat acrimonious circumstances. This time, the psychic fallout didn't seem to be as intense. In retrospect, I can see why this was. By this time, this group was no longer my primary source of magical friendships, relationships and ways of doing magic. Not only had I met other magicians by then, but I had also begun to strike out on blazing my own trail in earnest. Also, both my work and geographical distance from them meant that I had only been seeing the group every few months or so, and had very little social contact, apart from the odd telephone call. And, after a short hiatus, I was able to find another group which had no links with the other one.

Some ten years later, I found myself in similar circumstances. Shortly after moving to London in 1991, I was initiated into a large, international magical order. At the time, about two-thirds of the magicians I knew in London were associated with this order. So, in addition to attending formal meetings, there was a good deal of socialising involved as well. Despite being associated with two or three other groups, this particular order quickly became my 'primary' focus of attention. I met my partner through it, and began to devote a great deal of energy and enthusiasm into initiating various projects in it. Being in something of a 'privileged' position, I was party to the various 'political' manoeuvrings within the organisation, and largely treated them as games—a necessary evil, perhaps, particularly if one wanted to get certain things done. In my enthusiasm, I recommended to various friends that they should join the organisation and tended to reduce contact with correspondents who weren't involved or interested—my rationale (to myself) being that I didn't have the time anymore, now that I was devoting most of my attention to this group. It wasn't entirely a 'rosy' picture however. Looking back in my diaries, I find that I was critical of many things inside the organisation (often openly so) and several times was on the point of leaving—but never quite went that far, always saying "I'll give it another six months." There was the added complication that I was involved with various publishing-related projects with fellow members and had built some strong friendships with fellow members, both in the UK and abroad.

By late 1995 I decided that it was time to leave this organisation and retired from it a few months later—initially taking a formal leave of absence, and then making it known that I had no intention of returning. My partner left a few months later. Once again I found that my dream-life began to reflect this: dreams of working rituals with people in the order, talking to various people, and even dreams where rituals were being done with me as the focus of the rite though I was not present. I am not for one moment suggesting that I was being 'magically attacked' here. My dreams were merely resolving and working through the various emotions and feelings I had towards this organisation and the people within it, particularly those I regarded as friends & magical colleagues.

Part of the problem of leaving, with respect to this organisation, has been that I still have a fair number of friends who are involved in it, to varying degrees, so it has been difficult to avoid discussing what various people are getting up to or what the current 'gossip' is pertaining to various internal politics. I've also found that whenever I get together with friends who have also left this group, it's difficult not to either reminisce or go over old battles/arguments—particularly after a bottle or three. Eventually, I have come to see this as a self-defeating exercise, only serving to keep the various emotions & feelings I had about the group and certain members 'alive.' This has resulted in my becoming 'drawn into' some of the organisation's current soap-opera plots—again something which I have come to recognise as my own tendency to want to keep particular personal axes grinding away. So, despite having to all intents and purposes 'left' this particular group, I have been, to some extent (perhaps unconsciously) maintaining my link with them.

I feel this is natural and to be expected. In retrospect, when I have left other magical organisations where close friendships and intense magical work (or even enmities) have not been a factor, there has not been any 'fallout.' In general, though, when a group has been a 'primary focus' as in the above instances, it can take some time to work through all the personal and interpersonal issues which are thrown up. It's natural for us to be concerned with what a group (or people we know in it) are up to, or to wonder how we are being perceived ("what are they saying about me"). This also works both ways. It is common for people who leave magical groups in somewhat acrimonious circumstances to go on to devote energy into slagging the group off, either in magical journals or, as seems more common these days, on the internet. Magical groups tend, naturally, to be sensitive to such criticism from former members, although over-sensitivity to criticism can be equally self-defeating. Over the years I have seen various groups and orders issuing lengthy 'statements' (either in broadsheets or latterly, on the net) concerning what various ex-members have said about them. This has occasionally spilled out into protracted correspondence in the pages of magical journals. Again, I personally do not feel that this is of any help. Silence is better than denial, which only gives cause for speculation on the part of others not involved. It would be better to recognise that when people do leave an organisation in less than happy circumstances, they might well feel justified in airing their grievances as part of their own process of resolution.

The Process of Demonization
    Another issue which relates more to the group rather than the departed individual is the process by which ex-members become 'demonized' by the group. This is a common response by a group to the occurrence of members departing. Some years ago, a friend became involved in a group in North Yorkshire. She became wary when she was informed by the group's leaders that a number of ex-affiliates had banded together and were now engaged in magical attack against the group! My friend put this down to ingrained paranoia and departed, and subsequently found that she had been tarred with the same brush. It seems that some groups require enemies to maintain a sense of cohesion, whether those enemies are former members, enemy magical groups, or the state. Occasionally I have heard the argument voiced that the enemies are 'within' the group—a preferable alternative to dealing with internal conflicts, it seems, is to make vague references to unknown enemies inside the group. Demonization can be a very subtle process. Former members can become scapegoats on which various unresolved issues within the group can be dumped, with the added fillip that they are unlikely ever to be in the position to defend themselves, if indeed, they are so

inclined. Of course, this can be a problem if the person in question still has some friends within the group. In this kind of situation, friends of the ex-member face the choice of keeping quiet whilst their friend is having ordure heaped upon them or speaking up, and of course, risking censure themselves. As we know from studies of group dynamics, there is a great deal of peer pressure to conform within groups—particularly to those norms of behaviour or belief which are below the surface, and often go unspoken or are assumed to be all-inclusive. A related issue is that if the group has invested heavily in the belief that they are the 'best' group in existence (and I have been in several where such a belief is an undercurrent—particularly when the grape begins to flow) then, of course, people who leave become 'second-rate.' And of course, since the group in question is 'the best' then they don't have to own any of the responsibility for the circumstances over which the person departed. There does seem to be some expectation on the part of the group members that the departing member will never amount to anything (at least 'magically') once they have left the group.

Scapegoating in Groups

This process of 'demonizing' ex-members appears to be related to the well-observed phenomena of scapegoating. Scapegoating is a process resorted to by a group whereby particular members of the group are blamed for what is happening in the group. When a scapegoat is identified, other members of the group are likely to feel a considerable degree of relief, as a source for whatever feelings of resentment, distrust and anger, etc., has been identified. As Douglas (1995) notes, this process seems to arise "without apparent conscious effort" on the part of members.

Scapegoating appears to be resorted to when there is a lack of cohesion in a group, as a 'safe' means of resolving conflict. It is important to note however, that although the scapegoating process appears to arise 'unconsciously' within the group, that the scapegoats themselves are selected. Factors which influence this selection include:

• Group members who are perceived as having little, or sometimes too much social power within the group.

• Those who possess recognised characteristics which give rise to dislike from others (i.e., appearance, non-conformation to group norms).

• Members who are identified with previous conflicts within the group (i.e., friends of people who have left under acrimonious circumstances).

• Individuals who appear to demonstrate an ambivalence towards the dominant members of the group (i.e., being perceived as being overly critical or unsupportive of the group leaders).

• Members who demonstrate a strong tendency to be passive or lack self-confidence in speaking up for themselves.

Once a scapegoat has been identified (by the group as a whole or, as is more usual, by the leaders or dominant members) the group rallies to diffuse conflict within the group by censuring the scapegoat. This can range from 'formal hearings' with the scapegoat appearing before a tribunal to proceedings in absentia. In one notable occurrence, as the scapegoat refused to come to a group meeting, the High Priestess ordered that the individual concerned be summoned 'astrally' to the group.

There is strong pressure exerted on the scapegoat to accept and conform to the role which has been thrust upon them. When, as sometimes occurs, the identified scapegoat refuses to conform to the group expectations, further conflict ensues. Once a group member has been identified as a scapegoat it is extremely difficult for them to disassociate themselves from that role. Whilst the initial aim of the group may be to move the scapegoat to the periphery of the group until they 'recant' for their errant behaviour, if the scapegoat brings about further and prolonged conflict, (i.e., by refusing to recant) they may well end up being forced out of the group or being considerably marginalised (i.e., withdrawal of social support or notification of group events).

As there is a common tendency in such situations to avoid open conflict within the group, scapegoats tend to find it difficult to gain support from other members, particularly if other members are passive, acceding to the dictates of the dominant members. The scapegoat is generally perceived as endangering the existence of the group, not only in terms of its social cohesion, but possibly also in terms of its magical belief structures. I have occasionally heard group members censured in terms that their behaviour is "endangering the group egregore." Whenever sources of conflict in a group are elevated into magical or spiritual issues, the feeling of being threatened on the part of other members of the group tends to be heightened considerably.

Evidence of Transgression

An element shared by both the processes of scapegoating and demonization is that of the identification of transgressions on the part of the individual concerned. Here, any instances of perceived asocial behaviour (no matter how apparently trivial), including behaviour beyond the immediate group, is re-interpreted by group members as further 'evidence' to support the perfidy of the transgressor. Taken objectively, such 'evidence' may seem to be tenuous, but for those members projecting the scapegoat/demon role onto the individual, they are enormously helpful in terms of providing a focus for strong emotions which are deflected onto the member concerned. Instances of transgressive behaviour are seen as reinforcing the individual's deviant status rather than in terms of their historical context or the other member's perception or memory of the event. It is not unusual for the current transgressor to be blamed for previous conflicts within the group, particularly when these have been unresolved or the reasons underlying them remain ambiguous. Personal dislike and prejudice towards the transgressor is also re-interpreted as evidence of their deviant nature.

Group Responses to Departure

Just as a departing individual works through a process of personal resolution towards the group they have left, the group must also go through a similar process of resolution. A useful term from workplace studies is "organisational healing"—which denotes how a company deals with sweeping changes such as the downsizing of employees. I have observed that when individuals who have high status or who have been given a key task within a magical group suddenly up and leave, or if internal schism results in a large number of people to depart at once, the group needs time to 'heal' from such situations.

It is possible that defence mechanisms such as the demonization of departing members (not always viable, depending on the perceived status of the persons concerned) are short-term measures, (though they can of course become habitual if the group has a culture of paranoia[1]) relatively speaking. The problem with such defence mechanisms is that they only defer resolution of conflicts and interpersonal issues. Just as an individual's post-departure 'demonization' of a group seems only to continually recycle their own feelings about and towards the group, I would propose that any demonization of individuals by remaining group members does the same. Of course, this is a difficult proposition to test, as it unlikely that any magical group is going to admit that they use the demonization gambit in the first place, much less that the departure of any member (even after years of involvement) is in any way problematic for them, either individually or collectively. Indeed, from my own experience of magical groups it seems more usual that there is a common tendency

---

[1] The phrase "culture of paranoia" refers to a dynamic whereby the group members appear to be highly sensitive to criticism both from within and externally to the group. From my observations, this is something which grows over time and tends to be (perhaps unconsciously) expressed by the leaders or dominant group members. Factors which influence this include: the degree to which group members identify as being 'outsiders' in society and must therefore guard against intrusions by the state, media or government agencies; the injunction that what occurs within the group must be kept 'secret' at all costs from outsiders (which again can reduce individual member's ability to establish external peer networks); the recent history of the group (in terms of previous conflicts and how they have been resolved) and the common perception that any criticism levelled at the group is also direct personal criticism of those concerned, including criticism of their 'magical abilities.' Although such a 'culture' is not uncommon in small groups, it is particularly notable (in my experience) in larger organisations and networks where there is a tendency for subgroups within the overall structure to become suspicious of each other—particularly when geographically distanced or where there is a wide divergence of opinion among group members over beliefs, magical approaches and the direction the 'whole organisation' should be taking. A quotation passed to me in reference to a pagan network I was involved in for a while sums this attitude up: "Those people in Leeds—I don't know what they're doing—but whatever it is, I don't like it!"

to 'explain' why members leave in terms of it being due to their own personal difficulties and shortcomings, and whatever dissatisfactions that individual has expressed towards the group are ignored or at best, made light of. It should be noted that the group's recent history (in terms of prior conflicts) is likely to influence future situations of a similar nature. For example, a group which is still recovering from a recent upheaval is less likely to tolerate any behaviour from individual members which appears to diverge from the group's norms and values.

A common gambit used to by magical groups to 'heal' themselves is to resort to a ritual aimed at restoring 'group balance.' This may well be effective in the short-term, bringing members together for a common purpose and giving rise to a shared feeling of unity, but tends to serve to 'close' a period of conflict without dealing with the deeper issues of members' dissatisfactions and anger. This might well temporarily discharge feelings of tension within the group—effectively 'banishing' them—but unresolved issues have a habit of creeping back, and tend to recur when the original sources of dissatisfaction reassert themselves.

To summarise so far then, I would say, based on my own experiences and observations that individuals may encounter problems in leaving a group when:

• The group in question has been a 'primary' focus of attention.
• The individual concerned has established friendships which might be threatened by their leaving the group.
• Some personal connections remain which relate to the group.
• The group places high expectations upon its members which may lead to feelings of guilt or having somehow failed the group (NB: group values can quickly become personal values).
• The individual has been identified as a scapegoat by the group or is perceived to be allied to a previous scapegoat/demonised member.
• The group has hitherto provided the individual's main source of contact with other magicians & occultists.
• The group has been the individual's primary source of 'magical training.'

These last two points are significant as individuals sometimes feel hesitant to leave a group if it provides their primary source of contact with other occultists—particularly those who share similar interests. One of the most commonly-voiced reasons why people join groups in the first place appears to be that of meeting like-minded individuals.

The Importance of Support

The tension experienced as a result of leaving a group might well also be heightened if the individual concerned has no support network to turn to. It is often difficult for occultists to discuss such matters with non-occultist peers. In my own experience, I have found it to be very helpful to have magically-oriented friends whom, whilst not involved in the groups I have been in, have enough of their own experience of groups to understand my feelings in this regard. Having someone to talk through one's feelings with is highly beneficial to any process of resolution. Of course, in the case where the group has provided the primary source of peer relationships (as in the instance of my first departure from the coven, described above), this is difficult to obtain. I have met other magicians who, though voicing strong dissatisfactions with the group they were in, appeared to feel that there was 'nowhere else for them to go.' It does appear that the strong inclusiveness in many magical groups (the sense of 'we-ness') which acts as a bonding agency (shared interests, belief & common experiences) can serve to isolate individuals against making contacts with other groups & individual magicians. Other factors which can influence this include: geographical location (i.e., it is often harder to diversify one's range of contacts in a small town rather than a large city), and the suspicion which often exists between magical groups— particularly when an individual is 'crossing' from one belief system to another, or to a 'rival' group within the same genre. The diversity of belief and approach which characterises pagan and magical genres is generally regarded as a strength; however, it can also make the transition between different affinity groups and peer networks a difficult process, particularly if the individual concerned is already feeling isolated and wary from the break-up of their previous association with a group.

Conclusion

In joining any group, the individual is taking personal risks. Although magical groups have some unique characteristics which distinguish them from other types of groups, they are, of course, subject to the general dynamics which have been observed in all kinds of social organisation. As with other kinds of groups, it is important to be able to identify the processes which underlie situations and events, and this understanding is often difficult to come by. One reason being that the more one is emotionally attached to a situation, the harder it is to step back and uncover the underlying dynamics which contribute to the situation. Another is that there is a general lack of awareness of group processes within magical groups (at least in my experience—the one notable exception being a group which largely consisted of educators and health care professionals), coupled with a lack of awareness that being a member of a group requires the exercise of interpersonal and observational skills. Indeed, there seems to be a common assumption that being part of a group is easy and requires little effort. This lack of awareness is thrown into sharp relief when conflict occurs—in fact the very idea that conflict is an inevitable consequence of membership seems alien to some groups I have been involved with. The result being that processes for apportioning blame to individuals tend to be resorted to rather other forms of dealing with problems which arise. The problem with both scapegoating and demonization is that these processes quickly become habitual patterns for the group and are highly distressing for the individuals concerned. This in turn feeds the 'culture of paranoia' both within the group and how the group regards the external environment, again making it less likely that the group will explore other avenues of conflict resolution.

Reference

Tom Douglas, *Survival in Groups,* Open University Press, 1995

PONDERING DAILY PRACTICE

[*Pondering Daily Practice* was written in 2009 and appeared on *enfolding.org*. This is a short reflection on bringing esoteric practices into one's day-to-day life, of being open to surprises and taking advantage of opportune moments to cultivate skills and sensibilities.]

A central theme in my approach to tantra is "Awake-Awareness."

One way of explaining this concept is being awake to what's going on around you in the present moment, rather than becoming caught up in future fantasies or mulling over past events. A lot of our general practices aim at extending our capacity to be "awake-aware" and so can be done anywhere, as we go through our busy daily lives—rather than distinct practices that we set aside time for. We don't make the distinction that you'll find in a lot of western magic between magical v. mundane, spirit v. matter, lower v. higher, etc.— we don't compartmentalise different aspects of life that way—and quite a few of our exercises can be done anywhere, anytime you have an odd moment, rather than having to set a special time aside. Whilst we do encourage people to try out various types of daily practices, we're also very aware that people who have busy lives can't always do this. Tantra is not so much about pursuing a distinct set of practices, but living one's life in a particular way.

The idea of Awake-Awareness is related to the practice of locating yourself in the immediate present—of not being continually pulled this way and that by worries about the past, the present or anticipation about what the future may bring. Of course, this is very difficult, as we tend to find ourselves caught up in all kinds of mental turmoil. This is natural. I find that it's important for me not to beat myself up when I catch myself doing this, but to try to relax and just be aware of what's in my immediate environment. If all else fails, I try to focus in on how I feel in my body: How I am sitting, how I am breathing, how my clothes feel against my skin. Closing my eyes momentarily may help. Our bodies are the best teachers in this regard, so this kind of practice is sometimes referred to as paying attention to the wisdom of one's body.

Another thing which is central for me is the idea that we come closest to our sense of the god's presence (to the divine) when we experience wonder, joy, surprise. Any activity which cultivates those emotions is to be embraced, from the apparently simple to the profound. In one sense, tantra is a way of living that allows a person to make joy and wonder the ground-state of their being.

Joy can be very simple. I often find moments of joy just walking to work along the bank of the Thames. In the play of sunlight in a puddle of water, the smile of a passing stranger, just feeling the wind buffeting me. Looking at a chart I've just spent the last hour or so redrawing and finding a quiet satisfaction. I'd say for me, part of Awake-Awareness is about being open to joy, wonder, and surprise from any direction. Again, this takes time to cultivate.

Many years ago, I used to teach relaxation exercises in a hospital. One of the first shocks I had to come to terms with was that many people just did not know how to 'relax'—it was an effort for them—they had no conscious experience of the body sensation of relaxation. In modern culture, relaxation has become a form of 'work.' It's very difficult to simply "do nothing"—even if your body is not occupied, then the mind is whirling away. So learning how to do nothing can be an 'exercise' in itself. I've spent hours just sitting under a tree, thinking of not much. If you consider that we are perpetually bombarded with the urge to be busy and doing things and going places (either physically, mentally or developmentally), not doing things can be a magical practice. Of course, this can be read as a recipe for laziness—many books on magic will tell you that you have to cultivate self-discipline and willpower—but why? Everywhere I look on the web there are people bemoaning the fact that they aren't doing as much "daily practice" as they feel they should be doing. This looks to me like "spiritual-development-as-work." Why not take a playful approach? In the past, I've occasionally said to people that I'm not seriously practicing—I'm just "playing around."

Again, a component of Awake-Awareness for me is not forcing myself into an artificial regime. I get enough regimentation at work, and don't see any benefit in replicating that regimentation elsewhere in my life.

It's very easy to get into a cycle of thinking "I must do a daily practice" and then, once the initial enthusiasm wears off, of just stopping and then beating yourself up for not keeping it up. I know this very well from my own experience of setting myself impossible schedules and then failing at them.

So, Questions: Why do you "have" to do a daily practice? Is it necessary? What do you hope to achieve?

It may be that "daily practice" isn't really what you need right now. Maybe you need to rethink what constitutes a "daily practice" for you. Whilst we do recommend various daily practices, I also think it's important for people to find their own "beginning" as it were. If, for example, you find it difficult to sit still for any length of time, then a practice that involves lots of sitting still is going to be difficult. Again, a lot of our practices are things you can do anywhere, rather than having to set out a separate time and place for them. Practice can be about cultivating attitudes—such as open-ness to joy and wonder in the world. Doing rituals, repeating mantras, meditating, etc., are just aids to this process. Of course, it is good to do a daily practice in the sense of doing a special exercise—but I think one has to be "ready" for that—to look forward to it, to let it shape your day.

For me, things I try to do every day are:

• relaxing into the immediate present when I find myself getting caught up in mental whirlings
• paying attention to my immediate environment
• noticing how I'm breathing
• being open to wonder & joy
• being aware of my body

These are more like habits of mind rather than "special exercises."

TANTRA

Introduction

My engagement with Tantra began with a dream—a dream of Kali. In 1982, I was living in rural Lincolnshire, cut off from occult friends and contacts, and decided that this was an ideal opportunity to take a break from magic for a while. Although I thought I was done (for the moment) with magic, it seemed that magic was not done with me. One night I dreamt of meeting the Indian goddess Kali in a cremation ground. It was vivid. I woke with the memory of her eyes burning into me. The following night I had the same dream, and this continued for another three nights. I wouldn't say that I had never heard of Kali, but at that time I felt no attraction towards anything Indian. Of course, many occult books were peppered with references to mantras, chakras, and various Indian deities, but I certainly did not expect to have such a direct, intense, and recurring dream-encounter. At the same time it felt significant in a way I couldn't quite put my finger on.

Lacking anyone to talk to, I wrote the dream down, and turned it into a kind of pathworking, which I would run through before going to sleep. Unsurprisingly, the dream came back, and if anything, intensified. It was this recurring dream of Kali that first put the hook in me, but without anyone to talk to about it—to help me make sense of it—I did not focus on it.

A year or so later I moved to Nottingham to train as a psychiatric nurse and became involved with an experimental drama group. During this period, I was able to reconnect with many of my occult friends. Some of my Wiccan friends "explained" my newfound interest in Kali in terms of having had a past life in India, but I was rather sceptical about such assertions. It was around this time that I first started to try to read up on the subject of Tantra. There didn't seem to be much available. There were some New Age and "Sacred Sex" books, as well as one or two works written by Western Occultists who tended to treat Tantra as a variant of the Kabbalah, but nothing which dealt with ritual or how one might begin some kind of practice—which, of course, was what I wanted. I did read some of the writings of Sir John Woodroffe (aka "Arthur Avalon"), but found these largely incomprehensible.

My first big break came when I moved to York, having made the decision to switch from Psychiatric Nursing to Occupational Therapy training. This three-year diploma was, in itself, a major influence on my later approach to magic, as it included intensive training in both group dynamics and drama-therapy, as well as a multi-disciplinary approach to therapeutic techniques which later influenced my take on Chaos Magic. One of the students in my intake was a woman—Raven—who had spent some time in a Siddha Yoga Ashram in India. Raven seemed to me to be very knowledgeable when it came to Tantra and Yoga (she was a qualified Yoga Teacher), and she was also interested in Wicca. We formed a magical partnership, and she attended some meetings of the covens I was then involved with (one in York, and another in Macclesfield). It was an intensive, and rather stressful relationship, because we felt we could not share our mutual occult interests with other friends. It was through Raven's influence however, that I was able to make sense of my Kundalini experiences in 1984.

Kundalini is a difficult subject to write about at the best of times, as just about every occult author seems to have their own views on the subject and its significance as a magical or spiritual experience. At the Autumn Equinox in 1984 I was given my second degree initiation in Wicca. A few weeks later I began to experience bouts of vertigo, a sense of bodily dislocation, and odd sensations at the base of my spine. On more than one occasion, these feelings became overwhelming to the point where I was almost having a fit of sorts—my teeth chattering, feeling both hot and cold, and experiencing involuntary muscular contractions. I did not know what was happening, but Raven calmed me down and told me that these sensations were related to the awakening of "the fire-snake" Kundalini. These intense experiences seemed to occur with increasing frequency. Here is an extract from my magical diary of the period:

> "It began as a scream in my head—Kali's scream, I thought. It echoed on and on until I no longer 'heard' it. I felt it like a white light which shot down my spine, coiling around muladhara, which opened with a blaze. A cold fire, like every nerve was alight, spread around my body. I could feel it glowing from my fingertips. I began to tremble and twitch and felt a very jarring disorientation which worsened

to a whirling if I closed my eyes. These unpleasant sensations lasted well over an hour and I struggled to remain in control."

It's hard to communicate how scary and discomforting these experiences were for me, having very little in the way of a framework with which to make sense of them. I had read some books that dealt with Kundalini and chakras and so forth, but had come away with the definite impression that this kind of experience only happened to advanced magicians, and whatever pretensions I had about myself, I did not think of myself as being an advanced practitioner. Raven was the only person that I could really turn to, and her interpretation that this was a 'kundalini experience' seemed to me to be appropriate, given what I'd read and my recent initiation. She felt that milestone, together with the intense ritual and personal work I'd been doing, had triggered the rising of the snake.

This led me to rethink my relationship with the authority of occult texts. Up until that point, I had more or less taken what I'd read in occult books at face value and not really questioned them. I'd begun to be skeptical of some people's pronouncements of occult fact, but I still had a kind of reverence for text, particularly some of the older authors. I began, from this point, to gain a sense of discrimination—and perhaps a healthy scepticism—towards the pronouncements of occult authorities. Rather than just passively absorbing and internalising what I was reading in occult texts, I started to gain confidence in my own opinions and ideas. As the years have passed, I've been more and more inclined to treat these experiences as just something weird that happened to me, which had, at the time, quite a profound effect on me, but no more than that. Were they "authentic" kundalini experiences? In some ways that doesn't really matter. One can generate a great deal of spiritual social capital in staking the claim to have had a kundalini experience, but this has never really interested me. It seems to me that intense experiences are simply par for the course if one is pursuing an occult trajectory, and it doesn't do to read too much into them or interpret them as indicating having attained any degree of proficiency.

In 1986, I moved to Leeds. Leeds was a melting pot for me where various strands of my occult interests came together in new ways. Leeds had a thriving occult scene which had grown considerably since I had first encountered it in the late 1970s. Much of it was centred around Leeds University Occult Society, where I would later deliver my first lectures. Not only were there Pagans, Chaos magicians, Thelemites and people interested in doing things magically with Lovecraftian entities, but it was through the University Occult Society that I met my tantric teacher, Vishvanath, who was a member of AMOOKOS. After attending a lecture which Vishvanath gave on Tantra one evening, I was determined to find out more from this man, who seemed not only to be knowledgeable about Tantra, but also to have a sense of humour—something I often found lacking in people who professed to be interested in Indian spirituality. After a year of intense conversations and many night walks through the green places of Leeds, Vishvanath gave me an initiation, and I began working through the AMOOKOS grade papers under his direction.

AMOOKOS—or to give its full title, the "Arcane Magical Order of the Knights of Shambhala"—was a hybridised magical group which drew influences from primary tantric material, together with the writings of one Shri Gurudev Mahendranath, commonly known as "Dadaji". Mahendranath, originally Lawrence Miles, was a "white sadhu"—an English occultist who had lived in India since the late 1950s, adopted the lifestyle of a renunciate, and claimed to have been given initiation, and more importantly, the spiritual authority to transmit the lineage of the Uttarakaula Tantric tradition. Much of the AMOOKOS material was created by Mike Magee, who had been a member of Kenneth Grant's Typhonian O.T.O. and was translating primary tantric works into English.

I continued the practices I'd learnt from Vishvanath and AMOOKOS throughout the 1980s and into the mid-1990s. Gradually though, a sense of dissatisfaction came creeping in. An idea which was very much in vogue—particularly in Chaos Magic thought—was that all magical systems were essentially similar, and that cultural context and history were not particularly important. I'd accepted this view for a long time, but increasingly came to question it. I began to realise that in focusing, for the most part, on the similarities among the Western magical practices I was used to, and what I knew of Tantric magical practices, I'd ignored the differences—and the cultural and historical contexts which had shaped them. I tended to find that, whenever I gave lectures on Tantra, that the dominant assumption was that it was "all about sex," and I began to wonder where these popular assumptions came from. I became fascinated with how Western perceptions of Tantra were related to ideas which arose in the colonial period, and how much of Western occultural accounts of Tantra perpetuated and recirculated colonial tropes about India. At the same time, I discovered that there was a wealth of information to be had from scholarly material. Tantric Studies was now a recognised field of enquiry and that many tantric texts were now available in English. Engaging with this material was something of a revelation, and I became increasingly interested in trying to puzzle out how Tantra, as a cultural and historical phenomena, fitted into the larger picture of Indian religion and social life. I began to take up the position that to understand Tantra, it was actually very helpful to my own practice to gain an understanding—however incomplete and fragmentary that might be—of history, culture, language. At this point, I more or less stopped reading Western occultural explanations of what Tantra was supposed to be about, and instead started trying to read the dense, often confusing presentations by scholars, and the translations of the source materials.

In so doing, I began to change my perception of my own practices. I began to see that whereas I had tended to view the practices I'd engaged with (and those of my peers) as unproblematically "authentic" in a way that, for example, Neo-Tantric New-Age practices were not, that I had been, to an extent, playing the authenticity game which is all too common amongst occult practitioners of any tradition. I'd invested a great deal in this self-perception, and it took some time for me to disabuse myself of that attachment. I had to accept that my understanding of Tantra will always, to a degree, be fragmentary, partial, and unfinished—and that was okay.

In a way, I'd come to Tantra via Witchcraft, and what united both strands for me was the love of Goddesses, and the place made for wonder, mystery and epiphany that I had encountered first through Witchcraft, and then in Tantra. I was also intellectually stimulated by the challenges of Indian history and philosophy. I'd been used to the idea that practices were basically things that were active: rituals, meditations, and so forth, and that simply reading a book on say, Indian theories of poetics, wasn't as important as taking one's trousers off and doing something wacky. I began, though, to understand how the one aspect fed the other. If I was reciting, for example, a translated Indian hymn in praise of the goddess Durga in a ritual, it actually deepened my awareness of the meaning of that hymn to know that some elements of it were stock poetic metaphors, and some elements a reworking of earlier traditions. I began to think of myself as practicing a hybridized approach to Tantra—one which drew on those elements of the textual and oral traditions which I found stimulating, whilst acknowledging that I cannot (and in fact don't want to) escape my intellectual and cultural heritage.

Kundalini: A Personal Approach

[*Kundalini: A Personal Approach* was first published in issue 3 of *Chaos International* magazine in 1987. This essay grew out of a lecture given to Leeds University Occult Society in the previous year, and was an attempt to deal with my own 'kundalini' experiences whilst studying for a diploma in Occupational Therapy. Part of the diploma coursework was the study of brain neurochemistry, and together with some work placements in hospital units specialising in a variety of neurological disorders, very much coloured my approach to the subject at hand. There's also a leaning towards Timothy Leary's eight-circuit theory which I'd completely forgotten about having any interest in.]

<hr>

"I am the flame that burns in every heart of man, and in the core of every star.
    I am Life, and the giver of Life; yet therefore is the knowledge of me the knowledge of Death."

— *Liber AL,* II: 6

The Awakening of the Kundalini or Fire-Snake is a central feature of contemporary Magic, which has assimilated the concept from its original Tantric source. Although the concept of Kundalini was first introduced to Western occultists by Theosophists such as Alice Bailey and C.W. Leadbeater, it took the more detailed writings of Arthur Avalon and Aleister Crowley to launch significant numbers of Western occultists in search of this experience. It was Crowley in particular who provided a synthesis of Western and Eastern magical practices and left for future occultists an integrated approach towards Kundalini experience, identifying it as the central 'magical power' in the human organism. Crowley's (enthusiastic) experiments with both drugs and sexual magic were a far cry from the "spiritual asceticism" expounded by many of his contemporaries. While "spirituality" was generally seen in terms of philosophies that reject the bodily or somatic experience, Crowley laid the foundations of a Western approach to development which integrated both the psychic and somatic areas of experience. It was not until the 1960s, and the arrival of the "Psychedelic Era" that such an approach received widespread (and serious) attention. The 1960s ushered in the beginnings of what Timothy Leary terms "hedonic technology"—the discovery of pleasure over restriction via drugs, sexuality, dance, music, massage, yoga and diet. The "Psychedelic Era" also brought with it a great "Occult Revival," with particular interest in hedonistically-orientated magic, such as Tantra and Crowley's cult of Thelema.

Out of this explosion in consciousness came the developments in magical thought and practice of the 1970s, particularly Kenneth Grant's exposition of Crowley, Tantric doctrine and the works of Austin Osman Spare. Thelemically-oriented magazines such as *SOThIS, Agape* and *The New Equinox* provided focal points for the evolution of magical techniques and consideration. Awareness of the physiological nature of intense states of consciousness was growing, and magic was increasingly becoming viewed as an approach to development that integrated both inner, mental experience and bodily awareness. The placing of "potentia" was within the individual rather than any external power.

Since the 1960s, the "awakening" of Kundalini has become an experience that many Westerners seek. Magic is one of the major routes, yoga another, also ecstatic cults presided over by various gurus. There is a great deal of Information written on the subject, ranging from extremely technical writers such as Kenneth Grant, to popular works on Kundalini-Yoga and Tantrik-derived sex-manuals. Like many other occult subjects, there are now many books written "from the armchair," where a writer perpetuates a particular view of a subject, rather than writing from direct experience. This has led to much confusion and misconception concerning the whole nature of Kundalini and its attendant experience. The power of the experience to transform consciousness in varying degrees seems to be almost universally recognised, but some writers warn against practising Kundalini-yoga, whilst others give the impression that little more is required than a few basic yoga asanas, and a willing partner of the (usually) opposite sex. Is your Kundalini rising or are you just pleased to see me?

So what is meant by the term Kundalini experience? Kundalini is a Sanskrit word that can be translated as "coiled up." Kundalini is represented in many Tantric illustrations as a sleeping serpent, coiled three and a half times, at the base of the spinal cord. The popular view of Kundalini is that it is a dormant power that lies waiting to be unleashed by means of various practices. The "serpent power," once awakened, is coaxed up the central channel of the spine, entering the chakras (psychic energy centres) until it reaches the Crown chakra— and the yogi achieves "illumination."

Sounds straightforward doesn't it? But the Kundalini experience is a much more complex phenomenon. There seems to be no general consensus view of Kundalini, once one begins to delve into the subject. Western scientists and Eastern mystics, ancient sages and modern researchers all have produced widely-varying explanations of what Kundalini is all about.

As with any other kind of "occult" experience, the most useful way to proceed is from personal experience; and for Kundalini, direct experience of it changed my attitude towards it (and many other things besides), and set me on the track of finding my own answers. When I first encountered the subject of Kundalini in the writings of Kenneth Grant and Gopi Krishna, I developed the misconception that this was something to definitely avoid until I was "more advanced" as regards magical and yoga abilities. So what happened? I had a Kundalini experience. Shock-Horror! It came following a long period of Bhakti-yoga upon the goddess Kali, which culminated in a vivid "death-rebirth" vision of being burned alive on a stone slab, then being remade anew.

The Kundalini experience occurred seven days later. I had been experiencing acute discomfort all day without being able to pinpoint any particular source. In the evening, I was meditating with the Priestess Raven. Suddenly I experienced what I can only describe as a fit—muscles went into spasm, my teeth began chattering, I felt hot and cold flushes, and, with spine arching backwards, began to hyper-ventilate. Raven held me down and helped me to relax and "go with it." The "fit" lasted for about twenty minutes, and as it faded I felt quite weak and dizzy. Raven, a qualified yoga teacher with over 20 years of experience in Hatha and Raja yoga, remarked that she thought it was "the Serpent beginning to shift."

This occurrence was abrupt, extremely physical, and beyond my conscious volition. All the preconceptions I had about Kundalini (and about being in control of experience) were suddenly shattered. Underneath all the confusion though, there was an intuitive certainty that what was happening was "right."

Over the next 28 days both the Priestess Raven and I experienced "acute" Kundalini activity—characterised by muscular spasms around the base of the spine, euphoria, out-of-the-body experiences, and hallucinations. Here is a report of one of the most disorientating experiences (5/10/84, beginning approx. 11:30 pm):

> "It began as a scream in my head; 'Kali's scream' I thought. It echoed on and on, for what seemed like forever, until I no longer heard it but felt it and saw it—a white light which shot down my spine into the base chakra, which opened with a blaze. A cold sensation spread slowly around my body—it felt like each individual nerve was alight. A very 'jarring' sense of dissociation built up. When I closed my eyes, this rapidly became a sensation of whirling at high speed, accompanied by swirling patterns of colour. I was soon oblivious of other people in the room and adopted the lotus asana as the best posture to keep myself 'together.' This went on for over an hour."

Roughly at the same time, the Priestess Raven experienced a vision of Kali, coupled with a feeling of extreme rage. She "heard" wolves howling, and her cat became terrified of her and would not approach her.

***

Once the acute phase of Kundalini had abated, we then had to try to make some sense of it, which led me to examine Kundalini in a new perspective.

The first point to be made is that Kundalini isn't an isolated area of occult experience—though it is often written about in a way that suggests this. That Kundalini can be "awakened" through a variety of techniques (such as yoga, dancing, drumming, intense devotion [Bhakti], sexual asanas, various meditations, and use of psychoactive agents), indicates that it is a core feature of magical/transformative experience. When I had my first acute Kundalini experience, I hadn't been working for such an event, so it must have been "triggered" by other factors.

A close study of tantric texts reveals that Kundalini is, rather than being a dormant "potentia" sleeping until consciously raised, rather a kind of organising principle that maintains systems in equilibrium at all scales—from the subatomic to the cosmic. In the *Sat-Cakra-Nirupana*, Kundalini is referred to as the "world-bewilderer"—the root of the physical world. Kundalini is seen as a particular form of Shakti (energy) with dominion over matter. "Coiled" Kundalini is often referred to as "sleeping"—but sleeping as in the sense of Sushupti—the thought-free state of no-mind. It is coiled Kundalini which maintains the physical universe. The activity of Kundalini in individual systems (i.e., organic beings) is guided by the Jivatman—the embodied life-spark. To use a holographic analogy, the Jivatman is a holographic encoding within each individual system to replicate the holoverse, or Brahman in Tantrika. It is the Jivatman which carries the evolutionary "program" for each individual entity. So it is the Jivatman which "rules" Kundalini activity, not the "earthbound" ego-complex. This could account for the many instances where individuals pursue Kundalini experiences through yoga and other means without ever getting any spectacular results, while the sceptic next door can have a powerful "bliss" experience whilst hanging out the washing.

Many Eastern yogis do, in fact, warn Western students against trying to consciously "raise" Kundalini as a specific end. Sri Aurobindo's *Integral Yoga,* for example, is concerned with "living appropriately" and transformation *within* the physical world, rather than rejecting it. *Integral Yoga* is not concerned with seeking "liberation" from existence, but fulfilment within the world, whereby Kundalini rises "in its own time."

This idea bears out my own experience. The only times when I have used exercises specifically designed to affect the Kundalini (such as Crowley's *Liber SSS)* is during periods of acute Kundalini activity, when the experience became too disorientating. Any kind of occult practice or powerful transformative event will affect the Kundalini. It "awakens" when conditions in the system it organises become conducive to its arousal.

Many models which seek to explain the phenomena of Kundalini posit the existence of cosmic inner planes and psychic centres—the chakras. Kundalini, in these systems, is conceptualised as a "spiritual awakening." Fair enough, but such models as expressed by Western authors (such as C.W. Leadbeater and Alice Bailey) tend to maintain the spiritual-mundane/mind-body division, exhorting students to reject the material and seek the "spiritual" life. I find this idea somewhat suspect, preferring not to make such distinctions. At the time of my initial Kundalini experience, I was studying neurological medicine and consequently became interested in evolving a neurological (and later, neuro-magical) model of Kundalini activity.

In describing the onset of intense states of awareness, many people use the word "trigger" to attempt to explain how the experience came about. Trigger factors do not *cause* the experience in the usual linear fashion, but somehow facilitate it. When such an event occurs spontaneously, we can only perceive it, and are not aware of the microscopic patterns of which it is the peak. The trigger to a Bliss/Kundalini experience could be the final push which allows all the various microscopic interactions in the individual system to pass a critical threshold, thus bringing about a change in awareness.

Bliss researcher Nona Coxhead has investigated trigger factors in transcendental experiences and outlined some commonly-occurring situations:

Listening to Music	Sensation	Suicidal Feelings
Response to Nature	Relief from emotional pressure	News of terminal illness
Childbirth	Achievement	Grief or loss
Sports	Acceleration	Life-threatening situations
Devotion and worship	Happiness	Clinical death

To these can be added the techniques of yoga and magic: the various ways of achieving gnosis; protracted bodily exercises such as Hatha Yoga or Tai Chi; visualisation; ritual magic; contemplation; meditation; use of drugs; and others. The transformative experience (of which Kundalini is one conceptualisation) can occur spontaneously, or in relation to a systematised set of practices.

Intense emotional arousal, any technique to focus awareness upon one stimulus, and extreme physiological states appear to be key factors. Kundalini-related experiences are intensely body-oriented, with subjects reporting muscle spasms, spatial disorientation, and feelings of being filled with energy. Many people, such as Gopi Krishna, report strange sensations around the base of the spine—the site of the root-chakra Muladhara (root-support). Kundalini is often spoken of in poetic or mystical terms as moving up the spinal canal, entering the spinal chakras in turn. I, however, am more interested in what could be happening within the Central Nervous System.

During periods of intense Kundalini-arousal I experienced great "rushes" of energy moving up the spine. Looking at what occurred during such episodes in physiological terms, I was struck by two points: firstly, that my body seemed to be showing the kind of involuntary muscle patterns displayed during orgasm—only much more pronounced; and secondly, showing an extreme stimulation of the autonomic nervous system—hence the hot and cold flushes, for instance. Just because one feels "strange sensations" at the base of the spine does not necessarily mean that what is occurring originates in that area. Kundalini arousal could be an entirely neurological event which gives rise to a variety of bodily sensations.

So how does this relate to or trigger factors? The kinds of predisposing factors outlined above all have a powerful effect on the human nervous system. It is interesting to note that many ways of achieving gnosis are also used in torture and brainwashing—such as sensory deprivation, sleeplessness, fasting and pain. Aldous Huxley, in his book *Heaven and Hell* (1956) points out how the spiritual disciplines of mystics affected their biosystems:

> "...it is a matter of historical record that most contemplatives worked systematically to alter their body chemistry, with a view to creating the internal conditions favourable to spiritual insight. When they were not starving themselves into low blood sugar and vitamin deficiency, they were beating themselves into intoxication by histamine, adrenalin and decomposed protein in uncomfortable positions in order to create the psychophysical symptoms of stress."

It does appear to be the case that some psycho-technologies (such as magic) replicate, in a more controlled and volitional manner, the kind of intense states of arousal brought on by emotional stresses. Emotional arousal brings about fluctuations in both endocrine and nervous systems to such an extent that the changes can become a permanent pattern, with subsequent effects on perception, thought patterns, and behaviour. Perhaps, in terms of Kundalini-type experience, the trigger factor(s) relate to the individual's current neurological state at the time of the experience's onset. The trigger factor for my first Kundalini experience was a dyadic meditation performed with Raven, aimed at blanking out the mind. Predisposing factors could be both long-term influences, such as general and magical development, and more "recent" influences, such as the developing relationship between Raven and myself, the prolonged Bhakti on Kali and the death-rebirth vision, and work stresses. I don't believe that such experiences happen "by accident," but that the patterns leading up to them are not always immediately obvious.

The neurological basis of meditation has been well-researched by neuroscientists who have produced some intriguing accounts of how meditative techniques affect the brain. In particular, there is the phenomena of "habituation." Habituation is a neural response to the repetition of one particular stimulus. Focusing awareness on a single input (be it a visual or mental image, sound, chant or pattern of ritualised movement) dampens down sensory input and serves to inhibit the activity of the cerebral cortex. A simple example of habituation at work occurs when you go into a room where there is a clock ticking. At first it is a new stimulus so you will hear it clearly. Eventually, especially if your attention is taken up by something else, you "stop" hearing it. The neurons firing in response to the clock ticking have effectively become "bored" and the sound slips below conscious awareness. Inhibition of cortical neural activity leads to the inward-turning of awareness. The habituation response is mediated from a group of cells in the brainstem known as the Reticular Activating System (R.A.S.). This group of cells serves to 'censor' sensory input so that only "meaningful" stimuli reach the cerebral cortex (which relates to conscious awareness). A similar state can be induced by intense emotional arousal or shock, as if all inputs are momentarily 'frozen' by the R.A.S.

As noted earlier, Kundalini awakens in its "own" time—when the human biosystem/bodymind complex reaches a certain critical threshold. Some modern researchers into Kundalini experiences are trying to understand this process in terms of the build-up of key levels of chemical transmitter substances (both endocrine gland secretions and neurotransmitter substances) which relate to the physical and emotional stresses that the individual is undergoing. An allied theory is that of "neural coherence." This theory posits that conscious experience is generated by the highly complex activity of millions of neurons in the brain; conscious experience depends on the coherence and patterning of this activity. The more ordered the neural activity across the cerebral cortex, the stronger (more intense) the conscious experience.

We know that a great deal of information processing within the brain does not reach waking consciousness. Two factors that mediate this selection of stimuli could be the reticular system discussed above, and the level of "noise" in the brain. Noise, in cybernetic terms, is random background activity as opposed to coherent "signals." A high degree of noise across the cortex means that the individual is only aware of the strongest signals, such as sensory information. Signals that are less strong will be masked by the noise. Any kind of situation which "clears" the cortex of a large degree of stimulus input reduces the general level of neural noise. Any kind of activity which produces the kind of neural activity characterised by the habituation response therefore reduces neural noise. As this occurs, patterns of neural activity that are usually masked by noise come into conscious awareness. In other words, we become aware of more subtle aspects of experience which do not necessarily depend on our space-time bound senses. This could include psychic perceptions, and the core mystical experience of being enmeshed within a large "whole"—be it characterised as God, the Tao or Chaos. Also, we become aware of aspects of somatic experience that do not normally pass the threshold of awareness.

A difficulty with using "spiritual" models of Kundalini-type experiences is that it is often difficult to account for spontaneous experiences (such as happened to Gopi Krishna) and also, drug-induced states. Basing all such experiences within a neurological framework is not merely an exercise in reductionism, but an attempt to provide a basis of understanding which includes these two situations (and others).

Many self-proclaimed authorities decry the idea that drug-induced states are as powerful (in spiritual terms) as those attained through more long-term techniques. Writers on the occult often warn against using drugs as a "spiritual short-cut." However, research into LSD and similar agents indicates that subjects do, as a result of drug-induced experience, go through the profound life-changes—change in aspirations and "spiritual" awakening that occurs as a result of more orthodox disciplines, or traumatic life-events. However, an American researcher, W.N. Pankhe, notes that:

> "The hardest work may come after the experience, in the effort to integrate the experience with everyday life."

This is probably true for "trippers" who do not have a coherent belief-system with which to make sense of the experience—witness the number of "acid casualties" who end up as born-again Christians. This is also true for those who have "spontaneous" experiences.

The major distinction between the drug-induced experience and the "disciplined" approach is that the latter is much slower, and usually more controlled. Moving back to the "critical threshold" hypothesis at the beginning of this section, I would suggest that psycho-technologies such as magic or yoga, over time, produce changes in the human biosystem that eventually trigger the Kundalini experience. These changes relate to the establishment of patterns of neural cohesiveness—so that the practitioner becomes increasingly aware of the subtler aspects of experience and changes in other internal systems. Long practice of breath control, for example, lowers the CO_2 level in the blood, which also "smoothes out" cerebral activity across the cortex. Although the hardware of body organs doesn't change, the software does: i.e., the patterns of neural activity, chemical messengers, and transport of vital substances. All these factors can equally, of course, be affected by life-stresses, emotional trauma and repeated drug experience.

In these terms, Kundalini could be an organising principle that maintains the harmonious interaction of all human biosystems. When we become more aware of it, we are becoming more receptive to the internal dynamics of our own systems and, at the same time, opening (as Aldous Huxley put it) the "Doors of Perception". It's less that we "awaken" Kundalini, more that Kundalini awakens us. The riot of body-systems going into extreme activity often experienced as a part of early Kundalini "shifts" could be a result of the progressive software changes discussed above. It could represent a "peak" in the internal evolution of the bodymind complex, establishing new patterns of neural organisation in the brain. In subjective terms, this replaces previous "imprints" about the world and ourselves with the awakening of intuitive faculties, psychic perception, creativity, new aspirations, and a sense of being a part of a greater whole.

I do feel that my own Kundalini experience in 1984 marked the turning-point in my own development. I had to throw out many previously-held conceptions and learn to listen to and trust my own intuition. Acute peaks in Kundalini activity since that time have not been so disorientating, but have still released further potentia for activity and creative output. Indeed, during such periods of activity, I have found that the best way for me to manage the 'energy' is to direct it towards some kind of project, rather than "bottling it up" with meditation and yogic practices.

Kundalini activity in Tantric cosmology relates to the evolution of physical forms, the maintenance of the physical universe, and the spiritual evolution of entities in their return to Brahma—the noumenal source. It is the Jivatman, the spark of Brahman within each individual, which carries the instructions for our spiritual evolution.

Some Western scientists now regard the DNA-RNA structure as the genetic equivalent of the Jivatman. It has been suggested that the capacity to have Kundalini and similar experiences is encoded at the genetic level. Surprisingly, this hypothesis has come from research into schizophrenia. Research in the last ten years into the various syndromes collectively referred to as schizophrenia indicates that the subjective states reported by sufferers of the illness are similar, in many ways, to those reported by individuals undergoing "mystical" experiences. An individual's liability to develop schizophrenia is partially genetically determined. It has been said that schizophrenia is a gun primed by genetic factors, loaded by upbringing, and fired by some kind of trigger experience. Why such genes have survived is a puzzle, but it could be that the same genes which predispose towards schizophrenia also mediate the internal evolution of consciousness. Mystically-oriented commentators on schizophrenia such as R.D. Laing and C.G. Jung have drawn attention to the links between madness and the psychic-transformative journey. However, while the magician or shaman is "swimming," the schizophrenic is "drowning." If the genetic coding of such experience is the case, there are a multitude of other factors which impinge on the individual to facilitate neurological evolution: "illumination," neurological systems crash, schizophrenia, or many shades of either extreme.

Many people now believe that the next evolutionary step for humanity will be the evolution of consciousness. This is extant in current magical ideas such as the "gestalt consciousness" of the Ma'at Current, and in "new age" scientific paradigms as developed by Rupert Sheldrake (Morphogenetic Fields), David Bohm (Holoverse) and Timothy Leary (S.M.I^2.L.E. formula). Leary's 8-circuit model of neurological evolution in particular provides another way of interpreting the kind of process I have discussed. Briefly, Leary's theory states that since the design of the nervous system is encoded within the DNA-RNA structure, then the evolution of human beings in neurological terms is also contained therein. As the individual develops, there occur critical periods during which the brain accepts imprints which then become core elements of subsequent learning. The first four circuits ensure genetic transmission and variability, establishing humanity as a continuing species. The next four circuits are the DNA-RNA "Keys" to species evolution and adaptation. These "higher" circuits are opened when internal conditions are conducive. They represent states of consciousness which, after a certain intensity of experience, are reached (either by repeated access to them or by a very powerful single experience), and become hard-wired programs—a new basic 'reality' from which the individual acts. Once a circuit "opens" in this way, it becomes a powerful motivator for further development. For example, once bodily rapture (circuit V) has been experienced, it gives the individual a foretaste of what is beyond the basic survival circuits and their attendant conditioning. This could spur the individual on to accessing and imprinting the "higher" circuits.

This sounds similar to the Kundalini cycle, doesn't it? It is certainly an area which merits further investigation, and some magicians are now turning to neurologically-based models to integrate and understand their experiences.

Although much of what is presented here is done from a scientific viewpoint, much of it is built from very tenuous findings—there is still a long way to go in understanding Kundalini in neurological terms. It's a start, however. My own attitude towards Kundalini remains along the lines of, "Well, it happens, and then I have to integrate and evaluate the experience after it passes." I still don't work actively for Kundalini experience since I now hold the view that any kind of magical work will do this, and I find it more appropriate to work for specific projects and goals. Peaks in Kundalini activity, with their attendant changes in awareness, do result in the kind of new imprints that Leary is talking about. I have tended to find that whatever "map" of this experience you impose over it—whether this be Leary's model, Qabalistic power-zones, Hindu chakras, or Taoist chi-zones, the experience will fit them. This leads me to feel even more that the brain is the central area of the Kundalini experience. Kundalini is, indeed, the root magical power, since it is the potentia which can take us, once we are aware of it, beyond the limitations of cultural conditioning and space-time.

Sources

Arthur Avalon, *The Serpent Power*

Nona Coxhead, *The Relevance of Bliss*

Kenneth Grant, *Aleister Crowley and the Hidden God*

Aldous Huxley, *Heaven and Hell*

Timothy Leary, *Exo-Psychology*

Mary Scott, *Kundalini in the Physical World*

John White (Ed.), *Kundalini, Evolution and Enlightenment*

THE MAGIC WONDERLAND OF THE SENSES

[*The Magic Wonderland of the Senses: Reflections on a Hybridised Tantra Practice* was written in 2010 and appeared in the anthology *Pathways in Modern Western Magic,* edited by the late Nevill Drury (2012, Concrescent Press). This was the first I'd published something on Tantra for some time. I wanted to get across how I thought of my practice at the time, and again, some of the historical and cultural complexities that, I feel, have to be taken into account when trying to get to grips with Tantra as a practice. This essay is much more successful, I feel, in not only describing aspects of my practice, but my feelings about the practice as a whole; why I engage in it; what I get out of it; how exciting I find it. The ritual described and commented on is something that I've been practicing, in various forms, for well over a decade.]

———✦———

Introduction

Tantra, as Herbert Guenther put it, is "one of the haziest misconceptions the Western mind has evolved." The idea that Tantra exists as a monolithic and separate category to other forms of South Asian religious practice, is itself a product of the Western scholarly (and occult) imagination (see Hugh Urban, 2003, for an overview; also Padoux, 2002). Seeking to understand the manner in which Tantra has been 'imagined' and represented in scholarly, popular and occult discourses has also been a concern of my practice.

Within the subculture of contemporary occultism, this takes a particular form: Tantra is treated as essentially similar in practice and goal to Western Esotericism—at least once its content has been successfully re-interpreted by an author. Generally, there is an emphasis on Tantra as a set of 'techniques' or a 'sacred science' which is open to individuals to varying degrees. The figure of the Tantric practitioner is often portrayed as a kind of Nietzschean superhero, engaging in 'transgressive' practices which serve to take him or her beyond the limits of conventional society.

There is, however, very little attention (if any) given to Tantra as a *social* practice—the practitioner belonging to a particular group; that group's relationship to the wider culture; and the relationship between Tantric practitioners and the state (Tantrics and king-making, for example, or instances where Tantra became a 'state religion'). Often, Western occult authors find it necessary to reinterpret Tantra so that it becomes familiar—e.g., comparing it to the Qabalah—or occasionally re-representing Tantric concepts in entirely Western terms. This statement from the late Christopher Hyatt is not atypical:

> "Thus, do not expect a series of foreign words (some might call it 'Hindu babble') strung together as an answer to a question. To us, such approaches are nothing more than the refusal to answer the question by making the simple complex—for the benefit of the writer's ego. It would be ridiculous for us to answer questions by employing esoteric Eastern concepts. If we did, this book would be of little use for the Western practitioner. We do not pretend to be experts in the phraseology, language, culture, etc. of the Eastern path. What we are expert in is the utilization of their techniques to accomplish the desired ends.
>
> In many instances we will deliberately use Western methods and symbols as they are easier for the Western collective unconscious to assimilate and integrate."[2]

I find this approach to Tantra problematic, as it reduces Tantra to an exoticized support for Western understandings of magic and ignores much of the rich cultural and theological diversity present in South Asian forms of religiosity. Moreover, it presupposes that 'techniques' can be lifted or adapted from one cultural context to another without considering how those 'techniques' are enmeshed in, and reflect particular cultural practices and understandings. Furthermore, there is a tendency to assume that 'Western' and 'Eastern' paths are fundamentally incommensurable—which ignores the influence of esoteric concepts on Western esotericism over the last two hundred years or so, and takes no account of global exchanges between cultures.

---

[2] Christopher S. Hyatt, *Tantra Without Tears,* The Original Falcon Press.

I take a different approach. I work from the premise that the historically-originated South Asian practices loosely organised under the category of 'Tantra' are very different from what might be thought of as contemporary Western magic, and that to understand and enact them one needs to try to get a handle on the context in which they are embedded. This does require an active commitment to engage with 'phraseology, language, culture' (and much more). I generally refer to this approach as a 'hybridised' Tantra—one that draws from a series of interrelated historically-located practices/texts (notably the South Asian Sri Vidya, Kaula, and Trika currents) and from contemporary European philosophers (Merleau-Ponty, Deleuze and Guatarri, for example) who are concerned with challenging the binary divisions which have come to dominate our understanding of the world. The tendency to divide mind from body, self from social, subject from object—which has become so central to the Western enterprise—is simply not present in South Asian religiosity.

Rather than attempting to impose a linear structure on this essay (as in proceeding outwards from a definition) I want instead to discuss some key themes which weave in and out of Tantra that are important for me, and which may help with understanding the example of a Tantra practice which follows.

Wonder

The cultivation of a sustained sense of Wonder is both a *means,* and to some extent, the *goal* of my Tantra practice. Wonder is often related to the perception of the novel, the unexpected, the inexplicable; it's been linked to what is being increasingly termed a 'spiritual' quest for increased connection—the feeling of belonging, of engaged participation. Wonder can be found in a small moment—the sudden unfamiliarity of any artefact and how it came to be. Wonder can be an exhaustive epiphany, something I feel throughout my whole body, something that stays with me. Wonder has been sidelined in contemporary discussions of magic.

Wonder is, in many ways, antithetical to utilitarian purposiveness, to the urge to categorise, to order. Wonder propels us towards the unfamiliar, to seek new relations, to revel in dizzying complexity and richness. Wonder pulls us into the world beyond a limited horizon, beyond the certain, the familiar, the possible. Wonder is excessive—

and its excessive quality is something that Western philosophy, trailing in the wake of Aristotle, has fought to foreclose, to rein in.

Embodied Practice

Tantra is an *embodied* practice: the body is the primary site for practice, and the means through which the fruits of practice are attained. To speak of the 'body' in Tantra, however, is not merely to designate corporeality—Tantric body discourse includes sense-capacities, feelings, thoughts, moral and ethical capacities; the sense of selfhood. The familiar dichotomy between body and mind is absent here. Tantric bodies are open, porous to the world; a body which is a multiplicity of affects; a body which reaches out and is reached out to—a body enmeshed and produced by other bodies through reciprocal relations. The Tantric body is the lived cosmos and it is through the body that the practitioner identifies with the transcendental source which is simultaneously within, without, everywhere—collapsing all distinctions.

Relationality

For me, Tantra is above all, a *relational* practice. At its simplest, it is concerned with how we relate to ourselves, to others (both embodied/unembodied), and to the world in general. To do this requires, I think, both attention and care towards our relations. Tantra's relationality is baroque in the extreme: every affect or capacity can become—temporarily—a person; a god-goddess; a transactional nexus for worship, reflection, interaction, the joy of self-recognition. Think of yantras, mandalas, mantras as modal states—yantras as shimmering networks of unfixed relational points—each point a Shakti with the potentiality for exploding outwards into her own yantra, on and on with fractal-like recursion. Consciousness as a flower endlessly unfolding with an infinite number of petals... To dwell within this perspective is to open up to the possibility of engagement.

What is important for me is how to carry these points into practice. What is perhaps central to this approach is the negation of the familiar 'magical-mundane' dichotomy. Although I may perform special rituals, alone or with friends, much of my Tantra-practice is done on a day-to-day, moment-by-moment basis. Being open to wonder, or being mindful of relationships can be done anywhere, at any time.

The Magic Wonderland of the Senses

What follows is an example of a particular Tantric practice—the Arrow-Shakti rite—which I shall use as a loose framework for discussing how this particular approach that I am developing plays out in practice. This short ritual utilises both external worship (bahiryaga) and internal worship (antaryaga).

In this particular instance we exteriorise the Sense-Shaktis to honour them and engage with them as we would another person, and at the end of the ritual, draw back the Arrow Goddess (who is their condensed form) within the heart-cave which, in some Tantric traditions, is the seat of self. Many Tantric pujas (rituals, worship) proceed in this way and make use of various practices and identifications such as mantras and nyasa (touching different parts of your body to 'place' powers there), and so forth.

Tantric puja is modular in its structure—each 'block' can be performed as a particular practice, and puja can be extended by adding further blocks. It is important to understand the underlying principles of the puja. Many texts stress that mere performance on its own is useless.

The central theme in this puja is the gift-exchange. Offerings are made to the Sense-Shaktis as goddesses and the Arrow-Shakti (Lalita) who arises out of the total experiences of the senses; the blessing of the deities is received in return—in the form of food or grace (Prasada) and through the inter-identification of practitioner and the deities. A central Tantric theme in ritual is that to worship a god one must 'become' a god:

> "To worship a deity, a man must become the Self of that deity through dedication, breath-control and concentration until his body becomes the deity's abode."[3]

The visualisation of deities is a central feature of Tantra praxis. There is no connotation that visualisation is primarily imaginative or

---

[3]From the *Gandharva Tantra,* quoted in Alain Daniélou, *The Myths and Gods of India,* Inner Traditions, 1991, p.377.

that it is 'less real' than sense perceptions, or that visualisations are separate to an 'external world.' Visualisation is an intensification of experience—a means of reinforcing and embodying the symbolic order of the practice. Through the visualisation (of deities, yantras, chakras, etc.) the practitioner inter-identifies the lived body with the symbolic order of the tradition. The basic idea of deity meditation is that by focusing/contemplating the form of a deity (either using an iconic image or a textual description), the practitioner comes to identify with that deity and eventually takes on that deity's qualities, or gains that deity's perspective. Generally speaking, there is a progression from meditating on the anthropomorphic image of a deity to meditating on more abstract qualities. In the non-dual Trika movement, visualisation—combined with other practices such as mantra, nyasa, etc.—is said to draw the deities near to the practitioner by coalescing their shape or form out of consciousness, whereupon they come to reside in the ritually-prepared body, particularly in the heart.

Aspects of Tantra practice are often denoted as being either internally or externally directed. Internal worship might involve, for example, visualising one's chosen deity taking up residence in one's body. External worship might involve worshipping a deity as present within an image. However, these should not be read as opposed practices, but as practices which synergistically support each other— internal practice (that might be construed as 'meditation' in the West) supports and enhances external practice (ritual).

Beginning

I begin by snapping my fingers to the eight directions, above me, and below me.

Western approaches to magic tend to make a distinction between 'sacred' and 'mundane' space—and ritual acts are very often presented in terms of marking a transition from one to the other. In contrast, this Tantric approach holds that all space is the body of the goddess; all space is Shakti (capacity, power); and ritual acts to further condense or coagulate that Shakti. The emphasis here is thus on the intensification of present power. The attention to the eight/ten directions is not concerned with establishing a boundary (as a circle in Western magic is often thought to be), but in reaching outwards and pulling inwards.

Traditionally, snapping the fingers or clapping the hands (accompanied by the appropriate weapon mantras) may have been performed to drive away uninvited or unwanted persons (particularly unembodied persons) from disturbing the ritual. In the present context, this is done to signal the intensification of feeling/attention for the duration of the rite. Clapping the hands or snapping fingers is also more than just making a noise; it's a signal to oneself and others—a signal for attention or invitation.

The directions (eight, nine, or ten) are presided over by groups of deities such as the Lokapalas, the Durgas and the eight forms of Ganesha (there are many more). Worship of these deity-groups could be added to this puja at a later stage, according to preference. Note that there is no correspondence made between elements and directions, as one finds commonly in Western esotericism. Eight is generally an auspicious number in South Asia and the eight-direction pattern can also be found in temple and city architecture, and in ceremonies related to kingship (where the ruler's body is ritually made the centre of the eight directions). The eight directions are frequently internalised—for example, as eight cremation grounds, or eight chakras.

Honouring the Guru
I honour my guru, the guru's guru; the Adiguru. I give attention to those who have been teachers for me.

This is a brief moment during the sequence where I acknowledge my debt and relationship to past teachers (and, often, friends who have died). It's an acknowledgement of the role that others have played in bringing me to this moment. One of the trickiest aspects of Tantra for contemporary Western practitioners is the whole question of having gurus. When I occasionally lecture on the subject of Tantra, I'm often asked if I think a guru is 'necessary' and I usually answer by saying that I don't feel that I would have gained the understanding of Tantra that I feel I have, without the person I refer to as my 'guru'. For me, the necessity of the guru underscores the relational aspect of Tantra practice. It is a practice which requires the presence and co-operation of other people—friends, teachers, even (if possible) a loose community or network of other practitioners.

As the *Kularnava Tantra* expresses it: "Experience and good company are the two clear eyes of the seeker." My relationship with the person who agreed to become my guru—to help me in developing my own practice and approach—is a kind of friendship. It has been intense at times, particularly when we lived in the same city and could meet up fairly regularly. Now we live at different ends of the Earth, and the relationship we have is, of necessity, different. It's not like he even tells me things I should or shouldn't do, or advises me on what to practice, or that we must agree on points of doctrine or theology. Frequently, we don't.

Nyasa

I salute Shiva Shakti in my heart
I salute Shiva Shakti on the crown of my head
I salute Shiva Shakti on the top of my forehead
I salute Shiva Shakti in my Kavacha
I salute Shiva Shakti in my three eyes
I salute Shiva Shakti in my yoni/linga

Nyasa ('placing,' 'stamping' or 'imposition') is a major element of Tantric practice, whereby the body is made 'divine' by touching different body regions, visualising a particular God/Goddess (sometimes a God and Shakti pairing, also constellations, planets, the letters of the Sanskrit alphabet, sacred sites) often accompanied by mantras. Some nyasa sequences are highly complex and can be likened to inscribing a yantra onto one's body. Nyasa can be performed as part of puja or as a practice in itself. The above is a very simple nyasa sequence.

In 'placing' Shiva-Shakti within the body, Shiva-Shakti resides there, and we remind ourselves that we are Shiva-Shakti—or that Shiva-Shakti is our 'source.' We become identical to, or are merged with, the substantive presence of the deity who is the subject of the puja. In this approach to puja, nyasa is one of the processes by which we identify with the subject of the puja—simultaneously making our bodies 'divine' and infusing them with the presence of the deity. Following nyasa, the deity is often meditated upon as forming within the 'void' in our bodies, and is then externalised (via an out-breath) into a form for worship—either as a visualised form, or a picture, statue, etc.

In this nyasa, the Heart does not refer to the anatomical organ, but to the 'centre' of the body—the dwelling place of deity. The term Kavacha ('armour') is used to denote a set of practices related to magical protection—sometimes using amulets, mantra and liturgy to various deities.

As to the Three Eyes—many Tantric deities are described in texts (and depicted in iconography) as having three eyes (Skt: Tryambakam lit: 'three-eyes'). In modern forms of Tantra this is often related to the popular occult notion of the 'third eye' and the Ajna Chakra. There are, however, other considerations. In Tantra texts there are many triplicities—inter-related concepts such as the three Gunas ('qualities'); three Shaktis (Jnana-Iccha-Kriya); three times (past, present, future); three functions (creation, maintenance, destruction); three lights (Sun, Moon, Fire); and the three worlds. These triplicities are often mapped onto or homologised within the body. There is a popular Puranic story that tells how Parvati, Shiva's spouse, once playfully crept up behind Shiva and covered his eyes with her hands, plunging the Universe into darkness. To save the Universe, Shiva opened a 'third eye' between his brows. Tryambakam signifies mastery or equipoise between the triplicities.

Eyes are tremendously important in Indian religiosity. Darsan (which can be translated as 'to see with reverence') is a central feature in many forms of worship and ritual. In meeting the eyes of a god or goddess (be it through a statue, an auspicious person, or a possessed devotee or a lover) one is said to receive the blessings of that deity. In traditional temple puja where deity-images are created, the figure's eyes are the last to be painted. Darsan is a communion— an exchange between devotee and deity or, for that matter, a place or an object.

Yoni/Linga in this context refers to the practitioner's sexual organ.

Shiva-Shakti, in the context of this nyasa, is seen as providing the union of consciousness and power. Various textual sources privilege either Shiva or Shakti as the prime cause of the universe, but there is a common tendency in both Trika and Sri Vidya sources to view

Shiva-Shakti as a dynamic continuum—reciprocally realising each other. Neither can exist without the other.

The Worship of the Sense-Arrows

I close my eyes and, picking up a freshly-cut flower, inhale its perfume. As I breathe in the scent, I feel close to me the arrow goddess of the delight of smell.

I reach out and take a grape into my mouth. As its juice floods my mouth I let form before me the shape of the arrow-goddess of the delight of taste.

I press the tips of my fingers together. I direct my attention to how my clothes hang on my body, the feel of the ground beneath me. As I feel these sensations I let form the shape of the arrow-goddess of the delight of touch before me.

I listen to the sounds around me, to the soft breath of those others in this room, to the ticking of a clock, the low hum of electricity, the rumble of traffic outside, the distant bark of a dog. Out of these sounds there forms the arrow-goddess of the delight of hearing.

I look about me, settling my gaze on as many places as possible: objects, their shadows, the glinting of lights, textures, surfaces, folds. As my eyes dart about I glimpse the fleeting form of the arrow-goddess of the delight of seeing.

Here, the senses are personified and worshipped as goddesses— the Arrow-Shaktis. In several Tantric texts (particularly the texts of the Sri Vidya movement) the senses are referred to as flowery arrows, shot from the sugar-cane bow (the mind) and piercing the objects of perception—recalling Puranic tales wherein the God Kama shoots forth an arrow which causes Shiva to be inflamed with desire, so that he acts towards the world. All sense-experiences are divine, opportunities for us to experience wonder, joy, delight. All sensations and all pleasures are emanations of the divine. In cultivating Tantric awareness, the aim is to develop a sensitivity towards the beauty of everything around us and, in so doing, move closer to the sustained awareness of the wonder of the pulsation of consciousness that pervades all experience.

Shakti

Shakti is often translated in popular/occult texts to mean 'energy'. However, it has a wide range of meanings—such as capacity, power, ability, potential. Its verbal root is sak—and in its broadest sense it refers to the power to produce an effect. There are a vast variety of ways in which Shakti is used. For example, in the Puranas, Shakti is often used to denote both a philosophical concept and a goddess simultaneously. She is both the power possessed by the gods and is the transcendental source of the manifest universe—from which all forms emerge and into which, ultimately, they dissolve. Shakti is sometimes paired with a male god and portrayed as her consort; at other times, Shakti is said to create her male partner from her own body. Shakti can imply a relationship between two (or more) points/processes. Shakti can be transmitted between persons (embodied or unembodied), and can be thought of as a medium of transaction or exchange. Shakti can be accumulated through practices—it has moral and ethical aspects. Although Shakti is intangible, the degree of Shakti a person possesses is said to be reflected in the body as evidence of a practitioner's devotion and self-control (see Alter, 1992). Shakti as female power is also related to the belief that women generate more heat than men.

All the powers/abilities of our body/mind complexes can be interacted with as Shaktis. The personification and worship of the Sense-Shaktis which take place in this puja are of a temporary nature. The forms of the deities for ritual and devotion can be abandoned at later stages of practice.

Worship of the Arrow-Shakti

Seated with the five Sense-Shaktis before me, they shimmer and merge in and out of each other, becoming a single figure—their unity.

Arrow-goddess of the five, clothed in space, of a hue as red as a dawn, drenched in the nectar of ecstasy, holding in her two hands, five arrows and five flowers. She smiles gently, radiating satisfaction and contentment.

I make offerings to the Arrow goddess:

- Om, this is water, this is for sipping
- Om, this is incense, this is for prayer
- Om, this is perfume, this is for enjoyment
- Om, this is food, this is for sustenance
- Om this is flower, this is for experience
- Om this is fire, this is for sacrifice

I contemplate this form, then breathe her into my heart and meditate upon her presence there.

Three handclaps to close.

The offerings made here are the offerings one would make to an honoured guest—they are transactions. The Arrow-Shakti or Arrow-Goddess is a form of the Great Goddess Lalita Tripurasundari, who is the central deity of Sri Vidya (see Brooks, 1992). She emerges out of the totality of all sense-perceptions. She is the totality of the sense-perceptions—she is the transcendent source of all experience and all experience is simultaneously a gift from Her and an offering to Her. She is the Dancing Queen. She delights in all experience and to experience that delight—that wonder—is to become Her. The worship of the Arrow-Goddess is a reminder—an invitation to contemplate that our senses are not separate from each other; they cross-talk, play with each other. As much as we think the world in pieces, we experience that which is around us very differently.

Following the offerings and the contemplation of the Arrow-Goddess as separate to oneself, She is—with an in-breath—drawn within, residing in the heart-cave of the self. The puja is ended, but the aim, after all, is to shift the practitioner's awareness to being more attentive (and appreciative) of everyday experience—to be open to the wonder of the world around us and through which we move.

> "Let my idle chatter be the muttering of prayer, my every manual movement the execution of ritual gesture, my walking a ceremonial circumambulation, my eating and other acts the rite of sacrifice, my lying down prostration in worship, my every pleasure enjoyed with

dedication of myself, let whatever activity is mine be some form of worship of you."[4]

Conclusion

I was first drawn to Tantra practice in the early 1980s, through a series of recurring dreams in which the goddess Kali loomed large. At that point in my life I was involved in Wicca, and it would have been easy to interpret my dreams of Kali within a Wiccan perspective. But I was looking for something else. Westernised accounts and appropriations of what Tantra is supposedly concerned with are legion. In many ways, one of the largest obstacles I have had to work around over the last thirty years or so, has been moving through the Western representations of Tantra (both occult and scholarly), and discovering the rich and diverse theological approaches in South Asian texts themselves. As I came to grapple with this material, I found that to understand it, I had to abandon the Western (imperialist) perspective that asserts that the practices of other cultures can be easily assimilated into Western universalised esoteric schemas and, instead, seek to understand how those practices related to the wider cultural formations of India—both historically and in the contemporary milieu. In doing so, I found myself not only abandoning much of my previous thinking about magical practice, but also focusing towards what for me were increasingly central themes around which I wanted to base my practice—the wonder of life, the act of living from moment to moment, and the myriad ways in which we can experience that through our relations with the world.

References

Alter, J.S. 1992. *The Wrestler's Body: Identity and Ideology in North India*. Berkeley, California: University of California Press.

Brooks, D.R. 1992. *Auspicious Wisdom: The Texts and Traditions of Srividya Sakta Tantrism in South India*. Albany, New York: State University of New York Press.

---

[4] From the *Saundaryalahari,* quoted in W.N. Brown, *Man in the Universe: Some Continuities in Indian Thought* University of California Press, Berkeley, California, 1966, p.96.

Brown, W.N. 1966. *Man in the Universe: Some Continuities in Indian Thought* Berkeley, California: University of California Press.

Daniélou, A. 1991. *The Myths and Gods of India*. Rochester, Vermont: Inner Traditions.

Hyatt, C.S. 1999. *Tantra Without Tears*. Tempe, Arizona: Falcon Press.

Padoux, A. 2002. 'What do we mean by Tantrism?' in Harper, K.A. and Brown, R.L. (eds.). 2002. *The Roots of Tantra*. Albany, New York: State University of New York Press.

Smith, F.M. 2006. *The Self Possessed: Deity and Spirit Possession in South Asian Literature and Civilisation*. New York: Columbia University Press.

Tigunait, R. 1998. *Sakti: The Power in Tantra—A Scholarly Approach*. Honesdale, Pennsylvania: The Himalayan Institute Press.

Urban, H.B. 2003. *Tantra: Sex Secrecy, Politics and Power in the Study of Religion*. Berkeley, California: University of California Press.

Weinstone, A. 2004. *Avatar Bodies: A Tantra for Posthumanism*. Minneapolis: University of Minnesota Press.

TANTRA, SEX AND THE TRANSGRESSIVE IMAGINATION

[*Tantra, Sex and the Transgressive Imagination* was written in 2013 and appears on *enfolding.org*. It was intended to be the opening post in a much longer series, but my interest strayed, as it so often does, to other matters. I may return to it some day. Transgression—and its relationship to Tantra (and indeed to magic in general)—is a subject that has occupied me time and time again over the years, beginning with my engagement with Chaos Magic, and running throughout much of my early Tantric practice. In a great deal of magical writing of the 1980s and 1990s—particularly of the genres associated with Chaos Magic—the Left-hand Path, and Westernized Tantra, is the pervasive notion that becoming an individual is a heroic, transgressive exercise. In this essay I deliberately used a series of advertising slogans to highlight that this injunction to be an individual has been, for some years, normalised, and indeed, an accepted feature in contemporary culture.

Also, by attending to one particular text (in this case, a Buddhist non-dual Tantra) carries across the nuances and difficulties in the interpretation of particular texts and the doctrines which inform them.]

━━◆◆━━

"Like the concept of the primitive or the shaman, Tantra is a profoundly Janus-faced category: attacked in some historical periods as uncivilised or subhuman, and celebrated in other periods (particularly our own) as a pre-civilised unsullied original state, a sort of Eden before the Fall when harmony prevailed, when sex was free and unrepressed, when the body had not been subjected to modern western prudishness and hypocrisy."

— Hugh Urban,
Tantra: Sex, Secrecy Politics and Power in the Study of Religion

Sometimes You Gotta Break the Rules (Burger King)

Almost from the beginning of its discovery by Europeans at the turn of the nineteenth century, "Tantra" as a concept has revolved around two major axes—sex and transgression—almost to the point that these two elements are often read as tantra's defining features, that is to say, they are key elements in the "brand image" of tantra. After all, transgression sells. Contemporary ideals of transgression shifts products; we are encouraged to be individual; to "break the rules"; to find and express ourselves as authentic, creative and liberated individuals through buying stuff—from cars to cologne, burgers to books. There's a whole genre, seemingly, of books—occult books in particular—that make a point of declaring how transgressive they are—as if otherwise, one might not notice this. Hugh Urban (2006, p.254) asks a pertinent question: "Does the quest for radical liberation from even the boundaries of the self really lead to any meaningful sort of freedom? Or has it simply transformed the ideas of "liberation" and "transgression" themselves into commodities that can be purchased for $19.95 from Amazon.com?"

Given the ambiguities of contemporary attitudes to "transgression," I thought it'd be interesting to have a look at some tantric texts where the references to sexual or transgressive practices are, seemingly, fairly explicit—although it does not follow, necessarily, that they are either easy to interpret or even, dare I say, of much use to contemporary practitioners.

No Boundaries, Make Everyday Exciting, Go Further (Ford Advert)

I'm going to take a brief look at the *Guhyasamaja Tantra* ("the secret union tantra") which is probably one of the most well-known (or infamous) of Buddhist Tantras, dated approximately to between the 7–10th centuries, of which only Tibetan versions have survived. The *Guhyasamaja Tantra's* notoriety stems from the fact that it contains passages such as this (Chapter 5, v.2–8):

> "Those who take life, who take pleasure in lying, who always covet the wealth of others, who enjoy making love, who purposely consume faeces and urine, these are worthy ones for the practice. The yogin

who makes love to his mother, sister or daughter achieves enormous success in the supreme truth of the Mahayana."

and in Chapter 7:

"Taking a girl of good fortune, fair-faced and very beautiful, meditating on the foundation of blessing he should offer the worship of essence, and taking semen he should eat, open-eyed, with composed mind; this is the worship of the Body, Speech and Mind of all Mantras. It is called the accomplisher of all mantra-siddhi, the secret of those who possess vajra wisdom."

It is passages such as these which have prompted many commentators to dismiss all tantric texts as indicative of widespread cultural and moral degeneration, or equally uncritically, embrace them as amoral and "transgressive." If we take the first statement above at face value—the author(s) of this text are saying that people who kill, lie, are greedy, enjoy sex, eat shit, drink piss, and commit incest— are those who achieve success in (spiritual) practice. These sorts of passages, which occasionally turn up in tantric texts, have led to a good deal of puzzlement over whether or not they are literal statements of instruction, "coded" passages, or something else entirely. The underlying problem is that tantric texts in general, address "practitioners" within the traditions. Unlike the kind of magical manuals we have become accustomed to in contemporary western occulture, they are not, by and large, interested in explaining practices to "outsiders" or beginners—often quite the reverse.

Most scholarly interpretations of texts such as these advise following the extensive commentarial traditions which sometimes accompany such texts. For example, Christian Wedemeyer (2002), drawing on extant commentaries on the *Guhyasamaja* explains that the references in the text to "taking life" indicate the dissolution of identification with the limited sense of selfhood; that the injunctions to "possess the wealth of others" is, in actuality, the grasping of the intuitive wisdom of the perfected Buddhas, and the injunction to commit incest points, rather, to the non-dual "union" which is the goal of this particular tradition of Buddhism. Miranda Shaw (1995) offers a slightly different explanation of the *Guhyasamaja's* preferment for incest—that "Tantric adherents formed voluntary and tightly knit groups bound by secret initiations and pledges" and that "Tantrics defined themselves as family members in relation to one another." In support of this argument she cites a quotation from the *Cakrasamvara-Tantra:*

> "Stay only with female messengers:
> Mothers, sisters, daughters, and wife.
> Practice in a circle, like this,
> And not in any other way."

In Shaw's view, the female companion of a guru is likened to a mother, a female disciple of the guru is a sister, a male practitioner's "own disciple" (presumably a female disciple) is a daughter, and a male practitioner's female companion is a wife or consort. Her argument is that Tantric injunctions to have sex with one's own mother or sister should not be read as "transgressive" instructions for incest, but rather, point to the idea of tantric clan-groupings, wherein sexual rituals occur only between initiates—practitioners who share the same lineage, initiation and perspectives.

Another point which Shaw makes in respect to texts such as the *Guhyasamaja Tantra* is that these apparently "transgressive" instructions can be thought of as means of scaring off the lightweights as it were—that outsiders to the tradition would be put off by such passages, whereas only "insiders" to the tradition would be able to interpret them properly. However, this does not mean that there is necessarily one "inner meaning" hidden within such statements— Tantric texts tend to be open to multiple interpretations—and Esoteric Buddhism, for example, developed several hermeneutical strategies for doing so. Texts would have been interpreted—and deployed—according to particular stages in a practitioner's degree of attainment—and subject to the guidance of his (or her) preceptor. Again, this is an idea frequently encountered in tantric texts—that practices which, for an ordinary person (or a low-level practitioner) would be defiling (or, in the Buddhist context, be causes of samsara) were, for advanced practitioners, sources of liberation.

Break the rules. Stand apart. Keep your head. Go with your heart.
(Vanderbilt Perfume Ad)

But let's go back to the *Guhyasamaja Tantra*. Much of this text is framed within the terms of a discourse between the Lord Buddha Vajradhara and an assembly of buddhas and bodhisattvas. Immediately after Vajradhara lays out his transgressive programme, as it were (the verse about lying, eating faeces and so forth quoted above), the assembled bodhisattvas are thrown into confusion. The text says: "Why does the blessed master of all Tathagatas speak such words which should not be spoken in the midst of the assembly of all the Tathagatas?" Vajradhara calmly replies that "this is the pure Dharma-nature of the Buddhas who embody the essence of wisdom." The response of the assembly to hearing this articulation of non-dual wisdom goes beyond consternation—the bodhisattvas faint with fear, and are only revived when Vajradhara enters "the samadhi called Vajra of undivided sameness with space" whereupon, touched by the radiance of this great samadhi, the bodhisattvas attain understanding, and "filled with wonder and awe and overwhelmed with joy," begin to sing a song in praise of Vajradhara and the non-dual Dharma which has been revealed to them.

Wedemeyer (2012) reads this sequence of verses as an example of "motivated discourse"—an attempt to stress the non-duality of binary categories such as pure-impure; sacred-profane; immanent-transcendent. As he points out, the same pattern can be found in Chapter 9 of the *Guhyasamaja* whereby five teachings are given concerning the visualisation of mandalas which "become" one of the five transcendent Lords. In the first practice, a "mandala of buddhas" is transformed into the Vajra Asobhya: "Visualising the Buddhas of the three times, crush them with the Vajra, and contemplate the Body of Bliss of Body, Speech and Mind destroyed and crushed by the vajra, this supreme meditation with which achieves the siddhi of Mind." Secondly, the Wheel mandala is transformed into Vairocana: "then visualise all the vajra forms of the Buddhas by means of the five jewels; imagine that you steal all these treasures and draw them into the threefold vajra..." so that these stolen jewels become "great sages." The third practice is "visualise the Lotus mandalam and transform it into Amitayus; fill it all with Buddhas, and by the practice of the four yogas visualise them all there in union with the forms of women, this is the supreme vajra way." The fourth visualisation transforms a mandala of Buddhas into Vajra Amogha, in which "the forms of all the Buddhas" are visualised as "the vajra dwelling of false speech" who are then lied to. The final teaching is a mandala of Vajra Ratnekatu, and "filled with all the forms of Buddhas" who are then verbally abused. Once more the assembly are amazed and taken aback by these words, but Vajradhara and the transcendent lords explain the appropriate attitude towards this peculiar dharma:

> "Family sons, just as smoke appears and causes fire from two pieces of wood rubbed together and from the work of a man's hands, but the fire does not dwell in the wood that rubs, nor in the wood that is rubbed, nor in the work of the man's hands, so, Family Sons, the vajra laws of all the Tathagatas should be understood, just as a coming and going."

The chapter ends with the proclamation: "Among the dharmas most wonderful, like space, pure, beyond thought, the relative truth is proclaimed."

What's interesting here is that the apparently "transgressive" teachings are more than defiant disavowals of what we might think of as "normative" Buddhist practices. I don't believe that these teachings are an attempt to mount a critique of orthodox Buddhist ideology, but rather that they are deliberate provocations—aimed at orienting the reader or listener towards a consideration of the non-dual via a deliberate—and knowing—inversion of Buddhist ethics.

There's no one way to do it. (Levi's Ad)

Of course, one might easily raise the objection that this kind of interpretation represents a kind of bowdlerisation or "sanitisation" of something that was originally transgressive. As I noted at the beginning of this post, both academics and popular authors alike have been arguing for years over whether tantric texts should be taken literally or figuratively. Frequently one encounters the idea that non-sexual passages "hide" a secret, "sexual" meaning via recourse to a "twilight" or intentional language, whereas explicitly "sexual" passages should be read literally. The commentaries which accompany the texts—which themselves frequently favour multiple interpretations of passages—have been themselves criticised as later attempts to sanitise an earlier layer of transgressive "outsider" practices. This is an argument I will revisit another time.

Wedemeyer (2012), however, points out that seemingly "transgressive" statements can be found in other—non-esoteric—Buddhist texts. The *Dhammapada* for example, contains a passage which states: "Having killed mother and father as well as the king and two learned Brahmans, and having beaten the kingdom along with its attendants, a man is called pure." Wedemeyer comments that this kind of hyperbolic excessiveness is commonly understood to refer to obstacles to sadhana rather than a literal injunction to kill one's parents. After all, a literal reading of the Buddhist *Samantapasadika*—which Bernard Faure (1998, p.65) refers to as a "kind of 'Hite report' on Buddhist sexuality" might bring one to the conclusion that Buddhist monks were overly occupied with highly creative acts of bestiality with frogs and millipedes. Rather, it is another instance of the kind of rhetorical flourish or excess (Sanskrit: atisayokti) which is a common feature of religious, didactic and poetic literature. As Patrick Olivelle (2011) points out, the use of hyperbole in religious and didactic literature is different from its use in poetics, but "neither can be taken at face value or read literally."

Sources

Ronald M Davidson, *Indian Esoteric Buddhism: A Social History of the Tantric Movement* (Motilal, 2004)

Bernard Faure, *The Red Thread: Buddhist Approaches to Sexuality* (Princeton University Press, 1998)

Fransesca Fremantle, *A Critical Study of the Guhyasamaja Tantra* (London, 1971)

Patrick Olivelle, *Language, Texts, and Society: Explorations in Ancient Indian Culture and Religion* (Anthem Press, 2011)

Miranda Shaw, *Passionate Enlightenment: Women in Tantric Buddhism* (Princeton University Press, 1995)

David Shulman, *More Than Real: A History of the Imagination in South India* (Harvard University Press, 2012)

Hugh Urban, *Tantra: Sex, Secrecy, Politics and Power in the Study of Religion* (University of Chicago Press, 2003)

Hugh Urban, *Magia Sexualis: Sex, Magic, and Liberation in Modern Western Esotericism* (University of California Press, 2006)

Christian K. Wedemeyer, *Antinomianism and Gradualism: the Contextualization of the Practices of Sensual Enjoyment (Carya) in the Guhyasamaja Arya Tradition* (International Journal of Buddhist Studies, vol.3, 2002)

Christian K. Wedemeyer, *Making Sense of Tantric Buddhism: History, Semiology, and Transgression in the Indian Traditions* (University of Columbia Press, 2012)

Sexualities

Introduction

My early experiences in occult groups (and reading occult books) with regards to sexuality were not, on the whole, without issues. The prevailing attitude I encountered in the UK occult scene of the 1980s was that if you weren't straight, you couldn't be a witch or magician. This attitude ranged across the entire gamut of occult genres— Witchcraft, Ceremonial Magic, Tantra. Even the Neo-Tantra/Sacred Sex movement, which began to become popular in the early 1980s shared this view. Nik Douglas and Penny Slinger's best-selling *Sexual Secrets* (first published in 1979) held the view that "homosexual freedom" led to the decline of empires and that gay men should use yoga techniques to suppress their desires and thus avoid "karmic consequences." Nowadays, it is easy to come away with the impression that the world of Paganism and the Occult has always been accepting of non-normative sexualities. If people aren't accepting, then it is often laid down to individual aberrations and not embedded culture. It's easy to forget that in the 1980s and 1990s (in the UK at least) it was not unusual to find people mouthing statements that we would now recognise as homophobic, and largely not being challenged or called out for doing so.

For me, and most of the queer-identifying friends of my generation, the reality of the situation is more complex, and it has been my experience that the acceptance of non-straight Pagans and Magicians in the mainstream scene is the result of a long battle which is still, to some extent, going on. In part, this battle has been one of challenging assertions such Gareth Knight's "homosexuality, like drugs, is a technique of black magic" or occult theories that ascribe non-normative sexualities to "blocked chakras," an "imbalance of yin or yang energy," "reversed kundalini." We have also had to contend with explanations of polarity which draw on electro-magnetism or just good old "plugs and sockets," and the bizarre view that homosexuals are simply "not human," but are elemental or demonic entities inhabiting human bodies for dubious purposes—all ideas I have found in a wide variety of texts still in circulation.

Reading (and hearing) this sort of thing in the early 1980s, as a young man struggling with my own identity as a gay or bisexual man (I wasn't sure, and did think of myself as gay for some years), was confusing, to say the least. I went through stages of confusion, depression, and finally came around to being *angry* about it.

Getting *angry* largely took the form of writing, lecturing, and having long discussions with other non-straight Occultists and Pagans—there weren't that many, initially. I also started being more 'out' at pagan and occult gatherings—on one notable occasion, swanning around a field full of pagans in Leicestershire in leather trousers, a dog collar, and a feather boa.

By the late 1980s I'd become active in PaganLink Network (see the section on Paganisms) and it was through PaganLink I became acquainted with Gordon "The Toad" McLellan. Gordon started a Network called HOBLink which was a network with the aim of getting Gay, Bisexual, Lesbian and Trans pagans in touch with each other. The initial focus was on correspondence, although we did have a couple of enjoyable meetings. When I moved to London in 1992, I helped start up a London HOBLink group which ran for a while, titled "Queerwolf: A Radical Sexuality Network". We placed an advert in *Gay Times* to try to draw in some interest, but many of the respondents clearly associated Paganism with orgies on Hampstead Heath, which wasn't really the kind of meeting we were looking for at the time! I produced a newsletter entitled *Queerwolf,* although there was only one issue.

Throughout the 1990s I met and corresponded with a wide variety of non-straight magical practitioners from various traditions and approaches. Although I occasionally heard stories about people who'd had to "hide" their sexuality in order to be accepted in occult groups, things were slowly changing. Most of the people I knew through the Illuminates of Thanateros (IOT) or the Temple of Psychic Youth (TOPY) had no problems with queer magical practitioners, but a great deal of homophobia dressed up as occult lore still circulated in occult texts from other traditions, and of course, there was always occult scene gossip to contend with, which sometimes became public. By the late nineties some LBGT/Queer occult practitioners were creating their own autonomous spaces.

Queer Pagan Camp (QPC) is a case in point. Established in 1998, QPC ran for thirteen years annually (and after a brief hiatus, is running again) as a Do It Yourself Queer Space set up and run by Queer Pagan and Magical Practitioners—something quite different to a largely hetero-normative Pagan event that might (with the best will in the world) struggle to be "inclusive" of non-straight participants and perspectives. Part of the impetus behind the setting up of QPC was to offer a safe space for queer Pagans and Magicians, but also to create something different.

What does Queer mean in this context? It strikes me that there are two related but divergent ways in which the phrase "Queer Pagan" can be thought through. Firstly, as a noun, "Queer Pagan" can be read as an umbrella term, encompassing a multitude of identity-positions where perhaps the only commonality is varying degrees of commitment to refusing/resisting the hetero-normative gender binary. However, it's the second usage of "Queer Pagan" which I want to focus on for now, where "queer" is a verb, signifying a radical process of disruption—where the focus shifts from Queer Pagan as an identity-position towards Queering-Paganism as *process*.

What does it mean to "queer" something? Queering can be thought of a process of disrupting, disturbing and questioning the normal—that which is "taken for granted." Queer sidles up to identities, ideologies—any category that has been taken to be timeless, solid, and foundational and exposes gaps, fissures, resistances, instabilities, different possibilities, and surprises. Part of this commitment to challenge, to uncover the hidden, to look backstage and discover how productions are produced is the commitment to keep "queer" fuzzy and indeterminate—a recognition of the importance of not slipping back into an "us-them" binary which privileges a heroic "transgressive" queer subject against those still bound up in normative relations.

Someone asked me a couple of years back if Queer Paganism could be thought of as a "tradition". It is an interesting question, which for me highlights how Pagans tend to conceptualise different categories of praxis into "traditions." It also begs a questioning of how the very concept of "Traditions" is used in Pagan discourse. "Tradition" is sometimes used to denote a commonality of praxis—which is to say that it often implies common practices, ideologies, political alliances—and often there is an implication that this praxis is historically located—a kind of sense that what we do now was done by our ancestors, sort of thing. Tradition can be thought of (simplifying hugely) as an appeal to unity to varying degrees—and can act as a boundary in making distinctions between one approach to praxis and another. But for Queer Pagan(ism) such appeals to unity can only be, I think, of a temporary nature. One thing I see as central to Queer Paganism is a commitment to diversity and difference—which involves allowing a place for dissent—and the understanding that dissent is itself productive, rather than a failure. Equally, making a case for a historical Queer Paganism is also tricky. Although we can talk (at length!) about celebrating queer ancestors, reading queerness into and out of histories, of uncovering the politics of dissent hidden behind monolithic accounts of the past, I don't think that's quite the same as rooting a Queer Pagan praxis in the deep, undifferentiated past. I think of Queer Paganism as something new—Queer Theory and Queer Activism both emerged out of the 1990s, and the kind of Queer Paganism being enacted at QPC has direct connections to Activist groups such as Queeruption.

If one can speak of "Queer Pagan Tradition" at all, then it is as something relational to particular alliances and networks produced within, and temporary to heterotopic spaces such as Queer Pagan Camp. Perhaps a sense of shared tradition emerges when Queer Pagans come together to laugh, celebrate, dance and argue, but outside of such spaces it recedes, dissolving like morning dew. Rather than looking at tradition as a boundary which encloses particular practices (such as theologies, rituals, etc.), what seems to me to be of more concern within a Queer Pagan space is a commitment to an ethic of mutual care and reciprocity—an invitation to play with boundaries and categories, to celebrate difference. It is this ethical openness—primarily towards sexuality and gender identification, but also other forms of difference—which I see as central to understanding Queer Pagan approaches. Queer need not be an either/or choice made in opposition to other identities, but (depending on context/situation) possibly a "both/and" choice, or even a "neither/nor" choice. Opening to the possibilities of fluidity entails an acceptance of multiple orientations and positions that shift according to particular contexts and situations. At QPC, being "queer" is a matter of self-identification. If you think of yourself as queer, regardless of how you frame or express your desires (or not), if you can empathise with the ideals of the camp, you're "queer." It's not just Wicca with added glitter or Shamanism in High Heels.

The essays I've chosen for the Sexualities Section date from 1988 to 2019, and I feel, expose a wide range of influences and perspectives.

LOVE UNDER WILL

[*Love Under Will: Sexuality, Magic & Liberation* was written in 1988 and was first published in *Chaos International* No.4. It's a kind of "review" of occult understandings of sexual magic and their limitations as I saw them at the time. There's a heavy Starhawk influence here, and also I can hear the echoes of the arguments of some feminist friends. My references to "Tantric Sexuality" are rather wince-inducing now as my understanding of what constitutes "Tantric Sexuality" have changed enormously over the last 30 years or so. As an appeal to developing a more nuanced approach to sexual magic though, I still think this essay has something to offer.]

⚬

"I am the flame that burns in every heart of man, and in the core of every star. I am Life, and the giver of Life, yet therefore knowledge of me is the knowledge of death."

— *Liber AL,* II, 6.

At a time when magic is (supposedly) undergoing a renaissance, with core ideas & techniques presented in a clear and open manner, sexual magic remains entangled in glamours and misconceptions. There is little published material, it seems, which deals with the subject clearly. It is usually the case that sexual magic is shrouded (sometimes "drowned") in symbolic asides and allusions.

To begin with, what actually constitutes an act of sexual magic? A broad definition is: that it is the harnessing of one's own sexuality with intentionality—literally "Love Under Will"—to bring about change. This implies a great deal more than the waving of rods, wands, cups and roses. Celibacy, as a conscious decision not to be sexually active, can be as much an act of sexual magic as any ritualised copulation or masturbation.

The basis of sexual magic is to understand and experience sexuality as sacred or "magical." Sexuality is probably the most powerful means of transformation, discovery and knowledge that humanity has. This is why sexuality is effectively put under 'lock and key' by our Society. The Judeo-Christian attitude to sexuality has become "embedded" in the cultural psyche, to the extent that many of us feel that sexual expression is "naturally" followed by shame and guilt. For orthodox Christianity, sexuality can never be entirely sinless, even within the confines of marriage. The onset of the "Permissive Society" is supposed to have freed us from past constraints and inhibitions, but has it?

Sexuality has become another brand of commodity, another source of status. Although we tend to regard our own sexual natures in terms of privacy and "naturalness," it is subject to a great deal of interference and manipulation from external agents. There is a media-borne cultural imperative that we must be good at sex; that success is dependent on the number of orgasms that we can wring from our partners; or, indeed, from the number of partners we have. For many of us, sexuality is a major means of gaining status and egocentric power, associated with imposing one's will upon others. The key factor in rape, for example, appears to be that of the male demonstrating his power over another person (woman or weaker male). Society acts to channel sexual energy into acceptable forms— those which maintain alienation; channels such as sentimental romanticism and pornography. More powerful and invasive than any medieval incubi are the neuroses, obsessions and acts of violence which seem to be the inevitable spawn of this sexual nihilism. A characteristic of this profoundly egocentric sexuality is that one's partner is regarded as little more than an instrument to satisfy one's own needs (be they physical or status needs). Human emotions are alienated in the scramble for consumer gratification—in goods, wealth, success and the conquering of each other's orifices.

These cultural imperatives—to be successful and goal-oriented in every area of life—are so deeply embedded that we only tend to notice the most obvious manifestations of them—with regard to work, for example. They can easily pass unnoticed in the very personal domain in which we place our own sexuality, and equally importantly, our sense of "spirituality." As a result of the cultural emphasis placed on goal-orientation, a good deal of what passes for Western occultism is also goal-oriented. Western sexual magic is no exception. There is a tendency to regard sexual magic as merely a 'better' way to acquire goods, "powers" or wealth, and there is great emphasis placed on the necessity of visualisation, inhibition of orgasm and mental concentration rather than bodily awareness and pleasure. This seems to be a rather clinical and narrow approach to sexual potential; as Zach Cox put it (in *Aquarian Arrow* 22) "like using a microprocessor chip as a doorstop."

Part of the problem that Western sexual magic suffers from is the enshrinement of the ideas of Aleister Crowley, who is often held up as a paragon of the 'new sexuality.' However, pansexuality such as Crowley displayed does not automatically imply total sexual liberation. Though a great innovator and synthesist, Crowley was unable to disentangle himself from the prevailing sexual mores of his time. His sexual philosophy displays a typical (and enduring) dualistic attitude towards women, placing his "idealised" women on a pedestal, yet seemingly unable to accept women as equals. Examples of his egocentricity are not hard to find:

> "At about 8.45pm I was on 34th St & Broadway, looking for a soulmate, a destined bride, an affinity, a counterpartal ego, etc.; and should have considered the conditions satisfied by any orifice into which I could plunge my penis at a cost not exceeding $2.50."
>
> — *Rex De Arte Regia*

Crowley's approach to sexual magic seems to have been almost totally results-oriented, with his numerous operations for money, fascination, success, youth and magical energy. He implies that the partner in such a working is secondary to the will of the Mage, the selection of an appropriate partner being left to unconscious caprice. Unfortunately for present-day occultists, there is little material available concerning the work and ideas of the women who followed Crowley's system. Doubtless much of Crowley's attraction as a guru-figure is the way his attitudes uphold male egocentric sexual values. All the material currently available on the subject of "suitability" of partners" is male-oriented, and serves to maintain a kind of imbalance On the one hand there is Louis T. Culling's attitude:

"Often, a woman who has studied occultism becomes impossible because she has too many preconceived ideas which are not in agreement with her role as a good, co-operative partner. If there is any possible rapport, the woman becomes responsive automatically to the aspiration of the male, and after this has happened, it would be very easy to give her an explanation and an understanding of the magical aspects."

— *A Manual of Sex Magick,* p.25

While on the other hand, there is Kenneth Grants implication that Tantra is well-nigh impossible nowadays, due to the lack of suitable partners:

"Western women who possess the required traits are rare, and as they have not the hereditary advantage of initiation into occult techniques—as have certain African and oriental women—the sudden impact of magical energy on their personalities tends to disturb their sanity."

— *Aleister Crowley & the Hidden God,* p.84

Grant notes that according to Tantric practice, woman is the initiatrix of the male, but seems to hold the opinion that such women are a rarity in the West. Although the bulk of his writing is set towards the task of producing a sexual metaphysic based on the "occult" properties of menstruation, it seems to be distant from women in that there are many references about women as the Priestess or Suvasini—but almost nothing from women themselves on this subject.

The focus of this issue of "suitability" is couched wholly, it seems, in terms of occult metaphysics. Nowhere is it mentioned that it is beneficial for all concerned to be working on their own sexual/emotional conditioning, or that empathic sensitivity to, and even understanding of one's partners' needs and feelings could be paramount. It is these ordinary, human qualities that are lost in the vast symbolic meta-structures that Grant erects. One has the feeling that those who are not party to the ramifications of these "secrets" are not worth considering in terms of degrees of initiation. Initiatory experience in areas of life other than the occult does not seem to matter. Given this attitude, it does not seem likely that "Priestesses," at least in the way Grant seems to be depicting them, will "re-emerge," since women seem to be tacitly excluded from assuming a coequal role with males—as it is the latter who have erected the metasystem in the first place:

> "As it is we can but preserve the formula, confident that the present magical revival will discover genuine Priestesses to serve our mass."
>
> — *Aleister Crowley & the Hidden God*

Given the current developments in male and female consciousness, it is more likely that the "Priestesses" are already out there waiting for us men to get our act together!

It does seem to be a feature of male-oriented magic that the emphasis is upon building these heavily intellectual metasystems, which are removed from 'everyday reality.' In contrast to this, "Women's Mysteries" seem to revolve around aspects of daily experience—birth, sexuality, creation, nurturing, menstruation and Death. It appears that "High Magic" is largely concerned with acting within an abstract "inner-space" that has few points of contact with the consciousness of daily experience. I feel that this distinction should be emphasised, as the whole character of magic is changing. There is a movement away from its being a kind of developmental process which is seen purely in occult terms, and that has nothing in common with other spheres of life. This traditional attitude is being supplanted by the idea of magic as a fully integrative process of self-transformation. There has been a rekindling of the power of magic in making connections—in communicating with, guiding, healing, and "reaching out" to one another, rather than an entirely personal inner-initiation. As the general emphasis of magic changes, so too has there been a shift in attitudes regarding sexual magic.

Intimations of this shift can be discerned in the writings of Dion Fortune. Her influence upon developing Western sexual magic comes from her novels rather than from her non-fictional output. The underlying theme in her works, especially *The Sea Priestess* and *Moon Magic* concerns the intense consummation achieved by the partnership between a man who is in some way "wounded" and a woman who, to further her own magical intent, takes on the role of the initiatrix. The Priestess "Vivien Morgan" chooses her partner, initiates him and then withdraws. Fortune's writing displays levels of feeling—of intuition and cycles—which was absent in the writings of her male contemporaries. There is a fine understanding displayed of how "magical" development blends with one's relationship to life-changes in general. Fortune's approach to sexual magic is concerned with interpersonal transformation rather than goal or inwardly-directed experience. Her treatment of Pan, for example, in *The Goat-foot God* is more concerned with the inspiration and awareness of "a Greater Whole" than the rutting, phallocentric Pan that typifies Crowley's approach to sexuality.

The Return of the Goddesses

Over the last two decades, one of humanity's oldest cultural influences has begun to be reasserted in the return of the Goddesses. Within the occult subculture, this has manifested as the growth of Wicca and Earth-based Paganism, and in the wider culture, of course, as the rise of Feminism and the articulation of female consciousness. Wicca places great emphasis upon sexual magic. Doreen Valiente, in *Witchcraft for Tomorrow* notes the similarities apparent between Witchcraft and Tantra—the emphasis on balance between the sexes, and the central role of the Priestess as initiator and Earthly representative of the Goddess. The focus of Wicca is directed outwards—into Nature and awareness of cycles (both intrapsychic and Natural rhythm)—rather than a highly abstract meta-structure. The emphasis upon Sexual Magic is towards fertility rites and participation in seasonal changes. Some Wiccan writers see their attitude to Sexual Magic as the Hieros Gamos, the sacred marriage between Gods and Humanity. There is also the idea of sexual magic as a means of "passing power from initiator to new-initiate" (Galadriel, in *The Lamp of Thoth,* Vol.1 No.2). Again, this shows a shift towards harnessing sexuality as a means to a process of engagement, rather than simply being another technique for acquiring results.

The rise of Feminism is also a very important factor in considering the shifting emphasis of sexual magic. John Rowan (1987) puts it in these terms:

> "...women starting to notice that the whole thing (i.e., the Sexual Revolution against Victorian attitudes) had been organised by men, with male assumptions and male values, for the benefit of men. The

way in which women had been supposed to participate was by being like men in every way."

— *The Horned God*

The growth of Feminist ideology saw women demanding self-definition in their own terms, and a recognition of a female culture that is as important as that of male culture. Awareness of the necessity of this process has been growing steadily, not only at the sociopolitical level, but also as a Spiritual endeavour. It has showed up the glaring omissions in the "traditions" of Patriarchy-derived Occult systems. There is now a resurgence of Women rediscovering and recovering their own "Mysteries" as evinced in the work of Lynn Andrews, Barbara Walker, Monica Sjoo and others. A particularly important crossover for the development of magic is the work of Starhawk, who provides a Feminist approach to spiritual & transpersonal development for both women and men. Her book *Dreaming the Dark* connects the values of Wicca with a developing Feminist/ Therapeutic current. Starhawk writes of the idea of the archetypes of Goddesses and Horned God providing possible re-evaluations of male and female—beyond the constraints of patriarchal culture. Exploring one's sexuality through these archetypes is a way of transcending our cultural mores about masculinity and femininity. Sexuality is here understood as "a deep connecting power." (Starhawk, 1982)

This is a far cry from the "traditional" ethos of sexual magic. The focus has shifted from a "bits" approach, to sexual magic as a distinct set of techniques, to an emphasis which regards sexuality as just one aspect of a whole process of transformation. This is very close to the idea of sexuality as a means to "Liberation" mentioned earlier. But of course, such Liberation is not only spiritual, but sexual, social and political.

Sexuality & Intimacy

Sexual Magic as a path to Liberation is a core idea within Tantric philosophy, but does not seem to have been widely explored in Western Magic. It involves the redefinition of gender stereotypes, exploring relationships beyond the cultural confines, and exploring personal sexuality. Exploring sexuality becomes a means to knowledge, both of self and others. This Gnosis (Knowledge of the Heart) can take us beyond our cultural norms and limitations, to actively engage in the realisation of the post-patriarchal individual.

Very closely linked with this process is the recovery of Love from its imprisonment in consumer-romanticism. Western ideas of Love have become gradually warped by the concept of Egotistical possession, so that the language of Love is equivalent, to a large degree, to the language of ownership. Love bound by rules, duties, morals and projected by television and commerce serves to maintain the alienation of men and women from themselves and each other. The transformational power of Sexual Energy thus becomes destructive, maintaining the wedge driven between self and other, mind and body, Ego and Exo.

However it is possible for Love to be discovered despite these cultural blinds. This is the experience of Love as a Spiritual, inwardly-felt quality. Again, this idea is emphasised in Tantra, but not in Western Magic (until fairly recently). It appears in the concept of Courtly or Sublime Love idealised by the European Troubadours, considered as heretical by the church. This Sublime Love is spoken of as a positive force that reaches out towards others, taking them on a journey of expansion.

The key to Sublime Love is the "Deep Trust and Intimacy" experienced by the partners involved. Again, this recalls a Tantric idea, that the partners in acts of Sexual Magic be beloved to each other. This recognition (when it has actually been stated in Western writings on Sex Magic) tends to have been formerly restricted to statements that Sexual Magic is only valid when carried out by long-established ("married") partners, or else it becomes somehow "Black." This refers, of course, to Sexual Magic purely in terms of genital activity.

However, when the focus of attention shifts from a narrowly-defined view of Sexuality, to one of intimacy (of which physical sex is only one aspect), there also opens the possibility of intimacy in relationships other than those of conventional exclusivity. Close intimacy can develop within a "closed" magical group, without it necessarily moving into what we would otherwise call wife-swapping or group sex. Intimacy and Deep Trust in a group setting are powerful generators of a Group Gestalt which acts as a tribe or clan to each participant. To the prurient, this will be dismissed as an excuse for orgia, but exploration of intimacy can lead to a greater sense of involvement in both the group and the wider process of transformation. The emphasis is shifted towards mutual growth and development, rather than the pursuit of sexual conquests that appears to be so rampant in modern Occult groups. Indeed, the exploration of intimacy could almost be a necessity for Magical groups, where the undercurrents of sexual dynamics (attraction, anxiety, jealousy, etc.) which develop when members become attracted to others outside their usual relationships, can quickly destroy a group's coherence. Ritualized Sex in a group setting is only destructive when there is a lack of trust and intimacy among those taking part.

An American Psychologist, Mosher (1980) researching into intimacy found that 'the level of intimacy a person experiences is related to the degree of expression, awareness and interpersonal contact that is experienced during sex.' According to Mosher there are three levels of intimacy: Ego-centred, Surface-centred and Core-centred. Ego-centred involvement only concerns Egocentric gratification— one's partner being at best an instrument to fulfil physical or status needs. Surface-centred involvement centres on sexual performance and pleasure, both of self and partner. Core-centred involvement, however, is typified by the desire to open oneself fully to the partner, or at its "peak" the experience of Bliss and loss of Ego-boundary. There is also the implication that once a new level (or depth) of involvement is attained, that those formerly experienced are, in future, no longer wholly satisfying in the way they might once have been.

It is this "Numinous" experience of sexuality which most closely corresponds to the Tantric experience of Sexual Ecstasy. But in Western Society, the energy liberated by such experience tends to be diverted into the culturally accepted channels of expression—those which maintain the boundaries of Egocentric involvement such as possessive attachment, with all its attendant anxieties and neurosis. If these constraints can be transcended (which obviously will take a long time and good deal of effort), then the intensity generated can facilitate a "breakout" from the inertia imposed by society. Lovers can find enough support and energy in each other to reject the cultural limitations and seek new forms of living, free to move in any direction. Obviously, blissful sex cannot of itself wipe away a life-time of conditioning, but it can be an impetus towards further development in all areas of awareness. Sexual bliss is a powerful Gnosis for imprinting a new vision of reality, as recognised by Timothy Leary in his theory of Neurological circuits. A first experience of the Numinous often marks the "trigger" for an individual's transformational journey, and each subsequent experience of bliss provides further impetus for the process. It is the "heat" generated by such alchemical processes which moves the psyche from a condition of static identification (Ego-centric) to one of engagement and flow (Exo-centric). Starhawk writes of this sexual alchemy as:

> "...an exchange of energy, of subtle nourishment, between people. Through connection with each other, we connect with all."
>
> — *The Spiral Dance*

It is important to note that psychic structures cannot be "wiped away" completely by the transformational process, but they can be built on, and replaced by structures that are more adaptable, open to uncertainty and change. For men this involves letting go of the male Ego, and what John Rowan calls "surrendering to the Goddess."

> "Experiencing the Goddess through us, completes men and brings them into our world."
>
> — Alathea the Shamoon

This surrendering—or willing sacrifice is the beginning of a process of psychic death, which leads ultimately to rebirth into a world of participation and engagement. For males, this psychic meeting with the power of the Goddesses—in the form of the Dark Destroyer (for example, Kali, Hecate or the Morrigan)—has a powerful transformative potential. The Goddess in her dark aspect is the gateway to the Underworld, the place of psychic dissection and restructuring. This aspect of woman appears in Patriarchal culture as the male fantasy of the sexually uninhibited woman also linked with the anxiety-creating image of woman as castrator and devourer.

If Will can be directed towards change, then any Magical process involving psychic restructuring can lead to change in outward areas of life—interpersonal and social. The power of the Goddesses (Shakti in Tantric terminology) as experienced by men, opens us to an experience of empowerment (power not couched in male terms). We can recognise that the possibilities of transformation lie within us, which should lessen the tendency to project Egocentric needs onto women. The reality of this Goddess-experience is difficult to deny or rationalise away once it becomes immediate and heartfelt. This experience of Devi must surely begin to loosen our cultural conditioning. It is part of the painful process of absorption and rebirth—a rebirth into participation.

The Way Forward?
Liberation implies the freedom of the whole being, at all levels and in all areas of action. It is a change which is fundamental and total. It is not enough to ignore or try to wish away our current situation. The necessity of "obedience to awareness" is brought home with every update on our headlong plunge to self-destruction. In many ways this essay is a statement of my personal views of Sexual Magic as a way of uncovering, energising and realising our potential to evolve as Humans. The insights gained through the process of transformation give us glimpses of future possibilities, which we can then attempt to live towards. At the moment, we know very little about what it means to be male or female, beyond the boundaries of Patriarchy. Growing up or evolving is a hard and painful struggle, but we cannot resist it forever. Magic is a possible avenue by which we may at first glimpse, then realise these possibilities. This to me, is the essential nature of "Love Under Will."

A CLAUSE FOR CONCERN

[*A Clause for Concern* was written in 1991 and appeared in *Moonshine Magazine*. In 1991, the UK's Conservative government was debating Clause 25 of the Criminal Justice Bill—which included a range of provisions which would have many social activities for Gay men effectively illegal. Thanks to a campaign run by Stonewall and other activist groups such as Outrage, these provisions were largely overturned. This is one of my *angry* essays, and, I think, is something of a coming out piece for me. I was identifying as Gay at the time although later become more comfortable with my bisexuality. Some readers might be surprised that Pagans in the UK did not necessarily think that Paganism had any relationship to matters of wider social engagement—such as politics or sexual preferences— but this was not an uncommon attitude at the time.]

Clause 25 of the Criminal Justice Bill is all set to 'criminalise,' for Lesbians & Gays, a wide range of social activities that other people just take for granted. Exchanging a kiss in public, holding hands, arranging a date via a friend, staying overnight in someone's spare bedroom. "So What?" you might think. After all, 'it's not natural'; 'it's disgusting'; it's not my problem. But how would you feel if, every time you wanted to exchange a kiss in public with your lover, there is a possibility of arrest, imprisonment, and even compulsory medical treatment? Alternatively, there would be as well, the very real threat of getting the shit kicked out of you for being 'queer.' Think this would affect your world-view? It does mine.

So why am I writing this in *Moonshine?* What has Paganism to do with sexuality, or politics for that matter? Well I can't separate them out. Being a Pagan helped me a great deal with coming to terms with my own sexuality. When I first began to come out as Gay, I received a tremendous amount of support from my Pagan friends. I find there's a lot of cross-over; being Pagan can lose you your friends, a job, or estrange you from your family, in the same way that declaring your sexuality can. Both require you to examine yourself—to look within and say "this is what I am"—and feel good about it, even if you can't always be open to everyone.

Clause 25, ultimately, will affect us all, regardless of our sexual orientation and politics. It affects us all because it will, effectively, legitimise homophobia, a name or word-virus which says that 'real' men can't be gentle, affectionate with each other, or treat women as anything other than objects to be 'screwed.' Homophobia is one of the basic control-codes that maintains Patriarchy by defining the limits of masculinity in such a narrow way that any man who tries to step outside it will be branded a 'faggot.' Interesting word that. Faggots are bits of wood that get burnt. This derisive word hearkens back to the 'burning times' when Gay men were burnt at the stake. The number must have been many for the word to get into popular usage. Historically, Homosexuals and Pagans are both 'heretics', and share a common heritage of persecution. Likewise, in Nazi Germany, Occultists were sent to concentration camps, and over a million Lesbians & Gays were gassed in the death camps.

And the witch-hunts continue. Interesting that the same people who stirred up the Satanic Child-Abuse scare are the ones who issue "Kill a Queer for Christ" bumper stickers.

On another note, an increasing number of Lesbians & Gays are becoming interested in Paganism and Magic. For me at least, being Pagan is about discovering my own individual path and exploring it in an atmosphere where people make allowances for individuals. It's a lot better than certain other religions where being Gay instantly means you're in league with the Devil, or damned. Like I say, largely my other Pagan friends have given me a lot of warmth and support. Which says more about them as people than Pagan beliefs *per se.* Why do I say this? It's because there is almost a complete absence of literature that takes a positive attitude towards Lesbians & Gay men becoming involved with Pagan or Occult paths. There is, however, a quite strongly expressed belief that homosexuality (particularly male) has no place in Paganism or Magic. I've heard this from Wiccans, Pagans, Thelemites, Kabbalists, Tantric practitioners, etc. A few writers such as Dion Fortune and Gareth Knight have stated that homosexuality is a form of 'Black Magic.' Outdated ideas? Perhaps so, but these writers' ideas are still being circulated as 'spiritual truth,' and when prejudice becomes legitimated as 'spiritual truth,' then the Pagan who takes on board such a belief is not a million miles away from the ranting Evangelist screaming "All witches worship Satan."

Well you might say, "Why don't Lesbians & Gays adapt what is written for the majority (i.e., heterosexuals) in books." Well we do. But if all books on Paganism were written for women, how would men feel about 'adapting.' What I would like to see happen is Lesbians & Gays weaving our own forms of spirituality that are pertinent to us, rather than 'fitting into' a spirituality which has no definite place for us. Again, with Clause 25 in the pipeline, such literature may be difficult to produce, especially if we want to look at our own sexuality. Can you imagine one of the popular occult publishing houses printing a book promoting Gay Magic? Okay, it is a minority subject, but occult publishing is all about 'minority subjects.'

A final point I would like to offer is that those who dare to face oppression by standing up and saying "this is what I am," are those who act from a mind-set of power-from-within. I've always kicked against the middle-class; safe, self-satisfied Pagans; and magicians who, to me, are simply buying into and reflecting a rose-tinted mirror of society as it is, not as it could be—if we dared to look beyond its walls. Magic flourishes amongst the oppressed because all normal channels are closed. It's the only option left. It's hard to have a benign spirituality when it's being hammered into you (sometimes literally!) that you're different—despised and abnormal. It's not the 'safe' expressions of spirituality that help us grow, it's the resistance to the claws which reach out for all of us. Look at the impact of the magic which has risen from Feminism and Women's Spirituality— rituals at Greenham and the works of Goddesses. So, too, the modern Gay Liberation movement grew from the Stonewall Riot, where for once, despised 'faggots' stood up to the truncheons and mace—a magical act, if you like. We can choose to stay safe, or we can choose to try to evolve—a dangerous undertaking to be sure, but worth it. As Pagans, we've dared to be 'different,' so where's the problem in recognising and empathising with others who've also dared?

Don't feed the beast; fight the Clause.

Sodomy and Spiritual Fulfilment

[*Sodomy and Spiritual Fulfilment* was written in 1995. It was originally intended for publication for a London-based magazine whose editors had asked me to write an article on sexual magic. However, they decided (for reasons which were never clear) that it was too "hardcore" for them, so it was published in *Chaos International* No. 11 instead. Re-reading it now, I feel there is a trace of defiance here. I wanted to get away entirely from abstract accounts of sexual magic and write directly from my own experience, but at the same time I was keenly aware of crossing a boundary in describing the *feeling* of being fucked. There's a clear influence of the writings of William S. Burroughs and Jean Genet here too, both of whom I'd been reading since my early 20s. The line about anal sex stimulating the muladhara chakra—not something you tend to find in popular works on the chakras—is probably influenced by a reading of Alain Daniélou's 1992 book *Gods of Love and Ecstasy* where he gives a rather convoluted (and I would now say, spurious) account of anal penetration as a means of awakening the Kundalini. At this point, I was still reliant on such accounts of Tantric sexual practices and hadn't really started to question their validity. I no longer recall whether I took Daniélou at his word or if this was just a satirical occult justification for the benefits of passive anal intercourse.]

———

I remember very well the first time I got fucked. Exhausted and relaxed after all-afternoon sex, I lay sprawled on my boyfriend's bed and uttered those fateful words, "Do anything you want with me." From the corner of my eye, I saw him pick up a glass bottle in the shape of a unicorn, filled with a yellowish liquid (sweet almond oil), and I knew what was about to happen. I had no fear, only a deep sense of relaxation. It didn't hurt, but at the moment of penetration, one self died and another was reborn. An 'initiation,' certainly, and one that gave me insights which I will now attempt to collect into a coherent article.

What feelings does being fucked stir within me? Two words perhaps, describe them best: abandonment and possession. In being fucked, I am abandoning my ego-defences, opening myself at a deep level to another person, and am able to cast aside the socially-crafted 'masks' I put on to deal with the world. I abandon myself to total pleasure and to the pleasure of my lover. I cross back and forth between the borders of ecstasy and agony, until I am moaning and crying uncontrollably; soft liquid fire in my belly and a fierce tingling that seems most vivid at my fingertips. To date, I haven't had an orgasm from being fucked alone, but then, ejaculation and orgasm are two different experiences for me much of the time, and penile ejaculation seems unimportant, compared to the sensations which threaten, it seems, to tear my body apart when a lover is inside me. A lover's orgasm within me brings about a feeling of deep peace and satisfaction. I feel as though I have been revitalised and can go forth into the world with an inner glow. I regret deeply, in these AIDS-conscious times, that I cannot receive into myself a lover's semen. Yet it is as though in abandoning myself to another, I reaffirm my sense of selfdom.

At the same moment that I abandon myself, I am also in a state of possession. This is more difficult to write about, but it is linked, I feel, to a common misperception about intercourse—the concept of 'active' and 'passive.' For myself, I prefer the words 'giver' and 'receiver.' Our miserable, patriarchal conditioning has given rise to the conception that 'active' = 'masculine' and 'passive' = 'feminine.' I have increasingly come to reject this sort of thinking. Just because one person (male or female) takes a lover's penis into their body, doesn't necessarily mean that they are automatically 'passive.' This is clearly illustrated into the Tantric icons of Shiva mounted by Kali. Societal conditioning is strong enough to make some Gay men feel that anyone who takes it up the arse is somehow less than 'male' because abandoning oneself to pleasure is not appropriate 'male' behaviour. Why not? Personally, I feel that being fucked is a celebration of my maleness. I hardly ever feel that I have relinquished my personal power to the other (unless of course there is role-play of 'surrender' as a sexual game).

I often feel a sense of power 'over' the lover who fucks me. His pleasure and ejaculation reaffirms my own inner power. Somewhere in his magical diaries, Aleister Crowley said something to the effect that he liked to think that "when a man fucks me, it is because I am beautiful." The exhaustive records of Crowley's sexual opera (such as The Paris Working) show that he much preferred to be the receiving partner when it came (pardon the pun) to homosexual sex-magic. Yet the importance of his sex-magic with partners such as Victor Neuburg has tended to be overlooked by those who have inherited his magical philosophy. Any ideas why?

The intensity of these feelings—of abandonment to pleasure and possessing another, and at the same instant of being possessed—I have encountered in another setting: that of the shades of trance, ranging from overshadowing of a spirit upon my consciousness to full possession by a spirit during ritual and dance. The possession-trance is dubiously regarded in western occulture, just as allowing another man's cock inside them is anathema to many men. In many ways, allowing my psyche to be entered by a spirit (Goddess, God or whatever) stirs the same feelings as being physically fucked. The key seems to be the conscious or willed displacement of the ego to another—of offering up my body as a vehicle for the transmission of energy. Crowley hinted of this in his essay on devotional magic (Bhakti Yoga), *Liber Astarte.* The ultimate in Bhakti is being entered by the spirit one is working with. One Beltain, I drew the Goddess Eris down from above me and Pan from below me—they met somewhere in the middle and I lost consciousness in their climax.

Jean Genet suggests that a homosexual relationship "obliges" men to discover the 'feminine' elements within the psyche, but that it is not necessarily "the weaker or the younger, or the more gentle of the two, who succeeds the better; but the more experienced, who may be the stronger or the older man." *(Querelle of Brest).* There is an element of truth in this, but it is equally true that both partners may delight in allowing free rein to the feminine aspects of psyche—at the same, or at different times. Here I might as well discuss the magical concept of 'polarity', which in its most simplistic form is the much-quoted idea of God and Goddess within the self. The problem of 'polarity' occurs when divinity is confused with conditioning and what are supposed to be 'masculine' and 'feminine' qualities. Thus we are told over and over again that fire is masculine and water is feminine; that the capacity to display emotions and be intuitive are

feminine and that intellectual analysis is masculine. Says who?
Feminist critiques of conditioning make the point that we only know
what masculinity and femininity are because they have been defined
in specific ways. Working beyond these limitations is surely a
primary task in the developmental process. So much of what passes
for 'occult laws' is just a 'spiritualised' justification of social conditioning and prejudice. For Gay men, polarity needn't be as simplistic
as one partner assuming a feminine role—you can acknowledge the
feminine and still give your penis to another man. You can celebrate
the masculine elements of psyche and still receive another man's
cock into yourself. Goddesses and Gods are not subject to the same
restrictions as humans—after all, what would be the point if they
were? Imposing our own narrow limits upon them is to miss the
point of the whole exercise of invoking them. I invoke upon myself
to go beyond my present limitations—to join momentarily with
something greater, or outside my ego. Sometimes my lover becomes
to me a God, or a Goddess—or is that too freaky for you?

An early conditioning-block that I had to deal with was the mis-
taken assertion that from a Tantric point of view, sex between men
had no value. However, as I became more comfortable with my
feelings and longings for sex with men, I soon disabused myself of
this notion. From experience, I can say that I have had equally strong
Tantric experiences with men as I have had previously with women.
Sensations such as the 'Bliss-wave'; seeing my lover bathed in gold
light; the total-body orgasm and increased sensitivity to kundalini
activity are just as possible in a homosexual partnership as a hetero-
sexual one. Anal intercourse is a very effective way of stimulating
the Muladhara chakra, despite what some sex-magic manuals might
say. Personally, I would say that my sexual experiences with other
men that have given rise to the experiences described in Tantric
Magic have been all the more powerful due to the obvious element
of catharsis—being able to actualise desires which have long been
repressed is generally a powerful source of energy, which can be
magically directed, of course.

Modern (post-Crowley) works on sexual magic seem to treat
homosexuality in one of two ways. There is either the admonition
that it is wrong—it blocks your chakras, 'reverses' the kundalini or
'creates a dark astral vortex'—or the more positive view that the

gender of partners doesn't matter, and that the 'energy' is the same. Obviously I prefer the latter position, though I feel that things are just not that simple. The writers that cleave to this latter view tend to stress that sexual magic only works properly within an established relationship, which is true to a point, but neatly excludes all the facets of Gay sexual culture which straight society finds so disturbing— anonymous sex, S&M, and group sex particularly. In the UK, at least, there seem to be few individuals or groups who are attempting to write intelligently (or more importantly, feelingly) about the possibilities of Gay-positive Tantra, and the only group which provides support and magical approaches specifically tailored for gay men is the international Voudou Network. Hopefully, as the issue of spirituality raises its profile within the wider gay community, and more gay occultists declare themselves, this situation will change.

To conclude then, I dare to assert that being fucked is, for me, an intensely sacred experience; that spirituality lies in the celebration of pleasure rather than the denial of the body. Giving my prick to another man is pleasurable too, of course, but of a different order, and my reflections on this will have to wait for another time.

QUEERING BAPHOMET

[*Queering Baphomet* was written in 2010, and appears on my blog *enfolding org*. This is a highly autobiographical essay; an account of my relationship—if that's the right word, with Baphomet and how I understood the deity at different times in my life, beginning with Wicca, moving on to Chaos Magic, and finally, towards a Queer relationship with Baphomet, influenced by Queer Theory and Continental Philosophers such as Gilles Deleuze. The ritual described, which took place at the 2004 Queer Pagan Camp, remains one of the most memorable rituals I have ever participated in. This essay moves beyond the perhaps limited scope of sexual magic and instead focuses on possession and queering deities.]

———•◦•———

"All the gods died of laughter to hear one among them proclaim himself unique!"
— Pierre Klossowski, *The Baphomet*

"A sexual being of no fixed gender, In constant flux: growing and changing shape like plants do. more like a habitat in bodily form; the embodiment of vegetal sensuality. In my representation...appears almost female but the features are ephemeral and transforming: the breasts are becoming phallic; the cleavage vulval and who knows what's going on down below or behind? The humanesque appearance is for our benefit; a form we can identify with. being immortal, procreation (an intrinsically mortal function) is totally irrelevant to...whose senso-sexuality is absolute...but...is far from infertile, quite the opposite; however, this fertility is that of lush and mouldering, exuberant bounty."
— Z*qhyoegm, quoted in Lou Hart, *Magic is a many-gendered thing*

My on-off affair with Baphomet began in 1983, when I thought of myself more or less as a Wiccan, although that self-ascription was already slightly fuzzy at the edges. I'd bought a statuette of Baphomet at an occult bookshop and placed it on my altar without quite knowing why. I often used to meditate, aping the position of the statue. By that time, I was giving myself strong doses of Kenneth Grant, backed up with whatever I could find in occult texts about

Baphomet—Levi, Crowley—that kind of thing. But I didn't really "know" Baphomet.

I was living in York when I first tried a ritual aimed towards Baphomet. Unfortunately, my diary entry for the event (9th June 1983) is fragmentary, but it would have been "wiccan" in structure, and my High Priestess (who was from Macclesfield) was present, as was one other woman. My diary records:

> "Baphomet appeared at the edge of the circle and wanted to come in. We denied him this and he began to mess about, first slowly peeling a large art poster (appropriately enough, a depiction of a witches' sabbath) off the wall, then causing a stack of milk crates to rock back and forth. The ritual was (hurriedly) closed and we left the room."

I didn't actually see "Baphomet" standing in the room doing these things; note, it was more of a communal "psychic" apperception of events—we'd invoked the force of Baphomet—therefore these events were down to Baphomet—QED. That was pretty much how I thought of things at that time.

By the early 1990s, I'd come back to Baphomet again, this time through a magical order called the Illuminates of Thanateros (IOT), for whom the "Mass of Chaos B"—a rather minimalist ritual which focused on one person becoming "possessed" by Baphomet—was a favourite ritual. Throughout this period, I saw many instances of Baphomet: fierce Baphomets who screamed abuse at those present; prophetic Baphomets who spoke in tongues and made absurd promises of future greatness; inspired Baphomets who poured their essence into a chalice for sharing. By then I was beginning to think of Baphomet as unfinished. Usually, with deities, one can get a sense of them with recourse to myth. If say, you are interested in Pan, you can, by trawling through the Greek myths or other texts in which Pan figures, get a "sense" of what he is, what he is "about" as it were. This was, by that time, very much the approach I had taken to working with deities for invocation or possession. But there was also another strand here—possession by "unknown" beings which I'd come at through experimental dance-drama & mask-work: entities who only came into existence during an event; who had "unformed personas" that only developed or "grew" over time and repeated performance. Unlike the "classical" deities of familiar mythologies, they had no role, no place in a pantheon, no easily-assigned "function." This was how I began to think of Baphomet—something that lived beyond the boundaries and routes through which I normally thought of entities in terms of magical work. I became less interested in occult analyses of what Baphomet "symbolized," rather to what Baphomet might "hint" towards. Less mask, more of a masque.

Having participated in a fair number of Baphomet possession-events—either as "horse" or celebrant—I began to think about how many different "Baphomets" presented themselves. It seemed to me that the Baphomet we "got" at any one event was very much a "product" of that event. By that time I'd moved away from a perspective that held deities to be singular and entirely separate from the participants/events in which they "came through" to a much more interactive perspective: that these possession events shaped the way in which the focus of the ritual—the person(s) who were possessed by Baphomet—behaved. In the Chaos Mass B, Baphomet is portrayed as a kind of exemplar spirit—the driving force—through the progression of Aeons:

> "In the first Aeon, I was the Great Spirit,
> In the second Aeon, men knew me as the Horned God, Pangenitor Panphage
> In the third Aeon, I was the dark one, the Devil
> In the fourth Aeon, men knew me not, for I am the hidden one
> In this new Aeon, I stand before you as Baphomet, the God before all Gods who shall endure to the end of the earth."
> — Peter J. Carroll, *Liber Null & Psychonaut*

(The Baphomet in this litany is presented as predominantly masculine rather than poly-gendered.)

Possession is the dominant route through which I have engaged-fused-danced with Baphomet. Possession—with its long association with "the primitive"; with the popular representations of Voudun, Santeria and the like; as well as films such as *The Exorcist* with its excesses of bodily substances and forbidden sexualities—has something of a strange position within occulture. It's a practice that moves diametrically away from the ordered ritual universe of the magus towards play and performance, the blurring of boundaries and distinctions, and the surrender of control to a panoply of powers who have their own desires and agencies. When I first began to experiment with group possession in the late 1980s, I couldn't get many of the magicians I knew interested; instead I hung out with a motley collection of improv performers, and we played with masks and sheets instead, producing a series of performances to "unformed gods" through mask-trance. Possession is often difficult to approach as, by its very nature, it collapses boundaries between the self-as-agent and that which has been "invited in." In an essay giving my reflections on being fucked for the first time (*Sodomy as Spiritual Fulfilment*) I likened the experience of being fucked to that of being possessed. Possession, in this sense, undermines self-possession. Possession is linked to queerness, and in some people's minds, as a form of demonic possession.

I had my first queer experience of Baphomet at a possession-event at Queer Pagan Camp in 2004. This brought me into a different perspective on Baphomet, and a rather different approach to possession. This was in the context of a ritual that was being facilitated by some friends, who asked me if I'd volunteer to "carry" Baphomet. I'd spent pretty much the whole day preparing for this ritual, invoking the preliminary deities (Pan and Eris) with whose power I inflame myself prior to offering myself to Baphomet, so by the time that the formal ritual proceedings opened, I was very much in a state of semi-possession anyway. This was, without a doubt, the most intense possession I've experienced so far. This was the first time I'd done a possession on grass rather than the floor of a room or concrete. This was one of the few times I've had a close friend act as an "anchor"—someone I trusted to pull me back, as it were—which allowed me to "go deeper"—to unresist the flood of alien presences. Also, there were "safekeepers" who managed the ritual space during the proceedings. It took nearly a day to "dive in" towards Baphomet; it took several days to come back to the surface.

Snatches of memory persist: I had a fairly clear post-ritual memory of being surrounded by trees. Gradually, this became clearer, and I recalled that at one point, a couple of the safekeepers had moved very close to me whilst "I/Baphomet" was crawling around on all fours. I also have 'flashes' of moving towards the altar at one point, but not of picking up a hot incense burner or of stroking my arm with a very sharp blade—both of which "I/Baphomet" did.

Becoming Baphomet, Baphomet-becoming. It was a multitude which tried to speak in many voices, which could not walk or slither, but staggered and crawled across grass, which cried continuously, wailing to be unchained, stuttering grief and fear. Drawn towards the bright objects flickering in compound eyes; reeling with the impacts of eyes which wanted it to be a singular thing. Wonder at the bright blade that unfolds flesh and wells warm blood; terror of being confined, we felt, by trees; ancient and newly-born. None of us wanted to be separated from each other; we all fought the leaving.

> "...the god of this world is not the monotheistic one; he is rather the Baphomet, the 'prince of modifications.' As Klossowski explains, the Baphomet presides over an unstable and polycentric universe, an anarchy of metamorphosis and metempsychosis. William Burroughs maintains the regulative principle that we must regard every event as being willed by some agency, as being the expression of an intention. Klossowski proposes a complementary principle: he suggests that every intention is an external event, a modification of my being, and hence a sort of demonic possession. Each thought or desire is an alteration of my previous state; it is an intrusion of the outside, a whispering in my ear, a breath that I inhale and exhale, an alien spirit prompting me from offstage or insinuating itself within me. Of course, not all intentions are carried through to their conclusions; but any intention is already in itself a kind of action, a tribute paid to the Baphomet..."
> — Steven Shaviro, *Doom Patrols*

How then, to Queer Baphomet?

> "Queer theory might better remind us that we are inhabited always by states of desire that exceed our capacity to name them. Every name only gives those desires—conflictual, contradictory, inconsistent, undefined—a fictive border."
> — Lee Edelman, *Queer Theory: Unstating Desire*

I return to my earlier thought, that Baphomet is "unfinished," a becoming in Deleuzian terms: Baphomet is a monstrous body; an assemblage with no real-world referent (images of carnival monsters); an excess of signs—goat-breasted-horned-fire-winged-phallus; a surface from which multiple abject forms—woman-satan-sabbat—bubble and froth. Between goat-horns blazes a fire; not the managed alchemical fire of science, more the fecund moist heat of the compost heap. Snake-entwined cock, hidden cunt. Implosion of possibilities; surfaces; sufferances. Baphomet pulses—is a pulsation of life unbound; the mystery at the heart of the sabbat; a blurred image at the edge of the firelight; an offering to the unspeakable. The heresies of the templars made momentarily manifest. The "spectre" of sodomy and all unmentionable acts; witch-trial given form. Not hermaphrodite; most definitely not the accepted ephebe-androgyne of the western imagination; a multiplicity of shifting planes and horizons; Baphomet as animal-elemental-fusion. Baphomet does not mean anything; cannot be chained by regimes of symbolic order. Baphomet calls to free-roaming desire as excess; polymorphous perversion without goal, purpose, product. Baphomet wears human bodies as a drag act; lingers on in fading trails of glitter and snail-tracks of secretions. In amorphous longings and moanings. Out there in the darkness, something emerges...

BIOGRAPHY OF A KISS

[Finally, there is *Biography of a Kiss*, written in February 2019 and published on *enfolding.org*. Again, this is a highly personal reflection—a rekindling of the memory of sharing my first public kiss with another man. Sometimes a simple act can have its own magic, and the repercussions—although perhaps not realized at the time—can be immense.]

When you kissed me, my world turned around.

1986. I'd come down for a coven meeting, but I don't remember the ritual. I just remember the kiss. You walked me to the station but I don't recall the conversation. I just remember the kiss. As I boarded the train, you reached up, threw your arms about me, and kissed me. No gentle peck on the cheek, it was full-on lips to lips. That kiss turned my world around.

You took your time, as though it was the most natural, the most normal thing in the world. As though the other people on the platform, on the train, weren't there. Or didn't matter. And whilst the station was not exactly heaving, it was not empty either.

It was a scene familiar from a thousand movies and tv shows— the parting of lovers. A script I never thought I could participate in, at least not with another man. We were not lovers—but that first public kiss, in the warmth and heat of a summer's day, turned my world around.

I sat on the train. It pulled out of the station. There was a guy sitting opposite me, his eyes wide as saucers like he couldn't believe what he'd just witnessed. The whole journey back he kept glancing at me, and I reveled in his shock. And the funny thing was, as it turned out, this guy was at the same college I was attending in York—albeit in a different department, and for the next few weeks, I kept catching him staring at me in horrified—or perhaps jealous— fascination.

I'd grown up kissing other boys. In school, playing at "Stingray" I usually got to play the part of Aqua Marina, the silent mermaid, which gave plenty of room for kissing. It seemed natural, until one day it wasn't, and the kissing stopped, and the name-calling began. I came out to my parents at age 21, to have the whole thing wrapped in a blanket of frozen silence. I'd shared furtive fumblings in the darkness of clubs and alleyways; explored the fringes of polymorphous pleasures, but was still not confident or comfortable with my self and my desires as they always seemed to escape or confound any attempt at being this or being that kind of person. I certainly wasn't "out" to most of my friends, although I suspect some of them were more aware than I supposed. Most of my friends at that time were occultists of one kind or another, and I was just beginning to get angry about the sweeping generalizations that were everywhere at that time—the "we don't want any kinks in our circle ho ho ho" kind of comments or the flat declarations that anyone who was gay, lesbian or bisexual "couldn't be involved in magic." I knew there was a gay world separate to the occult—I just didn't feel ready to be part of it. I hid and sought consolation in esoteric obsessions and fantasies of power.

But I remember the kiss. And that chance meeting, after 25 years of distance, brought it back. So I just wanted to acknowledge that. Because when you kissed me that morning, my world turned around.

Histories

INTRODUCTION

By the middle of the noughties, I discovered I had a passion for history. Prior to that, I hadn't really bothered overmuch with history, or where ideas came from. After all, I was writing out of my own experience, and considered this was enough. But my fascination with history grew, and I began to experiment with new styles of writing.

Something that occasionally irritated me as regards to occult writing was the lack of attention paid to source material and references. Of course, I was as guilty as many of my peers in this regard. But I began to see the value of giving references as I read more scholarly material as it makes it relatively easy to check a source to see if the author of a paper has made the correct interpretation (providing one has access to the source material). This is, I think, a better approach to writing than simply making broad assertions and sweeping statements. Of course in the days before the internet and the necessity for fact– (or quote–) checking, authors could get away with a great deal more in the way of generalisations and unfounded assertions.

So I began to write more carefully, paying closer attention to quotations, sources, references and notes. One way in which this interest in history came to the fore is that I began to take an interest in a variety of historical personages whose writings were popular during their own period—and whose work had influenced contemporary occultism in various ways, but who seemed to have been forgotten or neglected. The two essays I've chosen for this section—a look at the infamous 'Tibetan' author Lobsang Rampa and travel writer, translator and novelist Elizabeth Sharpe—reflect this interest. Their works and lives have been influential or intriguing for me in a variety of ways.

As I dig into historical material, chasing down forgotten texts, pursuing obscure references and performing extensive searches through online repositories, I find myself enjoying this kind of detective work hugely. But it is not merely an intellectual exercise; often the trigger is a by-product of meditation or ritual practice.

These are, for the most part, much longer essays than I've tended to write in the past, and as you'll see, I'm trying to be more careful in regard to references and giving source material.

THE FANTASTIC WORLD OF LOBSANG RAMPA

[*The Fantastic World of Lobsang Rampa* began as a lecture at Treadwells Bookshop of London and was first published in the journal *Abrasax* in 2009. It was serialised on *enfolding.org* between December 2013 and January 2014. I'd read some of Lobsang Rampa's books in the 1970s, and being in possession of a few academic essays on the Rampa phenomenon, I initially thought I'd be able to knock together a lecture quite quickly. It took nearly six months, during which time I read all 19 of Rampa's books, listened to audio recordings of him speaking, and hung out on a couple of Lobsang Rampa fan sites.]

⸺◆⸺

1956 saw the first British publication of a book called *The Third Eye*—described in glowing terms by the *Times Literary Supplement* as "becoming a near work of art" whilst *The Observer* called it "an extraordinary and exciting book."

The Third Eye was the autobiography of one Tuesday Lobsang Rampa. He was the son of a leading member of the Dalai Lama's government, and lived in a well-to-do home in Lhasa. At the age of seven, astrologers predicted the boy's future: he would enter a monastery, train as a priest-surgeon, suffer great hardships, leave Tibet, and live amongst strange peoples. Tuesday joined a lamasery, and in due course proved to be an exemplary student and was selected to receive the most esoteric teachings. On the boy's eighth birthday, priest-surgeons drilled a hole in his skull, to create a "third eye" which would allow him to see auras. After recovering from the operation, Tuesday was interviewed by the Dalai Lama who had investigated the boy's past lives, and reminded him of the role he would soon play in preserving the wisdom of Tibet.

At the age of twelve, Tuesday took the examination to qualify as a medical priest. This involved being sealed inside a stone cubicle, into which was passed written questions, which required written responses. The tests lasted for fourteen hours a day for six days.

After passing the exams with flying colours, Tuesday accompanied his tutor, the great Lama Mingyar Dondup, on an expedition to collect medical plants and herbs. During this expedition they visited a monastery where the monks build box kites that are large enough for a person to fly in. Tuesday made several flights and also made suggestions for the improvement of their design. On another expedition, Tuesday and his teacher encountered the Yeti and found a garden of Eden-like paradise in a lost valley. At the age of sixteen, he is examined once again, and achieved the rank of Lama.

The book closes with Tuesday receiving the rank of Abbot—undergoing "the Ceremony of the Little Death"—and departing Tibet for China, on the instructions of the Dalai Lama.

Publishing The Third Eye

The manuscript of *The Third Eye* was first given to several publishers such as Robert Hale & Collins—who rejected it out of hand. The publishing company E.P. Dutton, based in New York sent it to Hugh Richardson, a former officer-in-charge of the British Mission to Tibet, who had lived there for nine years. Richardson returned the manuscript with many corrections and offered the opinion that the book was a fake, using existing published works as a basis and "embellished by a fertile imagination." Dutton rejected the book on Richardson's recommendation.

The manuscript was then sent to Secker and Warburg. The story goes that the author met Frederick Warburg and impressed him by reading his palm and correctly divining his age and that he had been recently involved in a criminal case. Warburg obtained a copy of Richardson's report on the manuscript and further, sent copies to a battery of authorities on Tibet, including the mountaineers Heinrich Harrer and Marco Pallis, and respected scholars such as David Snellgrove and Agehananda Bharati. All declared unequivocally that the book was fraudulent.

In the preface to the first edition of *The Third Eye*, the publishers acknowledged the reservations of the expert readers but noted that:

> "On many points of his personal life he [the author] displayed a discretion that was sometimes disconcerting. ...But Lobsang Rampa assures us that because Tibet is occupied by the Communists, he is

obliged to maintain a certain discretion in order not to compromise the security of his family. ...We might sometimes think that that he stretches the limits of occidental credulity, although our understanding in this field cannot be held to be definitive. The publishers are nonetheless persuaded that *The Third Eye* essentially constitutes an authentic document on the education and formation of a young Tibetan in the bosom of his family and in a Lamasery."

The Third Eye quickly became a best-seller in twelve countries, selling some 300,000 copies in the first eighteen months of publication in the UK alone—and within two years, it had nine hardback printings. French and German editions also appeared.

The Scholars Fight Back

The popularity of *The Third Eye* drew an outraged response from the scholars who had given their testimony to the publishers. David Snellgrove described the book as "shameless." Marco Pallis stated that it was "a wild fabrication and a libel on both Tibet and its religion." Heinrich Harrer's review was so scathing that *The Third Eye's* German publisher threatened him with a libel suit. Hugh Richardson published a critical review of *The Third Eye* in the *Daily Telegraph* and the *Morning Post* in November 1956, declaring that "anyone who has lived in Tibet will feel after reading a few pages of *The Third Eye* that its author, T. Lobsang Rama, is certainly not a Tibetan..."

In 1958, Marco Pallis, acting on behalf of a group of European scholars of Tibet, engaged the services of Clifford Burgess, a private detective, to discover the "true identity" of the author of *The Third Eye*. After a month of investigation, Burgess revealed that the author was one Cyril Henry Hoskin, born in Plympton, Devonshire in 1910. His father was a plumber, and he was considered by those who knew him as "an odd child." He later worked for a surgical goods manufacturing company and as a clerk for a London company who offered education via correspondence courses. Burgess reported that during this period, Hoskin became increasingly "peculiar"—calling himself Kuan-Suo, shaving the hair from his head, and taking his cat out on a lead for walks. He then appeared in Bayswater in 1954, calling himself Dr. Kuan-Suo. Burgess stated that until he moved to Dublin there was no evidence that Hoskin had ever left the UK.

Exposure and Response

In February 1958, the *Scottish Daily Mail* broke the story with "Third Eye Lama Exposed as a Fake". The *Daily Express* followed with "The Full Truth about the Bogus Lama" along with an article by Frederick Warburg, who reported that he had had a Tibetologist phoneticize the phrase "Did you have a nice journey, Mr. Rampa?" which he read out to the author. When he did not reply, Warburg informed him that it was Tibetan. The author promptly fell to the floor in an apparent fit and explained to Warburg that he had been tortured by the Japanese and had hypnotically blocked his knowledge of Tibetan to the extent that he had never recovered his native tongue. Even hearing Tibetan caused him pain, and he had warned Warburg not to press him further.

In February 1958, *Time* magazine featured the story, "Private vs. Third Eye". Hoskin did not meet with reporters, it was claimed, because of his health, but his wife attested that her husband had written the book on behalf of a real Dr. Ku'an, whose family were in hiding from the Chinese communists. She later stated that these comments were a fabrication by the press.

When *The Third Eye* was reprinted, it contained a statement from the author which began: "In the East it is commonly acknowledged that a stronger mind can take possession of another body..." He went on to explain that, late in 1947, Cyril Hoskin began to experience an irresistible compulsion to adopt eastern ways of living. He changed his name to Carl Ku'an, left his job, and moved to a "remote location" where he experienced hallucinations and his own memories were gradually supplanted by those of an "eastern entity." In 1949 he sustained a concussion falling out of a tree, and after this had no memory of his own early life but gained the full memory—from babyhood—of a Tibetan. He claimed that he had papers which proved his identity, but that he had sent them away again so that they would not be "sullied" by those who doubted him. In response to the opinions of the "experts" he responded that no two of them had been able to agree on any particular fault, and in any case, none of them had lived in Tibet as a lama—or entered a monastery at the age of seven "as I have done." In closing, he states that there is a great deal of Theosophical literature on the subject of possession and that his publishers have a letter from a swami in India stating that possession is quite common in the East.

Hoskin's statement is reinforced by one from his wife, testifying that since 1949 "his whole manner and make-up have been those of an easterner," and that "his general make-up and colouring have also shown a marked change." The book also contains a statement from Hoskin that British and German newspapers had been conducting a campaign against him—and that he could not defend himself because of a heart condition. He states once again that all his claims are absolutely true and that he did not copy from other books.

But that was not the end of the story. Undeterred by the critics, two other books quickly followed *The Third Eye*. *Doctor from Lhasa*, published in 1959, picks up the story of Lobsang Rampa in China, beginning in 1927. His many adventures include being recruited into a special corps of medical airmen in the army of Chiang Kai-shek; flying an air ambulance during China's war with Japan; being caught by the Japanese (twice!) and tortured—although his training as a Lama allows him to resist this. He also enrolls in a medical college where he astounds his instructors by sketching a magnetic field, as seen through his third eye. He hopes, by combining his knowledge of Chinese and Occidental medicine, to reproduce a machine he once saw in the ruins of a prehistoric city in a hidden valley in the Chang Thang—a device for reading auras and predicting the onset of disease or mental problems.

The Rampa Story (1960) opens in Tibet where the High Lamas have discovered, through astral exploration, a secret network of caves, which they are using to prevent their most sacred artifacts from falling into the hands of the communists. The Abbots, having known of the impeding Chinese invasion through their clairvoyant powers, have been secretly preparing this for years. By now, Rampa himself is living in Canada. The Lamas contact him telepathically and give him the task of writing a book explaining how one person can take over the body of another—with the latter person's full consent. The book recounts that Rampa, after drifting across the Sea of Japan (which was where *Doctor from Lhasa* ended), found himself in Russia. He is drafted into the Russian army but later arrested by the security police and tortured in Lubianka prison. He is released and is deported to Poland, but on the way the truck he is travelling in crashes and Rampa is badly injured. Whilst in hospital, he travels to the "world of golden light" in his astral body, where he meets his former teacher, who has been murdered by the communists, and Sha-lu, a talking cat. The thirteenth Dalai Lama meets him also and urges him to return to earth and continue his work. The problem is that Rampa's body is in no fit state. The Dalai Lama tells Rampa that a body has been located for him in England, and that the present owner's aura has the same "harmonic" as Rampa's. He is warned however, that if he returns to Earth, he will face disbelief, hatred and hardship, which is due to the force of evil which tries to prevent human evolution.

Further adventures take Rampa across Europe to America, and then to India, where with the help of an old Lama he makes an astral journey to the Akashic Records to investigate the past lives of the man whose body he is to inhabit. He meets this man on the astral plane, and he agrees to allow Rampa to inhabit his body. A month later, Rampa visits the man astrally again, and instructing him to fall out of a tree, Rampa and three fellow Lama's sever the silver cord attaching the man to his body and attach Rampa's silver cord to the body. He does a variety of jobs in England, and eventually writes *The Third Eye.* After the completion of the book he has a heart attack and moves to Ireland—an island which was once part of Atlantis. His old teacher contacts him again once more and directs him to move to "the land of the Red Indians" where he has a final task to accomplish. *The Rampa Story* ends with the prediction of a Chinese nuclear attack launched from Lhasa.

Sixteen other books followed this initial trilogy, including *Living with the Lama,* which was written by (Mrs.) Fifi Greywhiskers, one of the Lama's cats. It has been estimated that overall sales of the Lobsang Rampa series topped four million copies worldwide by the time of Rampa's death in 1981. The Lobsang Rampa books remain in print to this day and there are several websites and internet forums devoted to the discussion and circulation of his ideas.

Rampa as a 'Mystifier'

The scholar Donald Lopez characterises Rampa as one of the great "mystifiers" of Tibet—in the sense that he "mystified Tibet, embellishing its various realities with his own mystical fancies," and that "he mystified his readers, playing on the credulity of the reading public." Agehananda Bharati, never one to mince words, writing in the *Tibet Society Bulletin* (vol.7, 1974) takes a similar stance:

> "Every page bespeaks the utter ignorance of the author of anything that has to do with Buddhism as practiced and Buddhism as a belief system in Tibet or elsewhere. But the book also shows a shrewd intuition into what millions of people want to hear. Monks and neophytes flying through the mysterious breeze on enormous kites; golden images in hidden cells, representing earlier incarnations of the man who views them; arcane surgery in the skull to open up the eye of wisdom; tales about the dangers of mystical training and initiation—in a Western world so desperately seeking for the mysterious where everything is so terribly accessible to inspection, where the divine has been bowdlerized or institutionalized, where it speaks with the wagging-finger lingo of moralistic nagging, the less hardy and the softer will seek that which is the opposite of all these turn-off factors."

Most of the critical scholarship on Lobsang Rampa deals with him largely in relation to western idealisations of Tibet, placing him alongside other "mystifiers" such as Madame Blavatsky. Lopez, for example, in *Prisoners of Shangri-La,* recounts how he gave The Third Eye to a group of his first year undergraduate students—telling them to read it, without giving any clues to its provenance. The students, Lopez says, were "unanimous" in their praise for the book, finding it "entirely credible and compelling." Lopez poses the question of just why Lobsang Rampa's books have been so popular despite the opprobrium of scholars, and frames his answer in a discussion of authority. Lobsang Rampa's initial authority rested in his being accepted as a Lama by his readers. Lopez says that once Rampa was revealed to be Hoskin, his authority would have waned, were it not for the fact that *Doctor from Lhasa* and *The Rampa Story* show how Hoskin has become Rampa. Lopez points out that by the time Rampa released *The Hermit* (1971) he simply states that his books are True and that "Some people who are bogged down in materialism may prefer to think of it as fiction" to which Rampa adds, "Believe or disbelieve according to your state of evolution."

In closing the chapter of *Prisoners* which examines the Rampa phenomenon, Lopez says that he has met many Tibetologists and

Buddhologists who told him that it was reading the Rampa books which gave them the initial fascination with the world he described that led to them becoming professional scholars, and that some said that despite his being a fraud, he had a "good effect."

Rampa as a 'Demystifier'?

Having spent the last few months reading through many of Lobsang Rampa's books, I think there is a good case to make for Lobsang Rampa as a Demystifier—of both Tibet, and the esoteric subjects that he deals with. One of the things that impressed me—if "impressed" is the right word here—is that Lobsang Rampa's writing style is very "down to earth" in a sense. Certainly, he describes a wide range of odd experiences, but he does so in such a fashion as to render them unchallenging. He makes the unfamiliar unthreatening, in a sense. When he explains occult concepts, he invariably does so with recourse to common-sense analogies which would be familiar to a general western reader, and uses very few recognisably occult "technical" terms. For example, in his foreword to *The Cave of the Ancients,* Rampa expresses his disdain for "mumbo jumbo" and states that this is "a simple book, without any 'foreign words' in it, no Sanskrit, nothing of dead languages in it." This, I feel, accounts for some of his appeal. The wisdom Rampa presents is remarkably self-contained—given "as is." He does not back up his statements by quoting other authorities (in fact, one gains the impression that apart from himself there are no other authorities), and although he talks about the importance of learning scriptures and studying esoteric books in Tibet in his autobiographical reminiscences, he does not provide references or refer to specific texts. Only occasionally does he recommend other books to his readers.

Rampa also gives his views on a diverse range of esoteric subjects, much of which seems to be in response to letters he has received. He does not approve of fortune telling, absent healing or meditation in groups, which should be avoided, as it can lead to nervous illnesses due to contamination from other—untrained people's—thought-vibrations. In fact, he recommends that his readers avoid cults or esoteric groups of any kind. Astrology, he asserts, is genuine, but most of the people who advertise themselves as astrologers are fakes. Similarly, spirit guides and mediums are the target of Rampa's scorn—he wryly comments in *Feeding the Flame* that "if everyone who claimed to have an Indian guide or a Tibetan guide was listed, there just wouldn't be enough Indians or enough Tibetans to go round." In *The Saffron Robe,* Rampa is told by one of his teachers "not to bother with yoga" and that it is "just a physical exercise, nothing more. Nothing spiritual."

Rampa is also rather dismissive of scientists and "experts." In a rare interview from 1958, he says:

> "One should not place too much credence in 'experts' or 'Tibetan scholars' when it is seen how one 'expert' contradicts the other when they cannot agree on what is right and what is wrong..."

In *Chapters of Life* he states that scientists have little or no imagination, and that the investigation of subjects such as the world of anti-matter should be reserved for occultists, as "...the competent occultist can leave the body and get out of the body, and out of the Earth as well, and once out of the Earth he can see what this other world is like—as I have done so very, very frequently." He reveals that it is the anti-matter world which is responsible for phenomena such as the Bermuda Triangle, or the mysterious loss of Flight 19.

Tradition/Modernity

Rampa's books can be seen as examples of books which glorify tradition and at the same time condemn modernity. The 1950s was a period of great change in British life, with the end of post-war austerity and the rise of the "affluent society"—which saw the rise of commercial television, colour magazines, cheap paperback books, and an increase in advertising of luxury commodities. Also, establishment values began to be increasingly questioned and ridiculed. Individual freedom and choice became an increasing cultural concern. Yet the new freedoms and liberties also brought uncertainties. Rampa's books, which span a period from the mid-1950s to 1980 (he produced one book a year between 1963 and 1973) articulate and express the tensions between tradition and individualism.

When not recounting his autobiographical adventures in Tibet or elsewhere, or explaining various occult matters, Rampa comments freely on the state of the world and what has gone wrong with modern society. Hence we discover that young people of today are "dimmer" than their parents, and he directs particular scorn for those with "long hair...and scruffy, tattered, rags of clothing." He blames the state of young people today on television, cinema, and both parents (particularly women) going out to work. He is irrevocably opposed to drugs such as LSD as they can damage the astral body irreparably. Also, Rampa makes it abundantly clear (in *I Believe)* that he has no time for so-called "Women's Libbers"—who are not really "women." He opines that the rot started in the First World War, when women went to work in factories. Women should stay at home and be wives and mothers—as Nature intended. He recounts that in the Akashic Records there is evidence of a long-vanished civilisation of people "who wore purple skins" which became dominated by women. Men were treated as slaves, or virile studs for the sole purpose of making babies. This matriarchy was "unbalanced" and so ended. In *Three Lives,* the "Old Author" (Rampa) recounts a dream in which a young woman, killed in an accident, finds out that because she is a "Women's Libber" she (like media people) is destined for the "hellish regions." Hell, in this narrative, has special "stockades" reserved for publishers, agents, members of the press, old Etonians and Women's Liberationists.

Rampa believes that modern society has reached a crossroads, and that the only thing which will ensure stability is the return to a religious life. It should be, he says, a "fresh" religion, as the old ones "have failed so miserably." In *Candlelight,* in answer to a question about violence in the world, he says: "People are being given false values. Religion is being torn down. People no longer believe in the simple things of life. They listen to the radio, they watch terrible things on television, and they read the gory details in the sensational press."

Although Rampa is critical of western science, progress and "fallible machines," it is noteworthy that the 'core' of *The Third Eye*—the "opening of Rampa's own third eye (chapter 8)—is a surgical procedure, involving an instrument "resembling a bradawl," rather than the result of spiritual discipline, as one might expect. There is a continued enthusiasm for strange machinery running throughout Rampa's books, and the device for reading auras (first mentioned in *Doctor from Lhasa)* becomes a central refrain—he states on several occasions that his *raison d'etre* for his writing is to create funds for his research into creating this device, to the benefit of all humanity.

Sheelagh Rouse, in her book *Twenty-five Years with Lobsang Rampa* explains that in pursuit of his research in Auric photography in Ireland, Rampa held that the female aura was "brighter" than the male—stronger colours—and it was necessary to find female models who were willing to pose nude.

Rampa on Homosexuality

Rampa uses characters to flesh out and give veracity to his opinions. In *The Thirteenth Candle,* for example, his views on male & female homosexuality are verified through the device of vignette "slices of life" from two sets of characters: Lotta Bull ("the epitome of the masculine woman") and her lover, Rosie Hipp ("all feminine, fluff, and froth with hardly a thought in her vapid, blonde head"); also Dennis Dollywogga and Justin Towne—who writes a letter to Rampa objecting to his remarks on the causation of homosexuality in his previous book *Feeding the Flame,* in which Rampa states:

> "Being born is a traumatic experience, it's a most violent affair, and a very delicate mechanism can easily become deranged. For example, a baby is about to be born and throughout the pregnancy the mother has been rather careless about what she was eating and what she was doing, so the baby has not received what one might term a balanced chemical input. The baby may be short of a chemical and so development of certain glands may have been halted. Let us say the baby was going to come as a girl, but through lack of certain chemicals, the baby is actually born a boy, a boy with the inclinations of a girl. The parents might realize that they've got a sissified little wretch and put it down to over-indulgence or something, they may try to beat some sense into him one end or the other to make him more manly, but it doesn't work; if the glands are wrong, never mind what sort of attachments are stuck on in front, the boy is still a girl in a boy's body.
>
> If a woman has a male psyche, then she will not be interested in men but will be interested in women, because her psyche, which is closer to the Overself than is the physical body, is relaying confusing messages to the Overself and the Overself sends back a sort of command, 'Get busy, do your stuff.' The poor wretched male psyche is obviously repelled by the thought of 'doing his stuff' with a man, and so all the interest is centered on a female, so you get the spectacle

of a female making love to a female and that's what we call a lesbian because of a certain island off Greece where that used to be 'the done thing.'

The vital thing is that one should never, never condemn a homosexual, it's not his fault, he is being penalized for something he hasn't done, he is being penalized for some fault of Nature; perhaps his mother had the wrong sort of food, perhaps the mother and the child were chemically incompatible. However, whichever way you look at it, homosexuals can only be helped by true understanding and sympathy, and possibly with the judicious administration of drugs."

To which "Justin Towne" replies:

"Most homos are not the little pansies you see on the street, they are not the ones the psychiatrists and doctors write about because those are the emotionally disturbed ones. Being an adventurer I have worked in cities, farms, some radio work, etc., etc., and I know homos in all fields who are as normal as 'blue-berry pie' so to speak. So, they can be very masculine, they can think and act like men and do NOT think and act like women or have any of the feminine characteristics which so many heterosexuals seem to think they do.

I wanted to stress TO the homo, what an important part he could play in this world, if he'd get off his behind and quit feeling sorry for himself. I don't believe in things like this 'Gay Liberation' thing where like all youngsters today they think they have to make a big issue of it, but merely go along and do one's own job well, with the tools they have (Being their own talents etc.)"

Romancing Tibet: The Third Eye as Travelogue

Cyril Hoskin/Lobsang Rampa was not the first case of an author becoming his literary personality. One might think of notables such as T.E. Lawrence or Richard Burton assuming the disguise of the native; or, indeed, Alexandra David-Neel disguising herself as a Tibetan in order to explore the forbidden kingdom. There is also "Grey Owl"—Archibald Bellaney—who was a best-selling author and public lecturer in the 1930s (now hailed as one of the founders of the conservation movement), exposed, after his death as an Englishman, rather than a Native American.

When Rampa's narrative turns to his life in Tibet, he is clearly drawing on what we would now recognise as cultural primitivist assumptions about the exotic nature of Tibetan culture—stereotypes existing in European popular culture, drawn from the writings of Theosophists such as Madame Blavatsky and Alice Bailey, and James Hilton's *Lost Horizon*—although Rampa always claimed that he had never read any Theosophical works.

The Third Eye paints a rather idealistic picture of Tibet as an idyllic utopia, untouched but cautiously aware of the materialism and progress of the west. Tibetans do not have wheels for example, because wheels represent speed, and "so-called civilisation." Similarly, in *Doctor from Lhasa,* Rampa recounts with amazement his first encounters with a "spring bed," running tap water, people smoking, and later, an aeroplane, which he first believes is "one of the sky-gods."

Donald Lopez's comments regarding scholars taking an interest in Tibet due to their reading of Rampa's books is interesting. In researching this lecture, and trawling internet search engines in search of how Rampa is treated on the worldwide web, I found several instances of Tibetan aid foundations and organisations where members stated that their interest in Tibet had been sparked by reading the Rampa books. In addition, I found that several of the large Rampa "fan sites" also had information about current events in Tibet and carried links to sites such as Tibet Online and the UK-based Tibet Foundation.

The Third Eye was written after the Chinese invasion of Tibet, but before the 1959 Uprising and the subsequent diaspora of Tibetan religious leaders to India and the West. To some degree, one might argue that the popularity of Rampa's works, and the late-1950s controversy around it, heightened public interest in, and the desire to access, Tibetan Buddhism. It could also be argued that Lobsang Rampa also provided a window into events in occupied Tibet. Although Rampa does portray a romanticised picture of life in Tibet, he at least does not depoliticise the country's history—*The Third Eye* mentions both the 1904 Younghusband expedition and the Chinese military attempt to control Lhasa in 1910. *The Rampa Story* contains some retellings of astral visions of Chinese brutality against ordinary Tibetans and executions of monks, and recounts stories of nuns being raped and burned alive. However, I have been unable to find any reference to the Tibetan resistance movements or the 1959 Uprising in his books.

In *Feeding the Flame,* Rampa opens chapter three of the book with an account of what life in Lhasa is like under the "terror" of the Chinese. He describes the "genocide" being practised upon the Tibetan people by the Chinese. However, he also takes this opportunity to express his dissatisfaction with the Tibetan government-in-exile. He had hoped to "speak as a representative of Tibet before the United Nations," but he feels that "high-ranking" Tibetans, now "living in comfort in India," are afraid to support him because of the way he has been portrayed by the press. In *As It Was* there is a long section dealing with "predictions" made about Rampa's life by the "Chief Astrologer" which at one point extols Rampa's own skill at predictions, which include:

> "He had made the prediction that there would be no real Dalai Lama after the Thirteenth had gone to the state of transition; there would be another but he would have been selected as a matter of political expediency in an attempt to assuage the territorial ambitions of the Chinese."

The Chief Astrologer says (of Rampa):

> "It will be considered to the benefit of a people as a whole that he be disowned, that he be not supported by those who should support him, by those who could support him, and I say again that these are probabilities because it is quite possible for our own people to support him and give him an opportunity to speak before the nations of the world, so that first, Tibet may be saved..."

It appears that the apparent refusal of the Tibetan government-in-exile to recognise Rampa as a spokesman for Tibet rankled deeply. In *As It Was* he comments that "it is mainly the *lower orders* [my italics] of refugees who seem to be opposed to me." He also claims to have a letter saying that the Dalai Lama is praying daily for his health.

His followers sometimes claim that the present Dalai Lama's "public denial" of knowing Lobsang Rampa is a sham, because he is "playing the political field, prosituting (sic) his religion trying to appease too many people who wouldn't support him if he did."

The UFO Connection

Lobsang Rampa also had an influence on the UFO scene. In 1966 there appeared *My Visit to Venus*—an "unauthorised" anthology of Rampa's early writings from the mid-1950s published by Gray Barker, author of *They Knew Too Much about Flying Saucers* (1956), and now recognised as the person responsible for introducing the "men in black" component to UFO folklore. Rampa gave Barker "permission" to continue to publish the book, provided he made some minor alternations to the manuscript, and sent 10% of his profits to the "Save a Cat League" of New York. The second edition of *Venus* also contained a foreword from John Keel. In *Venus,* Rampa recounts how he and six fellow lamas encounter a race of giant, telepathic humanoids in a lost city, which they discover half-frozen in a glacier. These humanoids, it transpires, have been overseeing the development of humanity, and they take Rampa and his fellows to Venus where they experience so many wonders that Earth seems a tawdry, drab place in comparison.

UFO-related themes continue in Rampa's books throughout the 1960s. There are, for example, "the Gardeners," a race of aliens who colonised earth billions of years ago, and who periodically come back to check on humanity's progress. The Gardeners 'seeded' Earth with the human race, and although they are largely benign, they do occasionally abduct people and experiment on them to "improve the race." Humanity regarded them as "gods from the sky."

There is also a race of advanced beings who live inside the earth, who sometimes explore the surface using advanced technology; and interdimensional entities which can only be perceived (by humans) as patterns of lights. Also, in *The Hermit,* as Rampa recounts what we would now recognise as a 'classic' abduction experience, complete with telepathic interchanges and bizarre experiments performed on him, there is a description of the now-familiar gray alien:

> "There I saw a most extraordinary thing, a dwarf, a gnome, a very, very small body, a body like that of a five-year-old child, I thought. But the head, ah, the head was immense, a great dome of a skull, hairless, too, not a trace of hair anywhere in sight on this one. The chin was small, very small indeed, and the mouth was not a mouth the same as we have but seemed to be more of a triangular orifice. The nose was slight, not a protuberance so much as a ridge. This was

obviously the most important person because the others looked with such deferential respect in his direction."

Rampa's books have undoubtedly influenced contemporary 'alternative science.' Themes relating to lost technologies; underground cities; "lost lands" such as Lemuria & Ultima Thule; and "time capsules" as well as 'conspiracies' to suppress or guard against secret wisdom becoming common knowledge are all featured in his books. Whilst some of these themes may not have originated with Rampa, he certainly helped popularise them, years before the publication of Von Daniken's *Chariots of the Gods* and later works. Indeed, the work of contemporary "alternative science" authors such as Graham Hancock is seen by adherents of Lobsang Rampa as validation and proof of his ideas.

Some Final Thoughts

Lobsang Rampa is often written off as a fraud, whilst those who follow his teachings believe him to be the psychically-adept Lama of his books, the 'truth' of whose writings has been suppressed by various forces such as the current Dalai Lama, various governments, the scientific establishment, or western "occult secret societies" who didn't like the truths Rampa was revealing. The impression I have of Rampa—from reading his books, and the testimonies of those who knew him—is that he genuinely believed that he was who he said he was—or rather, that he was "host" for the spirit of Lobsang Rampa. Sheelagh Rouse describes how the body originally owned by Hoskin was, over time, completely replaced Rampa's body—and explains that Rampa suffered from the tortures he had received at the hands of the Japanese. Her picture of Rampa is that of a spiritual adept, uninterested in having followers and disciples, and somewhat reclusive due to the persecution of the press and critics, yet willing to help the people who wrote to him with their problems and questions.

Rampa's works stand at the dawn of the 1960s when Western fascination with Tibet, 'Eastern mysticism,' and other forms of esoteric wisdom took on new heights of popularity. It is rather ironic that Rampa's first book, *The Third Eye,* has achieved something of an iconic status as a key text for 1960s counter-cultural mystical enthusiasts, since Rampa makes it plain in his later works that he had no time whatsoever for hippies, young people, or the changes sweeping through Western culture during his own lifetime. *The Third Eye* remains, to this day, one of the most popular and widely-read books on Tibet, despite continued scholarly opprobrium. At least some of the appeal of Rampa's texts is his ability to present 'esoteric wisdom' in a familiar, uncomplicated fashion, eschewing either complex terminology or conceptual formations, rendering both beliefs and practices into a simple approach that reduces uncertainty:

> "Occultism is no more mysterious or complicated than the multiplication tables or an excursion into history. It is just learning of different things, learning of things which are not of the physical. We should not go into raptures if we suddenly discovered how a nerve worked a muscle or how we could twitch a big toe, they would be just ordinary physical matters. So why should we go into raptures and think that the spirits are sitting all around us if we know how we can pass etheric energy from one person to another? Please note that we say here 'etheric energy' which is good English instead of 'prana' or any other Eastern terms; we prefer when writing a Course in a language to adhere to that language."
>
> — *You Forever,* p.102

All the reader has to do is follow Rampa's guidance—and believe that the exercises he recommends will work—and he or she, too, will be able to begin to access the abilities that Rampa displays in his books. Rampa's books also appeal to readers who are suspicious of authorities—'experts' (such as scientists, or occultists) often draw Rampa's disdain. He uses his cast of characters not only to illustrate his worldview (and demonise the targets of his ire, such as Women's Libbers and members of the Upper Class), but also to provide 'independent' assertions within the text that he is a sympathetic listener and can be helpful to those who feel at odds with their position in society. The interchange in *The Thirteenth Candle* between Lotta Bull and Rosie Hipp establishes that Rampa's opinions about homosexuality have helped Rosie understand herself—prompting Lotta to ask "Is he...ONE OF US—Homo?" Which of course, Rampa isn't, yet is deemed capable of offering useful advice.

Rampa's books also act to provide readers with a 'privileged access' to Tibet (and other countries). His is not the world of the ordinary Tibetan, but the special insight of a superhuman elite—he repeatedly uncovers an aspect of Tibetan wisdom which is inaccessible to ordinary people or so-called 'experts'—a Tibet that makes explicit the romantic imagination of an exotic, yet ultimately familiar locale. At times Rampa's autobiographical adventures in different parts of the world take on epic proportions—he could be likened to James Bond in his ability to move around the world freely, fighting the various forces of evil (such as the Japanese and the Chinese), and deploying special abilities and technologies. Like Bond, Rampa's adventures are set against the backdrop of the Cold War—both visit exotic locations and uncover secret schemes and technologies. Both belong to an elite class which grants them privileged access to secrets and intrigues. But whilst Bond's touristic adventures are set within exotic locations such as the Caribbean and the Mediterranean, Rampa provides a touristic gaze into spiritual geographies—hidden Tibet, the Akashic Records, other worlds—places which are inaccessible to ordinary travellers, perhaps all too conveniently so.

Given the scope and breadth of Rampa's adventures in various parts of the world, his eventual arrival in postwar Britain—into the body formerly occupied by Cyril Hoskin—is something of an anticlimax. The writing of *The Third Eye* seems to have been a 'last option' for the transmigrated Rampa, as his adventures in England are rather less exciting than fighting, flying aircraft and performing medical miracles—they are mostly concerned with his attempts to secure employment and his problems with the Labour Exchange. Rampa the international adventurer is replaced by Rampa the reclusive author and teacher.

It would be easy to judge Cyril Hoskin/Lobsang Rampa as a 'hoaxer.' However, I feel this is too simplistic. For one thing, he appears to have genuinely believed himself to be a Tibetan Lama inhabiting an Englishman's body. Moreover, his books were, and remain, popular for reasons that are more complex than mere credulity on the part of a supposedly uneducated and uncritical audience. Rampa's work played a key role in the formation of both the New Age movement and contemporary occultism. His place in history in the Western imagination of Tibet has already been assured. He also deserves more attention in his attempts to make the world of the occult explainable in everyday terms.

Sources

Books by Lobsang Rampa

The Third Eye (1956)
Doctor from Lhasa (1959)
The Rampa Story (1960)
Cave of the Ancients (1965)
The Saffron Robe (1966)
Chapters of Life (1967)
Beyond the Tenth (1969)
Feeding the Flame (1971)
The Hermit (1971)
The Thirteenth Candle (1972)
Candlelight (1973)
Twilight (1975)
As It Was! (1976)
I Believe (1976)
Three Lives (1977)
Tibetan Sage (1980)

Other Sources

Peter Bishop, *Dreams of Power: Tibetan Buddhism and the Western Imagination* (Athlone Press, 1993)

T. Dodin, & H. Rather, (eds.), *Imagining Tibet: Perceptions, Projections and Fantasies* (Wisdom Publications, 2001)

Christopher Evans, *Cults of Unreason* (Farrar, Straus & Girard, 1974)

Christopher Lindner, *The James Bond Phenomenon: A Critical Reader* (Manchester University Press, 2003)

Donald Lopez, *Prisoners of Shangri La: Tibetan Buddhism and the West* (University of Chicago Press, 1999)

Sheelagh Rouse, *Twenty-five Years with T. Lobsang Rampa* (Lulu.com, 2006)

ELIZABETH SHARPE AND "THE SECRETS OF THE KAULA CIRCLE"

[*Elizabeth Sharpe and "The Secrets of the Kaula Circle"* was written in 2013 and also published on *enfolding.org.* A woman living an independent life in India, a successful journalist and translator of Sanskrit texts—Elizabeth Sharpe is an author whom I feel deserves more attention. As I discuss in the essay, she is best known for her 1936 novella, *The Secrets of the Kaula Circle,* which features an account of a "tantric orgy" which emphasizes drunkenness rather than sex, plus a character who is clearly based on Aleister Crowley. The emphasis on a drunken orgy, rather than a sexual one, is interesting as some Tantric texts spend more time on the merits of alcohol than they do on sexual intercourse.]

———

Elizabeth Sharpe (1888–1941) is one of the "forgotten" writers on India of the early twentieth century. She seems to have spent most of her life in India, with a brief trip to England in the 1930s. She wrote several books concerning aspects of Indian life, including at least one work on tantra; translated Sanskrit texts such as the *Siva Sahasranama*; and had a passionate interest in the education of women in India. She is best-known for her 1936 novella, *The Secrets of the Kaula Circle,* a tale of black magic and left-hand tantric orgies which featured a rather unflattering portrayal of Aleister Crowley.

Very little biographical information is known about Elizabeth Sharpe. She was born in Bangalore in 1888, her full name Phoebe Elizabeth Lavender, and at the age of 17 in 1905, married an officer of the Royal Ordnance Corps, John Charles Sharpe (1877–1943). According to David Templeman (in his introduction to the recent Teitan Press edition of *The Secrets of the Kaula Circle),* although the two were never formally divorced, they led quite separate lives.

Elizabeth Sharpe was the personal secretary of the Thakur Sahib of Limbdi province (now part of Gujarat state) Sri Sir Daulatsingh

(1868–1940), of whom she later wrote a biography. She also acted as private tutor to his sons, and was a special adviser to the Thakur regarding the education of women. She is known to have corresponded with Gandhi, Rabindranath Tagore (he wrote the foreword to her biography of the Thakur), and A.C. Benson (Master of Magdalene College), mainly concerning matters relating to the education of one of the Thakur's sons.

Under the British Empire, Limbdi was classified as a "salute state"—a protocolary privilege by which the ruler would be formally greeted with a gun salute—the number of salutes reflecting the degree of prestige accorded to the ruler of a princely state. The 21-gun salute was the highest salute accorded to a local ruler. The Thakur of Limbdi was accorded a 9-gun salute. Sri Daulatsingh was considered an able ruler and administrator, particularly with regard to education and agriculture and was granted the titles of KCIE (Knight Commander of the Order of the Indian Empire) and KSCI (Knight Commander of the Order of the Star of India). He represented India at the state opening of the first parliament of the commonwealth of Australia in 1901 and was, by all accounts, very supportive of the British in the Great War, raising war funds and encouraging his subjects to join the armed forces. His predecessor, Maharana Sri Sir Jaswantsinhji Fatehsinhji Sahib (1859–1907) attended the 1887 Golden Jubilee celebration for Queen Victoria in London—and later in the same year, made a visit to the USA. He is particularly notable for being an influence on Vivekananda, is said and to have rescued Vivekananda when he fell into the hands of a "degenerate sect of sex-worshippers." Lord Willingdon, the Governor of Bombay, paid a visit to Limbdi in 1916, the day of the formal opening of the Lady Willingdon Girls' School—although the school seems to have been founded in 1859.

Elizabeth Sharpe published a number of books during the period 1924–1939. These were: *Shri Krishna and the Bhagavad Gita* (London: Arthur H. Stockwell, 1924); *The Flame of God: A Mystical Autobiography* (London: Rider & Co., 1929); *Shiva or the Past of India* (London: Luzac & Co., 1930)—which included translations of sections of the Shiva Sahasranama and Anandalahari; the aforementioned biography *Thakore Sahib Shri Sir Daulat Singh of Limbdi, Kathiawar* (London: John Murray, 1931); *The Tantrik Doctrine of*

Immaculate Conception (London: Luzac & Co., 1933); *Philosophy of Yoga* (London: Luzac & Co., 1933); *The India that is India* (London: Luzac & Co., 1934); her "semi-fictional" novel *The Secrets of the Kaula Circle* (London: Luzac & Co., 1936) which, of all her work, has received the most attention; *An Eight Hundred Year Old Book of Indian Medicine and Formulas* (London: Luzac & Co., 1937); *The Great Cremation Ground-Mahasmasana* (London: Luzac & Co., 1938); and *Indian Tales* (London: Luzac & Co., 1939), which included her translation of the biography of a 16th century Jain monk. She also wrote the preface to Swami Ramdas' *At the Feet of God* (1928).

Thus far, I have only managed to obtain two of Sharpe's books: *The India that is India* and *The Secrets of the Kaula Circle.*

The India that is India

The India that is India is a collection of essays, many of which had originally appeared in the *Indian Illustrated Weekly* or in the New York-based *World*. Sharpe's foreword relates that, "These articles were written of India and Indians, to prevent Europeans applying their own standards of judgement in solving problems which are essentially matters for the Eastern people alone. What the Western world itself feels about the matter is not the criterion best suited for a balanced judgement." Many of the book's essays reflect Sharpe's keen interest in the lives of women, from her descriptions of the life led by Indian princesses, the women of the Zenanas, marriage customs and a chapter on "The Education of Girls".

There is also an essay on Jains, and two chapters discussing "Fakirs and Sadhus". Sharpe explains that there are good and bad Sadhus; that some are solitary and lead simple lives, whilst others have become "very worldly" acting as though they were judges and barristers. Some sadhus, she says, are merely criminals in disguise, and there are those who practice "revolting austerities." She relates an incident where 5,000 Vairagis rioted at a Kumbha Mela "because they were disappointed about the distribution of food." She goes on to briefly discuss several of kinds of Sadhus—for example, the sword and rifle-carrying Nagars (i.e., Nagas). She then turns to the sects of Yoga ascetics, including the Kanphatas and their founder, Goraknath and the Aghories whom, she says, "are the most feared of all the Indian ascetics," going on to describe an encounter with an Aghori ascetic. In her chapter on "Religions and Fairs" she then turns to a discussion of the "Vamacharis (left-hand worshippers) of Shiva and Shakti." She opines that, "These exoteric worshippers have done more to bring the Tantras into disrepute than any other sect in India to-day." She briefly describes the "so-called kaula-circle" which culminates with couples retiring to a private chamber "where the man was supposed to have worshipped the woman as 'mother.'" She says that, due to scandals, this form of worship is now "held in considerable disrepute." She quotes a letter from a Sri Vidya adept which states that:

> "a genuine Shri Vidya Upasaka…must always have his lady, or her lord with him or her. Only the really initiated know the use of the other sex in these practices, which while on the border-land of sex, are actually entirely devotional, mystic and supremely holy. The least trace of evil, or sensual, sexual desire would turn the Sadhaka into a beast: in fact amongst Sadhakas there are many who prowl about and hide their sensualism in the maze of rituals and poojas."

This is somewhat reminiscent of Kularnava-Tantra 5.112: "One who experiences the bliss of union in sexual relationship as being between the Supreme Power (Parasakti) and the Self—such a person knows the meaning of sexual relations; others are inferior, indulging only to pursue women."

The chapter continues with a discussion of the worship of Krishna and Radha, the various temples and maths devoted to Krishna, and various Vaishvana sects of ascetics. In this section she briefly mentions the cross-dressing Sakhibhavas:

> "Certain Sadhus, called Sakhi-Bavas, go about in feminine attire, personating Radha, and worship Krishna thus attired. They hope, ingeniously, to win Krishna's favour quicker by this method, believing that He will be more attracted by a worship from one in the form of His beloved. …their numbers are steadily lessening; and they do not command the respect of the public that they did formerly."

The Secrets of the Kaula Circle

So, on to *The Secrets of the Kaula Circle* which has just been re-issued (2012) by The Teiten Press with an introduction by David

Templeman. Appended to the novella is a translation of a hatha yoga manuscript entitled "The Science of Breath".

Sharpe, in her introduction, explains *Secrets* as:

> "a history of fictitious people—many things are disclosed: there is a faithful account of the orgies practised, and the reason why the shibboleth used is retained is that the reader may recognise the methods used in capturing the imagination of the unwary. ...it is published to warn both the Western and Eastern worlds that the pure paths of worship retaining the good and the ideal are the best."

She follows with a note explaining that, "The publishers thought it advisable to omit certain portions of this book" which, although as she admits, results in a "certain disconnectedness" does not believe that it impairs the overall message. She also notes having "met with some unwelcome attention from various occult societies"—presumably from her previous writings.

Of course, exactly what was omitted from *Secrets* is unknown (unless the original draft of the book can be discovered). David Templeman comments that, "It is difficult not to speculate that the excluded material might have detailed the tantric sexual activities and the round of offerings and oblations that we know took place in the course of such gatherings." As he points out, such omissions were not unusual, particularly where publishers were wary of prosecution under the Obscene Publications Act.

Strange Rites

Without wanting to give too many "spoilers," the plot of *Secrets* concerns a woman named "Mary de la Mont" who fell under the sway of, and married a "Lama"..."a man of superhuman power." Mary recounts her adventures with the Lama and reveals some of the yogic practices she engaged in, and experiences of past lives.

The first chapter recounts a ritual "from an old book":

> "A young and lovely girl was brought to an altar, before which lay a sarcophagus in which reposed a very old man some thousands of years old it was believed.
>
> The girl approached the recumbent man and placed the nipples of her breast, first one then another, in his mouth. The corpse-like crea-

ture, whose mummified lips could not, at first, hold the firm nipples began suddenly to suck heartily and soon grew young.

He then tried to clasp the fainting girl in his arms; but she eluded him, floating far above the concourse of the chanting worshippers.

Returning to earth at last, she again allowed him to drink of her body."

The description of the "orgy" of the Kaula Circle comes in the sixth chapter:

"The "Kaula" circle is the circle of the worshippers of the left-hand path, whose secret none but they of this circle have known till now.

In this circle, the woman is the 'mother'—but all her desires are fulfilled: that is the vow.

Few women come through the ordeal pure, unstained: for it is believed that the husband is born of the mother, and the mother and the wife are interchangeable terms in the circle.

...Man after man, woman after woman passed by me, singing, reeling and dead drunk.

Later on, they would be forced to drink the forty-two bottles of wine prescribed by the rules of the ceremony: eat, drink and be merry and die: for their doom—poor fools—was already on them.

...I still remember that inner courtyard: stark-naked men and women, who, from time to time, with excruciating yells, leapt to their feet, shaking their heads backwards and forwards, the women with loosened locks falling in black disorder about their heaving, shaking breasts.

A voice would then cry out in deepest scorn the sonorous Sanscrit Tantrik verse: 'Let their desires be satisfied.'

And there would be a perfect orgy of bestiality."

This description warrants examination. It bears some resemblance to the popular descriptions of tantric orgies from the early nineteenth century, such as those given by William Ward or the French Abbé Dubois' "reported" account of Shakti-Puja:

"Among the abominable mysteries current in India, there is one that is all too well-known: this is the practice called sakty-poudja... The celebration of these mysteries, invariably foul as concerns their content, can at times vary in their form. In certain cases, the immediate objects of the sacrifice to Sakty are a large vessel that has been filled with local alcohol and a girl who has reached the age of puberty. This latter, entirely naked, stands in an altogether indecent pose. They then summon the goddess Sakty, whom they presume accepts their invitation by simultaneously establishing herself in the vessel of alcohol and that portion of the girl's anatomy which modesty prohibits me from naming. ...brahmans, sudras, pariahs, men and women all become drunk on the alcohol consecrated to Sakty, which they drink from the same vessel, touching it with their lips... The men and women then throw themselves on the food, avidly gobbling it down. The same chunk of food passes from mouth to mouth, and is successively chewed away until it has been entirely consumed... In this case, the people are persuaded that they are in no way sullied by eating and drinking in such a revolting manner. When they have at last become entirely intoxicated, men and women mingle freely and pass the remainder of the night together..."

— quoted from David Gordon White, *Tantric Sects and Tantric Sex: The Flow of Secret Tantric Gnosis,* 1998

Such accounts of "tantrik" orgies were fairly common throughout the colonial period.

What's particularly interesting regarding Sharpe's account is the stress she places on drunkenness (as does Dubois). It may be, of course, that this passage originally contained details of sexual rites— as Templeman suggests—which were removed by the publishers. However, I would draw the reader's attention to the recent work of Annette Wilke on Kaula texts, in particular her essay *Negotiating Tantra and Veda in the Parasurama-Kalpa Tradition* in which she asserts that:

"Singling out sexual rites from the integrated whole of the pancamakara may be a Western bias. In any case it is not by chance that alcohol is presumably called 'the first.' It is actually the most important ritual substance in the PKS (PKS = Parasurama Kalpasutra) as well as in the KT. (KT = Kularnava Tantra) KT 5.77 equates liquor with the god Bhairava and the goddess, that is, their self-revelation. Excessive drinking was apparently a form of possession trance. ...In singling out sexual rites, then, too much stress has been laid upon them. Indeed a stronger focus on alcohol than on intercourse is acknowledged in the commentary tradition too."

— Wilke, 2012, p.145

It is, of course, in the *Kularnava Tantra* that we find one of the most well-known set of verses on such rituals:

67. Intoxicated by passion, the women take shelter with other men, treating them as their own. Each man also takes a new woman and treats her as his own, when in the state of advanced ecstatic joy.
68. Seized by delusion, the men embrace other men...
71. O Shambhavi! The yogis take the food from each other's plates and dance with their drinking pots on their heads...
73. The women who are not in their normal senses clap and sing songs whose words are unclear, and they stagger while dancing.
74. Yogis who are intoxicated with alcohol fall upon the women, and the intoxicated yoginis fall upon the men, O Kulanayika! They are induced to perform such actions, to fulfill their mutual desires.
75. When this state of ecstasy is not accompanied by corrupt thoughts, the bull among yogis reaches the state of godhood (devata-bhava).

Also of interest is Sharpe's location of the origin of Kaula worship in Mongolia, and that the action of the novella is set in Tibet, rather than India. This, at first glance, seems peculiar, but given the increasing antipathy to Kaula and tantric practices in late colonial India, this can be thought of as a way of (geographically) distancing the degenerate practices of the Kaula circle from mainstream Indian culture—to which Sharpe, in her other writings, displayed a deep commitment. David Templeman, in his introduction to the Teitan reprint, points out that Vivekananda also located the origins of the "evils" of tantra in Tibet.

In addition to Mary de la Mont's Lama-Guru—and the mysterious figure identified by the numbers "666" (guess who)—the novella features the "Maharaja of X" of whom the narrator says: "This strange mixture of Dr. Jekyll and Mr. Hyde was, at one time, the main topic of talk of more than half of India: so extraordinary and so varied were his eccentricities; yet so perfect and so cultured were his views on life, modelled in phrases above reproach." It is possible that this is an oblique reference to the "Maharaja" of the 1862 Vallabhacharya scandal, which drew widespread comment in both India and Europe.

It's difficult to say how influential *Secrets* was. It seems to have received favourable reviews at the time of its publication, and it is occasionally cited as a reference in popular works on tantric sex to this day. One book which draws heavily on *Secrets* is Omar Garrison's 1964 book, *Tantra: the Yoga of Sex*—an important book in the twisted tale of western imaginings of tantra.

As far as I am aware, there has been little scholarly interest in Elizabeth Sharpe. Hugh Urban briefly discusses her (2003, 2006) in relation to *Secrets of the Kaula Circle*—which he describes (2003) as "one of the most vivid descriptions of the depraved rites of the Tantras" as part of a discussion of women romantic novelists of the late colonial period. Hopefully, Teitan's reprint of *Secrets* will inspire more attention to be given to this fascinating woman, her life and her writings.

Sources

Hugh Urban, *Tantra: Sex, Secrecy, Politics and Power in the Study of Religion* (University of Chicago Press, 2003).

Hugh Urban, *Magia Sexualis: Sex, Magic, and Liberation in Modern Western Esotericism* (University of California Press, 2006)

David Gordon White, "Tantric Sects and Tantric Sex: The Flow of Secret Tantric Gnosis" in Wolfson (ed.) *Rending the Veil* (Seven Bridges Press, 1998: 249–70)

Annette Wilke, "Negotiating Tantra and Veda in the Parasurama-Kalpa Tradition" in Husken & Neubert (eds.) *Negotiating Rites* (Oxford University Press, 2011)

FICTION

Introduction

On Fiction and Humour

I have always been fascinated with the way magical narratives can blur the distinction betwixt the apparently factual and the fantastic, and in so doing, create a space in which a reader's imagination can take flight. Fiction also helps to place the reader into a situation or place. When I first began to get interested in magic, it seemed only natural to draw on the fiction I was reading at the same time. Having recently discovered the horror stories of H.P. Lovecraft, and finding myself living in a village on the edge of a mountain range, I found that his depictions of a haunted and living landscape easily transposed itself from New England to the wilds of West Yorkshire. His fearful depictions of teeming cities which held both brooding terrors and hidden delights could find their echoes in Huddersfield, my first experience of living in a city, where miles of empty warehouses and factories were a mute testament to a vanished industrial past. Feeling a kind of kinship with a Lovecraftian outsider, in search of secrets and fitting together disconnected clues, I discovered new experiences and freedoms in the most unlikely or unlooked-for circumstances. What also attracted me to Lovecraft was that the mythos which had grown up around his tales was fragmentary and unfinished. It wasn't something I felt could be systematised or squeezed onto the Kabbalistic Tree of Life—although there were attempts to do exactly that! Rather, it was for me, a jumping-off point—a place to start from that might lead somewhere novel. In reading the fiction of Lovecraft, Dion Fortune or Lord Dunsany—all early and enduring favourites—I gained the sense of magic as a journey—as an unfolding into wider spaces and broadening vision. Listening to an audio recording of Lord Dunsany's *The Beggars* as I walk through London draws me towards an animist perception—an unfolding of the city's age-old secrets as I gaze around me with new eyes. Fiction opens us to new possibilities.

At the same time, reading fiction and bringing fictional themes into my occult practice led me towards the realisation of the importance of *emotional engagement* in magic. This is what brings both fiction and magic to life: the ability to be caught up in something, feeling terror for the victim on television drama, or weeping at a soppy film. Occult internet forums and Facebook groups resound with much debate and argument about the effectiveness (and appropriateness) of particular traditions and approaches. The time-honoured response is, of course, that "it works"—by which standard anything can be made legitimate. But with magic, *anything* can work—providing you have made an emotional connection to it. Whether a practice has the force of history behind it or has been quickly cobbled together over a pint and a pie in a pub and then glossed over with clever prose or marketing, it can be held to work. Providing, that is, someone has an emotional response to it—it resonates with them; they can find themselves within it. It makes sense. Whether or not a tradition is historically grounded is almost besides the point. I spent about a decade doing tantric practices that bore very little resemblance to the traditions as they are described in primary textual sources—but that didn't mean that the rituals or practices were not personally effective for me just because they were based on western imaginings of tantra as opposed to "the real thing." If what I was doing hadn't worked, I wouldn't have kept doing it—and it was the momentum gathered which impelled me to try to get to grips with the traditional material.

Writing fiction can be a way of revealing oneself to the reader, giving a space for the intrusion of inner dialogue, self-reflection, and perhaps most importantly for me, a sense of humour. Fiction or satire can be a useful way to poke fun at occult pretensions, particularly if it entails acknowledging one's own pretensions. Most of my attempts at fiction are grounded, I think, in the desire to undermine my own fantasies of being a powerful magical adept. It is all too easy to get caught up in the self-projection of being powerful, of having access to secrets and standing apart from the rest of humanity. When I began to write fiction and occult humour in the late 1980s, I was becoming increasingly aware of the pitfalls of such fantasies, and wanted to explore the vulnerabilities and weaknesses of the pose of the magician instead. Hence, in the three pieces of fiction selected for this section, one narrator is hiding from his own conjuration in a broom cupboard, a second is scared of wasps (and hippies), and the third is nervous about entering a gay bar.

Satire and other kinds of humour have their place, too, in occult writing, and I often feel that satire, in particular, is undervalued as a mode of expression. Gently poking fun at occult theories and fads can be as much an encouragement to critical reflection and challenging the status quo as any well-researched or argumentative writing, and in some ways, I feel, is more effective. If I want to be critical about an idea or perspective then it helps, I find, to get people on my side using humour. Laughter can build bridges among opinions, faiths and status. Laughing at and with those ideas we hold sacred is in itself a magical act.

PLAYMATES

[*Playmates* was my first attempt at short magical fiction. I wrote it in 1989, and sent it off to a Pagan fiction fanzine, the editor of which promptly rejected it, due to its 'sexual' theme. It first saw the light of day in the March/April issue 1990 issue of *Pagan News*.]

———◆———

...safe here I think. God, my heart's pounding. What if she hears it? Got to get a grip on myself... take a few deep breaths... pranayama... that's... that's better.

I can just about see out of the crack. A sliver of light, but maybe I'll be able to see her shadow... oh! Don't suppose she has a shadow. Damn!

I could open the door just an inch... better not... if she finds me, then... What's that smell? Shoe polish? Brasso? This must be the cleaner's cupboard. Maybe that'll put her off. Wonder what she'll do if she can't find me? Take it out on some other poor sod? No. She can't leave the house. That's the rule isn't it? They can't leave the place they're called into. Maybe she'll get bored and go away. Maybe she'll fade away. Maybe... if I could remember how, I could banish her from in here. Banishing ritual of the broom cupboard... it'd be funny if it wasn't so pathetic.

I could wait till Andrew gets back. He'd sort her out. But no, I wouldn't be able to look him in the face again. It'd be like being caught wanking. I suppose it is, in a way. He'd tell everyone, and it'd be all over the scene inside five minutes. I can just see that posing stud Brian smirking all over his face. Big Joke yes... on me.

Do I hear creaking? Is she coming downstairs? Then again, she can just teleport or project everywhere—she doesn't need to walk. Hang on tho', didn't it say in the book that sex makes them take on the semblance of solidity—helps them become individual personalities? No wonder she's so damned eager. Thought for a minute my head had come off. God, I'm hungry. I could murder steak and chips. It was my turn to cook tonight and all. Shit.

Well, isn't this cosy. Just me and the mop bucket. Wish I knew where she was. I wonder if ectoplasm washes out easily? Cavorting with demons. Mum would have a fit. At least I can't get AIDS or get her pregnant or something. Or could I? Maybe right now she's spawning hundreds of little pink tentacled things. I'll be followed 'round by a horde of elementals all mewling and puking. I suppose it's one way of getting a familiar.

God, I'm sore. She sucked me dry. Worst thing was her laughter. It was a game when it started, but I didn't think it'd be so demanding. I couldn't handle it. Or her. So much for being an adept, huh? Bet old uncle Aleister didn't have to hide from his own conjurings. He wouldn't be hiding in a cupboard with a rampant she-demon upstairs hell-bent on fornication. But then, he wouldn't have petered out after half an hour either. This is it, no more Left-Hand Path for me. It's Gareth Knight and his whiter-than-white rosicrucians from now on. Or maybe I'll become a born-again Christian. They don't seem to have sex at all.

Dark in here. I wonder where she is. I can just imagine her— faintly luminous, green eyes, red hair. Typical vampire. Very alluring... maybe I could persuade her to let me rest for a while... get my strength back... mmmm... she's certainly a beauty... if only I could...

Aaaaarghh!

"Aaah, there you are. Come and play..."

WITH BOTH HANDS

[*With Both Hands* was written in 1991 and was first published in the third issue of *Both the Ones,* a Temple of Psychic Youth magazine. Out of all these pieces, this is the most directly autobiographical, as at the time of writing, I lived in Headingley, Leeds 6, where this story is set. I'd also lived in a basement flat and had spiraled down into the kind of lonely, depressed state, that in this story is the effect of a spell. The character of "Jeff" is a composite based on some of the people I met on the magical scene in Leeds, and many of the places mentioned are real.]

———

Jeff was an ex-scientologist, an unlikely shaman, but so it often goes. The face he turned to the world was that of a drifter, buoyed up by a peculiar brand of techno-terms and salad of mixed metaphors. Jeff would have us think him a man of knowledge, forever hinting at secrets, conspiratorial asides and sidelong glances at his collection of occult books. He gathered secrets about him like a cloak, weaving them into the fabric of his clothes. It seemed at times, though, that the cloak weighed him down, dogging him with spectres of a dim and distant horror.

In the first flush of the Age of Aquarius Jeff had sought out the masters, both living and dead. Krishnamurti, Gurdjieff, Alice Bailey. He'd done the lot, from meeting Aleister Crowley on the astral plane to sitting next to Kenneth Grant on the tube. Eventually, world-weary with accumulated wisdom, he fetched up on the shores of scientology, cooling his heels at East Grinstead Manor. And from there, through a broken trail of years, fetched up in Leeds Six. A basement case; a mute testament to the dreams of the Sixties.

I first encountered Jeff at a party, having slunk in on the standard friend of a friend story. There wasn't much action and, not feeling up to worming my way into any of the tightly-knotted conversations, I headed for the kitchen. Someone (it was Jeff) followed, the penta-gram around my neck drawing him like a magnet. I watched him unfolding an introductory smile, and ran through the probable open-ing lines, marshalling my standby reactions. Was it to be drugs?

Worth the words if there's a score in the offing. Religion? Well my carefully-cultivated cynicism hadn't been fed for a while. A lot would depend on whether he was a Christian or a sociology student. Sex? I doubted it. But by that time, blurred by alcohol and spurred by nagging loneliness, well, you know how it is.

As it happened, it was none of these.

"Are you into magic then?"

I graciously assented.

"Are you any good?"

I shrugged, conveying at once that I was non-committal about such things, unconcerned maybe...but yes, I thought I was good.

Jeff studied me for a while, then reached for his address book. Ripping off a page, he stuffed it into my jacket pocket. "You'd better be, 'cos I'm going to kill you."

And with that, he spun on his heel and stalked out of the room.

I was surprised by the speed of the exchange, and not a little bemused. I shook my head and resumed my trip to the kitchen. Finding an almost-virgin can of lager, I drank the encounter away, washing away the brief flutters of fear.

"Just another acid-head," I thought, at that moment feeling eyes running down my back. Deliberately, in my head a sinister puppet, I turned around, expecting to find the "Acid-head". Instead, there was the flash of domino eyeliner, spiky black mop and a pink tongue, caught in the act of moistening purple lips. A surge of confidence swept through me, and eyes widening to maximum zoom, stepped forwards and closed in.

***

I'm lost. Confused, no longer sure what's happening. There's an invisible barrier in front of me. I'm...trapped. The air is stuffy and heavy. It's no good, no matter how hard I try, I can't get out. I'm trapped. I can see light ahead, but it's too bright. Vast shapes loom menacingly in the distance. It's like being on the other side of a wall, but it's so smooth. I can't grasp a purchase no matter how hard I try. I just end up slithering down the sides. My teeth feel awful. My throat's so dry, and there's a lingering taste like chewed wood. My head's buzzing so loud I can hear it rising and falling, like a thousand angry chainsaws. Across the barrier, a gigantic shape bends closer. A god, perhaps come to pull my wings off? There's a muffled booming from the other side of the barrier. Is that how gods laugh? I can't get out, I can't get away. Caught like a wasp in a jar. When I was eight, I caught a wasp in a jar. It got out and stung me and since then I can't stand to be in the same room as them. I'm trying to dig through the barrier, but my claws slide hopelessly across the glass. Catching a flicker of movement, I peer close to glimpse my own reflection. Understanding hits me like a kick in the crotch. I'm a wasp. I'M A WASP I'MAWASP I'MAWASPINAJAR OH GOD I HATE WASPS I'M A WASP I HATE THEM I HATE THEM I WANT TO GET OUT I'M A WASPWASPWASPWAZPWAZ-BWZBZBZBZZBZZBZZBzzzz...

And jerk awake, sweating, shivering, gibbering with fear. Oh god I'm so relieved. It's so good to be awake. And then the fear comes again. I strain my ears, waiting for the tell-tale buzz that will announce the presence of my nightmare's demon. Perhaps it was crawling into my ear as I slept—no, push that thought away. Waiting, but no buzzing comes, no rustlings against the curtain, no silhouettes inside the lampshade. Nothing.

The nightmare ruined my day, so I didn't go out. There wasn't much point. No letters, not my signing-on day, no pressing visits to make. I stayed in bed reading and daydreaming. No one came to call. I was in a basement room, so I didn't feel intruded upon by the world. Briefly, I thought of going down to the pub, but that took energy, and frankly, I didn't have any.

That night, I was almost afraid of going to sleep. I was sure I would wake to find some yellow and black-banded horror perched on my pillow.

The next day brought sunshine to Headingley, and the rays streaming into my room seemed to evaporate the nagging fear that hung in the air. It receded to the back of my mind and jostled for position with neglected bills and bank statements. Out of sight, out of mind. Or at least, conveniently forgotten.

Spring gave way to summer in fits and starts. For the most part, I was largely indifferent to nature's bounty. I'd occasionally walk through the parks and common ground, but never felt bound to flee the city for nearby moors or rivers. Invitations to a Beltain Bop passed unheeded. Instead, I sauntered down to The Royal Park pub, sank a few pints, and passed the time sitting with friends. But I couldn't join in the table-talk. I felt so distant. Part of me was still trapped in a jar. Or perhaps I wanted things to be like that.

I sat indoors reading a book. The same book. Over and over. Occasionally, the doorbell would ring and I froze, heart pounding, until the caller went away. Once a fortnight I would put on my overcoat and make the trip into town to sign on, nodding hallo to people. Faces I vaguely knew but whose names had long eroded from my memory. Leeds' town centre loomed oppressively around me, and it was always a relief to get back to my room. Fortunately, the local shops provided all my needs, so I hardly had to leave Headingley at all. My room became the centre of my universe. The hub on the wheel of life. I was becoming invisible, or perhaps fading would be a better word. The worlds of magic held no mystery and my occult books gathered dust on the shelf. Scrupulously avoiding people, I felt no longer taxed by the necessities of maintaining a social front. Washing went out the window, likewise dental care, hair brushing and eating properly. Yet I knew the merits of every asian-made samosa in the district. Custard and crisps took the place of cooked meals. And I fucked everyone I'd ever wanted to, alone each night in my bed.

***

The change came without warning. Three or four times a week, I had taken to walking down to the all-night garage for a three a.m. snack of sandwiches, chocolate and juice. I enjoyed these night walks as there were fewer people around, and I could feel a faint nostalgia for the company of others. I slunk through the streets evading any imminent presences, yet drawn by the lights and closed curtains. In truth, I was beginning to savour being an outsider. Or a ghost.

On this particular night, waiting for my order to be filled, I felt a presence behind me. Someone else queuing, probably. Eyes on my back—perhaps some former friend, but of course I wasn't going to make the first move. Picking up the plastic bag of junk food I turned to leave. A hand clutched my arm.

"I thought you said you were good."

I turned to stare at the owner of the voice. A typical Headingley hippie—he didn't look at all familiar.

"I'm killing you, you know. You're trapped in my web." "What are you... I don't understand..."

And then of course, I did.

"My name's Jeff," said the hippie. "We met at Ruffle's party. Don't you remember?"

"Y-yes. I think so. I was rather drunk that night. Why have you... how have you done this to me?"

"Don't you know? I thought you were the mighty magician?"

"You've put me in a pen—is that it? No wonder I don't like leaving this area. Everything...my thoughts...they're clouding over. What time is it?"

He laughed. "You're lucky you know what day it is."

"Are you going to stop now?"

"Why should I? Look, it's simple mister-so-called-magician. Either you die, or you fight to stay alive. Your choice. I'll be waiting."

I was rooted to the spot. Unable to move as he sauntered off into the night. And then my feet came free and I sprinted home as if all the devils in hell were after me. In the opposite direction to Jeff.

***

Back home, I looked, really looked at the tip I'd been living in. Saw the dust, heaps of magazines, overflowing bin-liner and stale-smelling dishes in the sink. And the grey duvet cover...hadn't it started off as white? I searched along the shelves and found some essential oil jars. The labels were faded but the oil went into a bath of hot water regardless. As did I. After a long soak (I had begun to avoid water), I returned, found the last of my clean clothes, and started a long-overdue spring-clean. Restoring order to the heaps of comics that had accumulated on the floor. Amongst them I found a couple of skin-mags and guiltily sneaked them into another tenant's dustbin. Then to work. Rooting through boxes I assembled candles, incense, altar-cloth and other magical bric-a-brac. The charcoal discs were damp, so I gave my fragrancer a quick wipe and blasted the room with Rosemary Oil—'it banishes the parts other incenses don't reach.' A feeble sally I know, but I was beginning to laugh my way back to some semblance of normality. I banished so hard my whole body tensed up as I viciously slashed the pentagrams into the air, hissing the words through clenched teeth, flooding the ether with the dazzling whiteness of Kether. This was better. I was alive again, and I was going to do my damnedest to make sure it stayed that way. Jeff was trying to keep me in, to keep me away from people, so it was to people I went. I crossed over into Woodhouse, only a few streets from the flat, but I almost felt like an explorer braving the jungle for the first time. I plucked up my courage and dragged myself to a friendly-looking door. I was received kindly and graciously by people that I had neglected to visit for weeks, who I had pretended not to notice on the street, and had played deaf when they rang the bell. They thought, so I learned, as apparently many other people did, that I had succumbed to a solitary street skag habit. They fed me. They fed me soup, bread and lentils; and better, they fed me with life. While my stomach was in shock from being crammed with food, I discovered what I had forgotten…what Jeff's spell (if such it was) had caused me to forget—that I hungered, too, for attention and affection. I talked for hours, amazed that I had let myself be turned away from the bright glow of company. I stayed late, and rather than go home, stayed the night.

And in the night, I dreamed.

I dreamt of walking along a seashore—the crash of surf and hum of distant traffic mingling in my ears. There was a pier ahead of me, and as I drew closer to the barnacle-encrusted girders, a figure detached itself from the darkness.

"Well, at least you're beginning to shape up." It was Jeff. "But you can't hide forever you know. If you want to play, you'll have to play to win. Otherwise you'll die."

"Why are you doing…?" But he was gone.

Back home, I began to try to sort my head out. Appalled at the blank pages in my magical diary, I set out a strict regimen of banishings, meditations and yoga. But I still had no idea why this Jeff person was trying to kill me. Had I insulted him or rebuffed an advance? He claimed that we'd met at Ruffle's birthday party, and my memory of that night was hazy, to say the least. All I could come up with were a few disconnected scenes, like a badly-spliced home movie. Standing on the edges of conversations, drinking god-knows-what concoctions, and finally, under the kitchen table, necking with someone of indeterminate gender. I had no memory of Jeff at all. And then it occurred to me that he had given me a clue. Dreams. He'd made himself a key to the backdoor of my mind and was sauntering in through my dreams. Whether I remembered them or not, he was in them, meddling and muddling my thoughts. That he could do this so apparently effortlessly, caused me to grudgingly respect him and to loathe him. But he was not the only person who could juggle dreams.

Since I couldn't consciously remember Jeff, I tried to recover the memory magically. A sigil did the trick. After six nights of mumbling a meaningless spell-phrase, I dreamt 'true' of that which I desired. I dreamt of Jeff.

I returned as an observer to Ruffle Bar's birthday party. It was shot in slow-motion and sepia, with no sound. I saw me thread my way across the conversation-scarred living room, only to be accosted by a frayed-at-the-edges hippie—Jeff. Suddenly, I spotted the movement and mentally 'paused' my dream VCR. I ran it back again, and saw Jeff pushing a piece of crumpled paper into my pocket. Success!

So now I had another clue. Another search commenced, this time through my clothes. Finally, I tracked down the garment in question—a black denim jacket, as yet unlaundered. Inside one of the top pockets I found a crumpled, knot of paper. This turned out to be a page from an address book. A hastily-scribbled note read 'Jeff Kirby, 221 Brudenell Terr, L6.'

Jeff's address.

This gave me a few options. I could go and confront him directly; I could try to get some of the more menacing squatters that I knew to break his arms; or…I could try to counter-attack.

The only question was, how? I knew that people like Crowley had fought magical battles with legions of demons, but I had no idea about how this could be done. If I tried anything simple, Jeff would probably wipe the floor with me. Yet I had to do something decisive before his spell gnawed away my resolve to resist. I had to do the unexpected. But first I needed to distract him. This proved to be simple. I sought out someone who knew someone else who lived in the same flats as Jeff and inquired of them if "that weird hippie" worked or not. It turned out that he didn't. Presumably, I thought, he spends all his time doing weird things to people like me. Well, if he wants to mess with my head, I'll mess with his.

In the next week, Jeff had visits from the fraudulent claims squad, drugs squad, had his dole cut off, and a whole string of people ringing his doorbell in the small hours. Small victories, but they all add up. My *pièce de résistance* was getting myself into the house where Jeff had a flat late one night and tying a piece of rope between his door handle & the stairwell.

Two nights after this, Jeff slid sideways into my dreams again. I'd been practising, and was learning to guard my back, so to speak. As he appeared, I snapped out of being a passive dreamer into being an active participant. Pointing a crystal-tipped wand at him, I tried to zap him with the destructive power of Khamael. It worked, but he didn't have the decency to stay zapped.

"Not bad work at all. You've covered your back and you're learning about weaponry. Also, if you want to survive, you'll have to occasionally resort to dirty tricks. Such a pity that it's all in vain."

With that, the dream cracked, I jerked awake. The wand that I had so carefully sanded down, lettered, and consecrated, had split down the middle. My first thought was to blame it on its proximity to the gas cooker, but the coincidence was too much to brush away. Things were getting serious. I was fighting to live, knowing with a sick certainty that if I didn't, then I would either die, or end up in some semblance of living which was possibly worse. Until now, I had approached magic as though it were a psychological head-game. I'd had some interesting buzzes from meditation and enjoyed path-workings & drumming sessions with some other people at the Solstices, but never had someone managed to demonstrate to me, so effectively, that magic was real enough to threaten my continued existence. Nothing I'd read or heard had prepared me for this, and so I was running on ingenuity and intuition. Know what? At times, I was enjoying it.

***

"Got you, you bastard!" I thought, lowering a borrowed camera. A long-range shot of Jeff entering his front door. A photograph and a sample of his handwriting—not much to go on, but perhaps enough. I started to grasp the situation and wonder how I could turn it to my advantage. Jeff had obviously established a magical link with me—a corridor through which he could reach into my mind. Maybe, I wondered, I could use that corridor as well. The hunted becoming the hunter, and all that. I read Kipling's *The Jungle Book,* watched a video of *The Company of Wolves,* and saw in my daydreams the figure of Jeff running, running through the streets of Leeds. Panic-stricken and pursued by wolves. At first this was perhaps nothing more than a morale-booster. It kept Jeff's spell from slithering back inside my head. I played with more sigils, and then I dreamt of werewolf time. The dreams came through stronger, and during the day, dogs began to howl when I passed them. There was a sense of something coming closer. What it was, I didn't know, but whatever lay in store, I was going to meet it face to face. On two legs or four.

Gradually, I grew stronger. I knew that Jeff had tried to box me into a limited space and sap my will. I knew what the boundaries were. I broke them, one by one. I spent more time in town and out of town. I visited friends and invited people to come around. I flirted outrageously with the most unlikely people, and generally acted the fool. My self-important arrogance dropped away. In short, I learnt humility, and eventually, humanity. I began to wonder how much of Jeff's spell was already lodged inside my head, waiting for a chance to spring out. Had he bound me using a web of lies that I had, for the most part, woven about myself? I looked around the flat—it was untidy, but not irretrievably so. I hadn't done my daily meditation yet, but there was still time to fit it in. In short, I wasn't yet perfect, but at least I was making an effort, and knowing that I was going somewhere.

This reverie was interrupted by a banging on my window. I walked upstairs and opened the main door. And stood staring. It was Jeff. Thoughts flickered wildly for a moment—a curse, a sarcastic put-down, a blast of psychic energy. I could even hurl myself at him and he'd fall backwards down the steps…

"Fancy coming out for a drink, then?" He smiled and held out both hands in a gesture of peace. I looked at him, with his long hair, straggly beard and faded flared jeans. Suddenly he didn't look fear-some any more. "Christ," I thought, "I've been afraid of someone who wears flares!" Then:

"Okay, why not?" And off we went.

Over the second pint he said, "Consider yourself initiated."

"Into what?" I said, suddenly suspicious again.

"Into yourself," he replied. "You needed to be goaded towards death so that you would begin to pay attention to life. You played at magic and you played at life. I only took away that which you hadn't learnt to appreciate and which you thought you could get by without. That's all."

"What happens now?"

"That's up to you really. We'll talk. I can't teach you, but we can learn from each other. Come around some time."

I did. He could sit for hours spinning tales of dreams, dope and dakini dancers. He could tell you the quality of an acid tab just by placing it on his fingertip. Like I said at the beginning, he drew secrets about himself. He'd done the seeker-of-wisdom trip to death. It gave him power, and he fed it further with other people's credulity. He knew how to make the right moves to the right person at the right time. Not quite knowing how things would come out, but knowing that it was necessary. He showed me death with one hand and gave me life with the other. Through knowing Jeff, I came to know a whole lot more people. But I'll never forget the first person he intro-duced me to—myself.

Astral Advertising: A Modern Occult Menace?

[*Astral Advertising: A Modern Occult Menace?* first appeared in the Jan/Feb 1991 issue of *Pagan News*. Written as a satirical news report, it uses some of the stock characters and phrases used by other *Pagan News* humorists. Written well before ideas such as spiritual consumerism had received much attention, it pushes popular occult theories into the realm of the ridiculous.]

The Occult community is becoming increasingly divided over a controversial development in modern magick—Astral Advertisements. In their recent Yuletide broadcast to all Witch Queens, Magi & Gurus, the Secret Chiefs departed from their usual message of world peace and harmony to urge the heads of all magical Orders to make voluntary cutbacks in the level of astral advertising.

One of our reporters interviewed a recent 'victim' of astral junk mail, The High Priestess of the New Reformed Orthodox High Church of Wicca (Wymeswold Branch), Marjorie Pebble.

"It's awful. Why only last week we invoked the Goddess, and instead of getting the advice I wanted to heal our Sharon's bad knee, all I got was a repeating message to subscribe to 'Occult News Monthly' or something. It's getting so bad that every time I meditate I get all these jingles running through my head selling Aeon-share holidays or ozone-friendly Demon-repellant."

Last month, a public meeting of occultists at Conway Hall was thrown into chaos when, following a Pathworking, several members of the audience complained about seeing 359 formation-dancing Angels advertising the new Qabalistic treatise by 'Z'em Bang Hafesh Wang'. Visitors to Glastonbury have also reported feeling a strange 'empty' sensation when climbing the Tor, which can only be assuaged by visiting Russell Wobble's Astral Health Food and Orgone-free Wine Bar. The problem appears to become particularly bad during the festivals, full moons, and in the run-up to Yuletide.

But some occultists, notably those in the business sector, are fully behind astral advertising. We spoke to Angel Moonflower of the 'Have A Nice Day' New Age Centre, Stow-on-the Wold:

"Well, I prefer to think that it gives consumerism a spiritual dimension. All our crystals have been charged with the messages 'buy me' and 'buy one more.' But really, you know you can never have too many crystals. I think that little blue one in the corner likes you..."

After a long and arduous ritual (including intermission & commercial breaks) we managed to find the inner-plane adepts masterminding astral advertising in the UK, the shadowy A...A..., Inc. They were out to lunch, but we left a message with the Guardian of the Threshold. Later, in a channelled interview through their solicitors, Shem, Ham & Phorash, the A...A... said:

"This is only the beginning. We can train a good neophyte in six months to project an image & soundtrack, and thanks to the Butterfly Effect it'll stay coherent on the astral for months. Of course, whenever someone accesses the advert, their contact feeds more energy into the thought-form. Our first takers were a consortium of Chaoists doing a special offer 'try our Chaosphere on the astral for 90 days before you buy.' Then the OTTO hired us to project an advert of Crowley endorsing one of his own books. Anyone doing the Gnostic Mass for the next few months should be able to pick it up. That's the beauty of it—not only is it cheap, but you can target your audiences. And it's not only occultists who are taking advantage of our services. A major soup company has offered us a substantial amount to market 'Olive Twitch's Instant Cook-in-a-Cauldron Noodles', using a doppelganger of Gerald Gardner and the New Forest Coven. In the next few months we're to begin beaming out a series of coffee ads starring several members of the Greek Pantheon. It's amazing what some of those old deities will do for a bit of media attention. We're particularly pleased with the one featuring Zeus, 2 Nymphs, several goats and a jar of Nescafé Gold Blend."

"But," we said, "isn't this getting a bit out of hand?"

"Not at all. The occult needs to move with the times, and we're using 1% of our income to help general spiritual enlightenment with sponsored pathworkings for minor demi-gods; posting 'Keep the

Planes Tidy' notices at all major portals; and computerising the Akashic Records."

But some traditionalists are not convinced. Hercules Wobble of the Order of the Nine Blades, head of the Surbiton Branch of the 'Clean Up the Astral' campaign told us:

"It's bloody disgraceful. Yesterday we performed a full evocation of Asmodeus and his 99 legions for a Channel 4 Astral Broadcast Unit, and all the little buggers turned up wearing 'Norse Gods Comeback Tour' t-shirts!"

Despite the controversy, it looks as though Astral Advertising is here to stay. Since we complained on behalf of suffering readers, the A...A... have generously offered a simple astral 'noise filter' meditation. It costs a mere £500 and is available from Mammon Investments direct. Simply visualise the A...A... logo—a dollar sign inside a triangle, and, on hearing the astral bell, simply chant your name, address and Karmacard number.

THE PIT

[*The Pit*, my only attempt so far to write a Lovecraftian pastiche (albeit a rather queer one), was written in 1995 and submitted to the editors of the Creation Press anthology *Starry Wisdom* who declined to publish it (they accepted "Cthulhu Madness" instead). Over the years this been my essay of choice to send in whenever asked to submit something to Lovecraftian magic-themed anthologies, but thus far, no one has wanted it.]

———

I suppose that it was curiosity that first drew me to the pit—that and a desire to reach into forbidden territory. I styled myself an outsider, an observer of men and their petty foibles. Rather than bow my head and accept the routine drudgeries of the world, I sought that which lay on the edges of society. Forbidden things, forbidden knowledge. Heretofore, I had spent my time in dim and darkened libraries, poring over ancient texts—books thought too awful to be released from their dusty tombs into the common world. Avidly I read, of acts that I had only suspected could take place, things of which I had only glimpsed in feverish dreams and nightmares. Now, the reality of these dreams was creeping slowly towards me, as step by faltering step I descended into the pit.

I had always felt myself 'apart' from my fellows. An alien perhaps, biding my time, watching the routines of the world through narrowed eyes. Biding my time. Waiting for the message to come through—the message that would bring forth my unknown, but foreshadowed purpose. That I was different from the rest, I had no doubt. But why? How did this come about? I did not know. Perhaps some rogue gene that, after lying dormant through generations, wakened in me, and coloured my soul with a flash of mutant awareness. In past centuries, I would have been feared as a sorceror or heretic. Occasionally, others would sense my 'alien nature,' if only unconsciously. This served only to reinforce my sense of standing alone in the crowd. As I delved deeper in forbidden lore, I came to know of the Pit. Quite what its significance was eluded me for some time, yet

I knew that, ultimately, I would be drawn to plumb its depths and discover for myself the heart of its mystery.

The air down here is thick. In the distance I can hear a dim cacophony, a muted babble of voices, strange unearthly music. The stone beneath me rumbles as though the very earth is warning me, testing my resolve to seek those unnamable experiences that I have for so long sought. But I will go on, I have held back for too long, seeking consolation in the feverish prose and paintings of those who shared my desires, who have already tasted the forbidden fruit.

Something squelches beneath my feet and...no I will not look down, I will not turn back to look. I must continue. I have come so far. I must prove myself and join the celebration which surely lies ahead. There are others of my kind, I am sure. Dreamers, outsiders, sensualists for whom the grey world above holds no lure.

The Pit beckons me, and I keep on walking.

A shaft of light cuts through the gloom, dust-motes dancing in the air before me. The door is ajar, and I can see the dim shapes, pressed close within the chamber. Dark and menacing. Hulking black-clad forms looming up at me in the darkness, pools of glowing luminescence throw up crazy glimpses of the inner room. My throat is dry. I am here! Nervously I thrust myself into the press of bodies. The music returns, jarring my ears, catching me in the stomach with its deep resonances. The air reeks with sweat and animal odours. Head down, I nudge my way between the hulking figures, making for the altar-like structure ahead. I must present myself before it. My coat snags on a chain, but with a jerk I am free and there! The sea of shapes opens to receive me, and I have achieved my desire. This is it! The bloated creature behind the dais turns slowly, regarding me with frank appraisal, and suddenly my throat is choked. No words come. And then...

"Yes love, what can I get you?"

"Er...a half of lager please."

"Haven't seen you before have we? Didn't anyone tell you Thursdays was Leather?"

fin

OTHER TITLES BY PHIL HINE

CONDENSED CHAOS
Introduction to Chaos Magic
by Phil Hine
Foreword by Peter J. Carroll

"... the most concise statement ... of the logic of modern magic. Magic, in the light of modern physics, quantum theory and probability theory is now approaching science. We hope that a result of this will be a synthesis so that science will become more magical and magic more scientific."
— William S. Burroughs, author of *Naked Lunch*

"*A tour de force.*"— Ian Read, Editor, *Chaos International*

PRIME CHAOS
Adventures in Chaos Magic
by Phil Hine

An overview of the fastest-growing school of modern occultism: Chaos Magic. Simple, effective techniques for becoming proficient in practical magic, including ritual magic, sorcery, invocation, possession and evocation. *Prime Chaos* also explores some of the lighter—and darker—aspects of modern occultism, and presents new ideas for developing magical techniques.

"I wish I'd written this book!"
— Peter J. Carroll, author of *Liber Kaos* and *Psybermagick*

THE *Original* FALCON PRESS

Invites You to Visit Our Website:
http://originalfalcon.com

At our website you can:

- Browse the online catalog of all of our great titles
- Find out what's available and what's out of stock
- Get special discounts
- Order our titles through our secure online server
- Find products not available anywhere else including:
  - One of a kind and limited availability products
  - Special packages
  - Special pricing
- Get free gifts
- Join our email list for advance notice of New Releases and Special Offers
- Find out about book signings and author events
- Send email to our authors
- Read excerpts of many of our titles
- Find links to our authors' websites
- Discover links to other weird and wonderful sites
- And much, much more

Get online today at http://originalfalcon.com